HEAVEN'S DESIGN TEAM

VOL.05

BY ▸ HEBI-ZOU & TSUTA SUZUKI

ART BY ▸ TARAKO

HEAVEN'S DESIGN TEAM

CHARACTER PROFILES

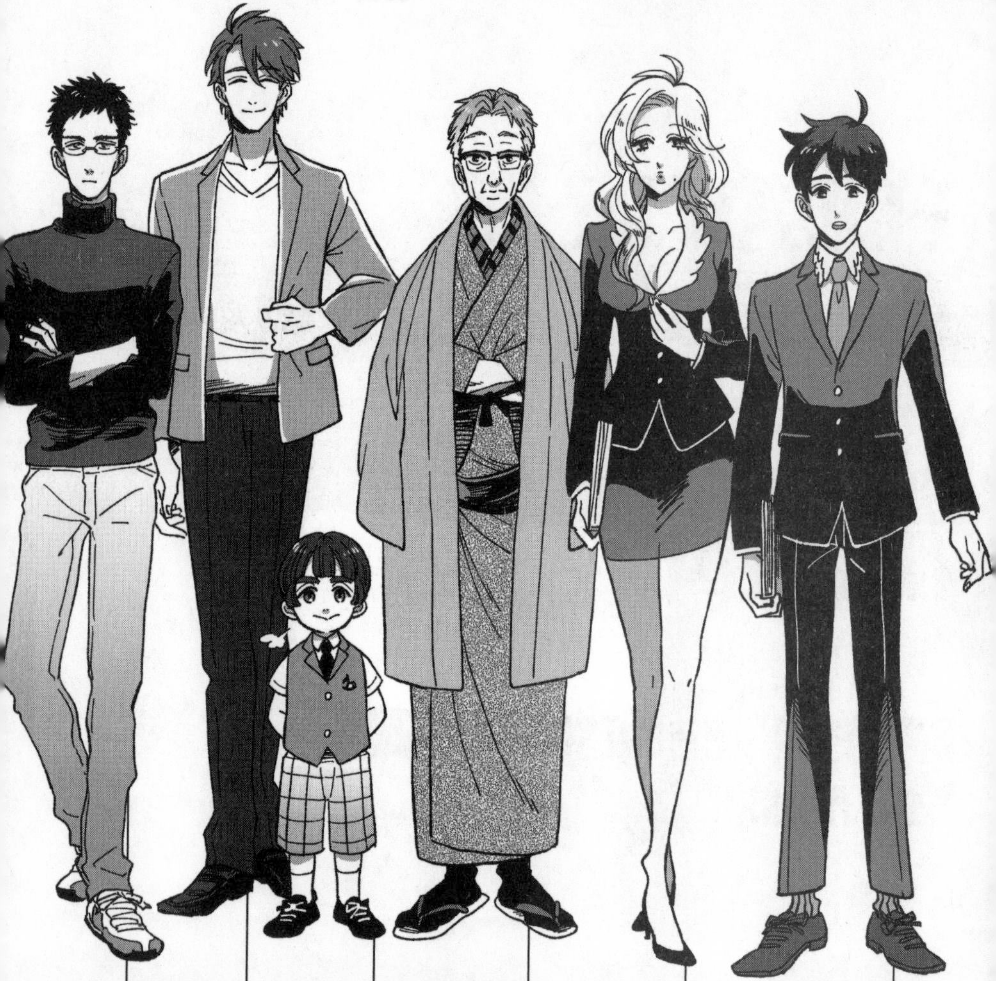

MERCURY
A designer. His masterpiece: the snake.

JUPITER
A designer. His masterpiece: the cow.

MR. SATURN'S GRANDSON
Mr. Saturn's grandson, Kenta. A horse fan, just like his grandpa.

MR. SATURN
A designer and the head of the Design Department. His masterpiece: the horse.

UEDA
Shimoda's supervisor. An angel who acts as a liaison between God and the Design Department.

SHIMODA
The new angel. Serves as the liaison between God (the client) and the Design Department.

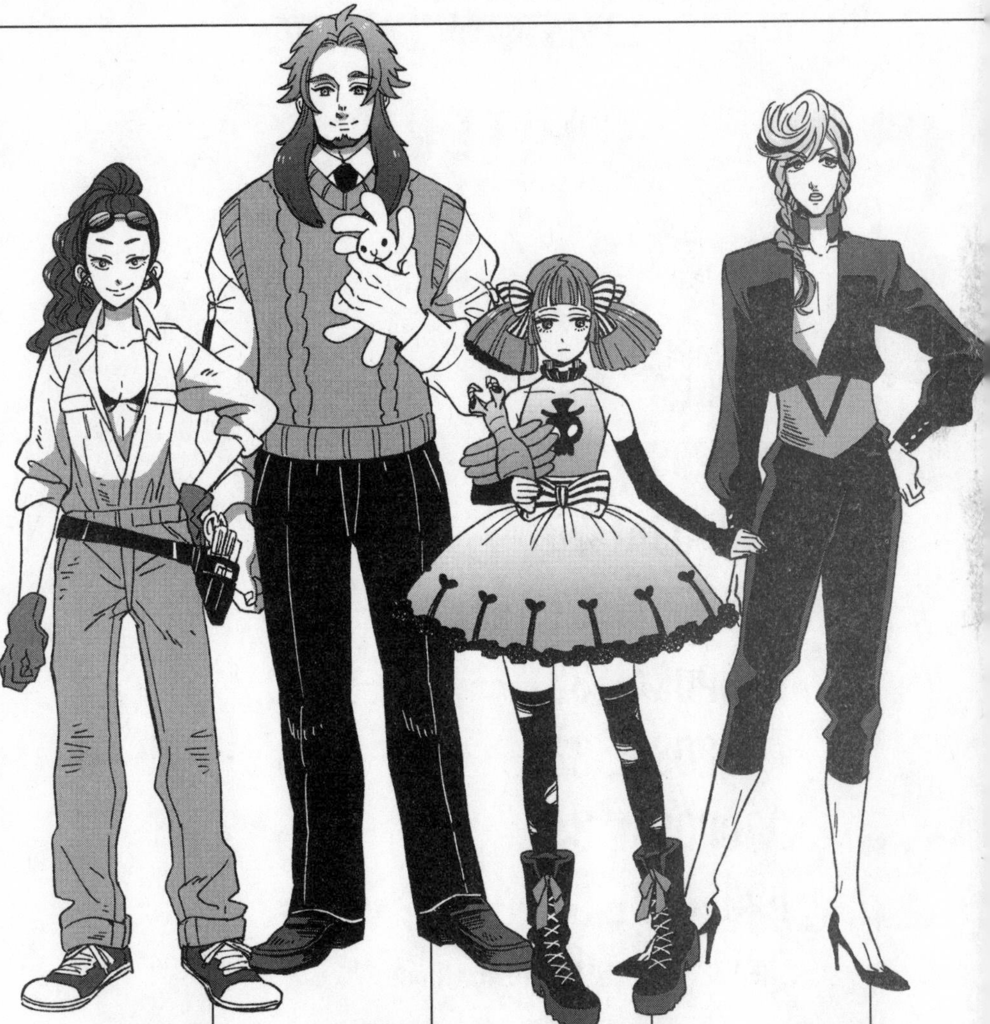

MARS

An engineer. Tests whether the animal designs will actually function in the physical world. The hardest worker in the office.

NEPTUNE

A designer. His masterpiece: the kangaroo.

PLUTO

A designer. Her masterpiece: the poisonous frog.

VENUS

A designer. Nicknamed "Ven." Their masterpiece: the bird.

HEAVEN'S DESIGN TEAM

CONTENTS

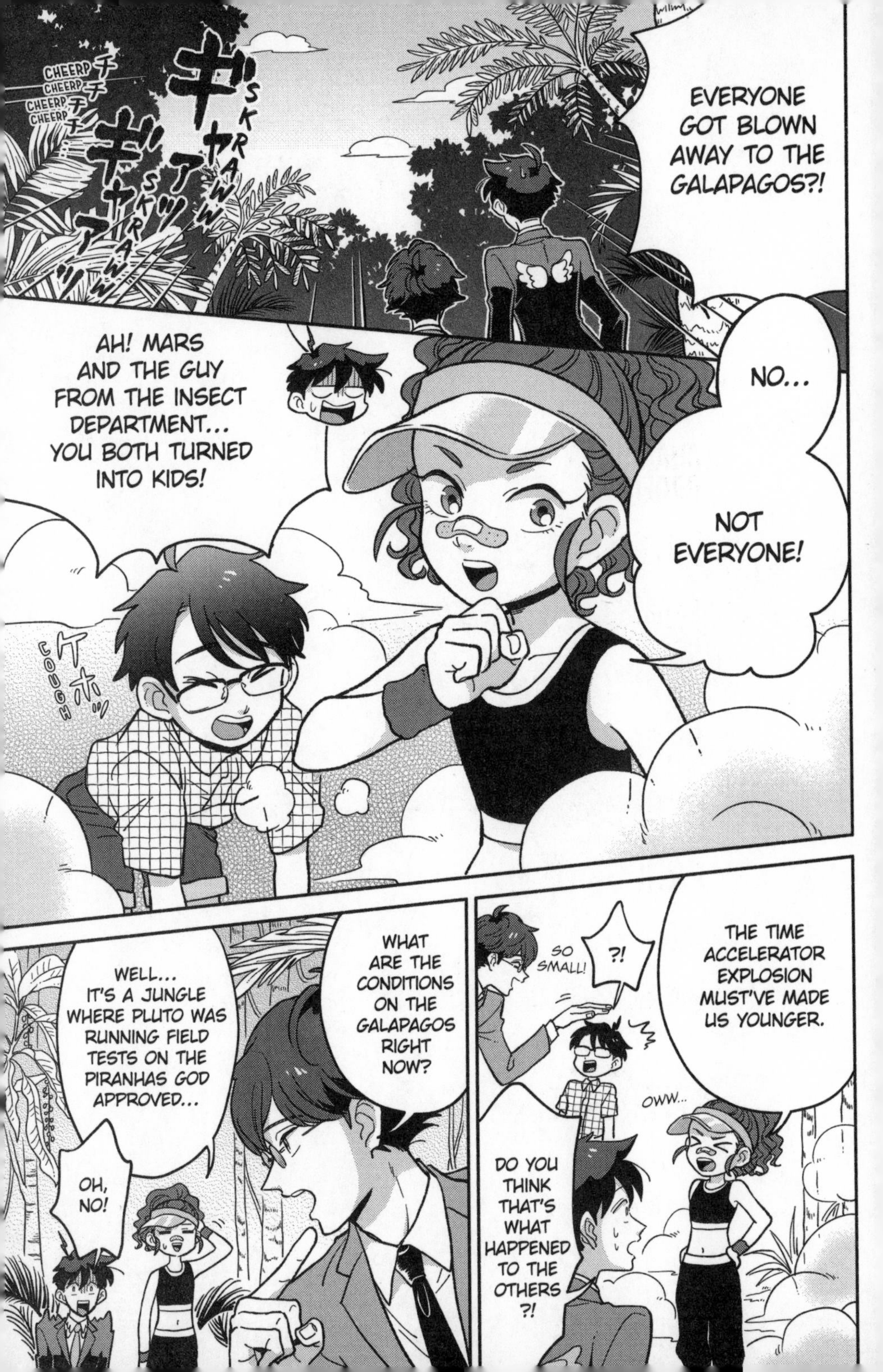
EVERYONE GOT BLOWN AWAY TO THE GALAPAGOS?!
SKRAWW SKRAWW
CHEERP CHEERP CHEERP CHEERP
NO... NOT EVERYONE!
AH! MARS AND THE GUY FROM THE INSECT DEPARTMENT... YOU BOTH TURNED INTO KIDS!
COUGH
THE TIME ACCELERATOR EXPLOSION MUST'VE MADE US YOUNGER.
?!
SO SMALL!
OWW...
DO YOU THINK THAT'S WHAT HAPPENED TO THE OTHERS?!
WHAT ARE THE CONDITIONS ON THE GALAPAGOS RIGHT NOW?
WELL... IT'S A JUNGLE WHERE PLUTO WAS RUNNING FIELD TESTS ON THE PIRANHAS GOD APPROVED...
OH, NO!

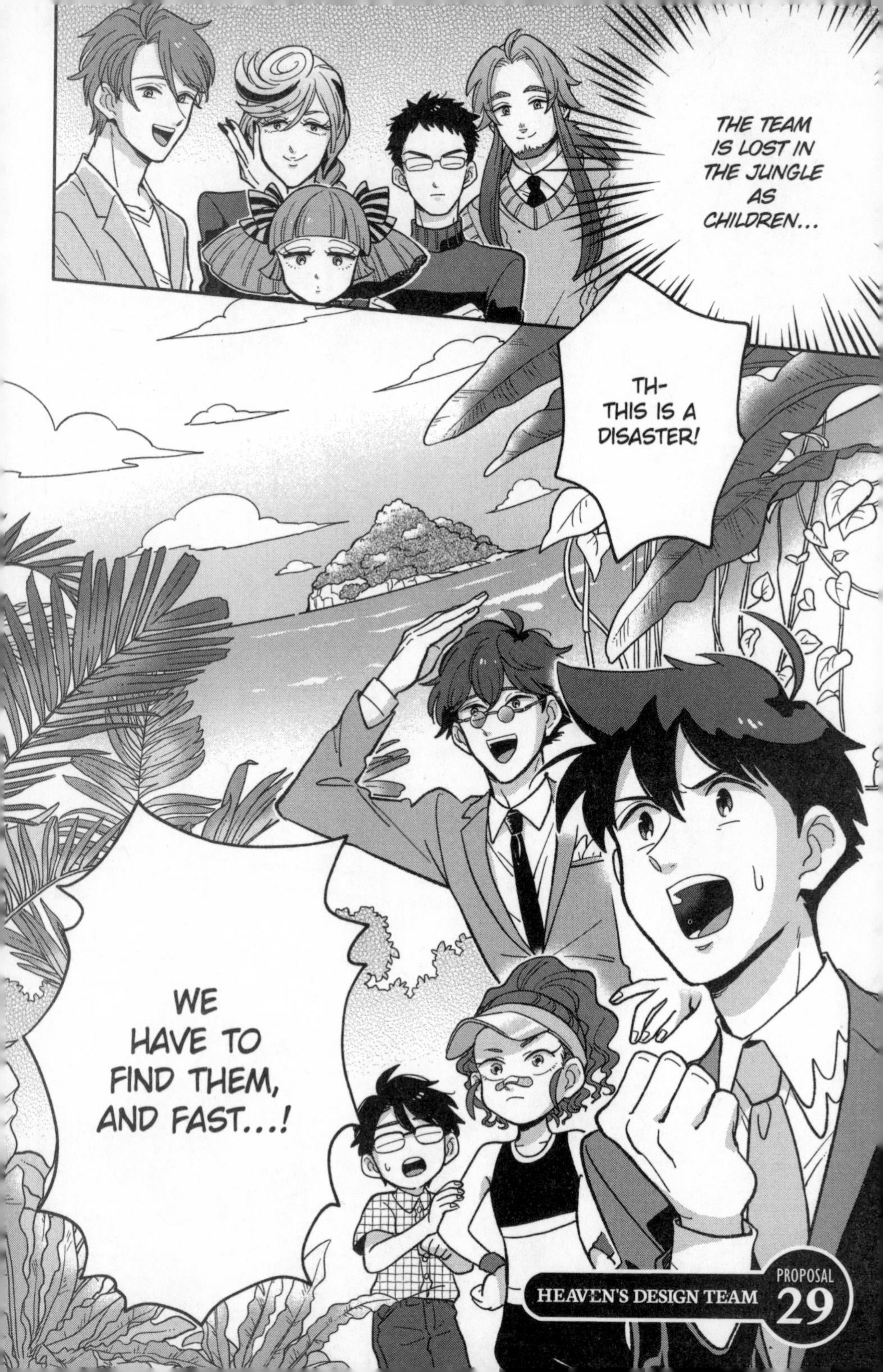
THE TEAM IS LOST IN THE JUNGLE AS CHILDREN...
TH- THIS IS A DISASTER!
WE HAVE TO FIND THEM, AND FAST...!
PROPOSAL 29
HEAVEN'S DESIGN TEAM

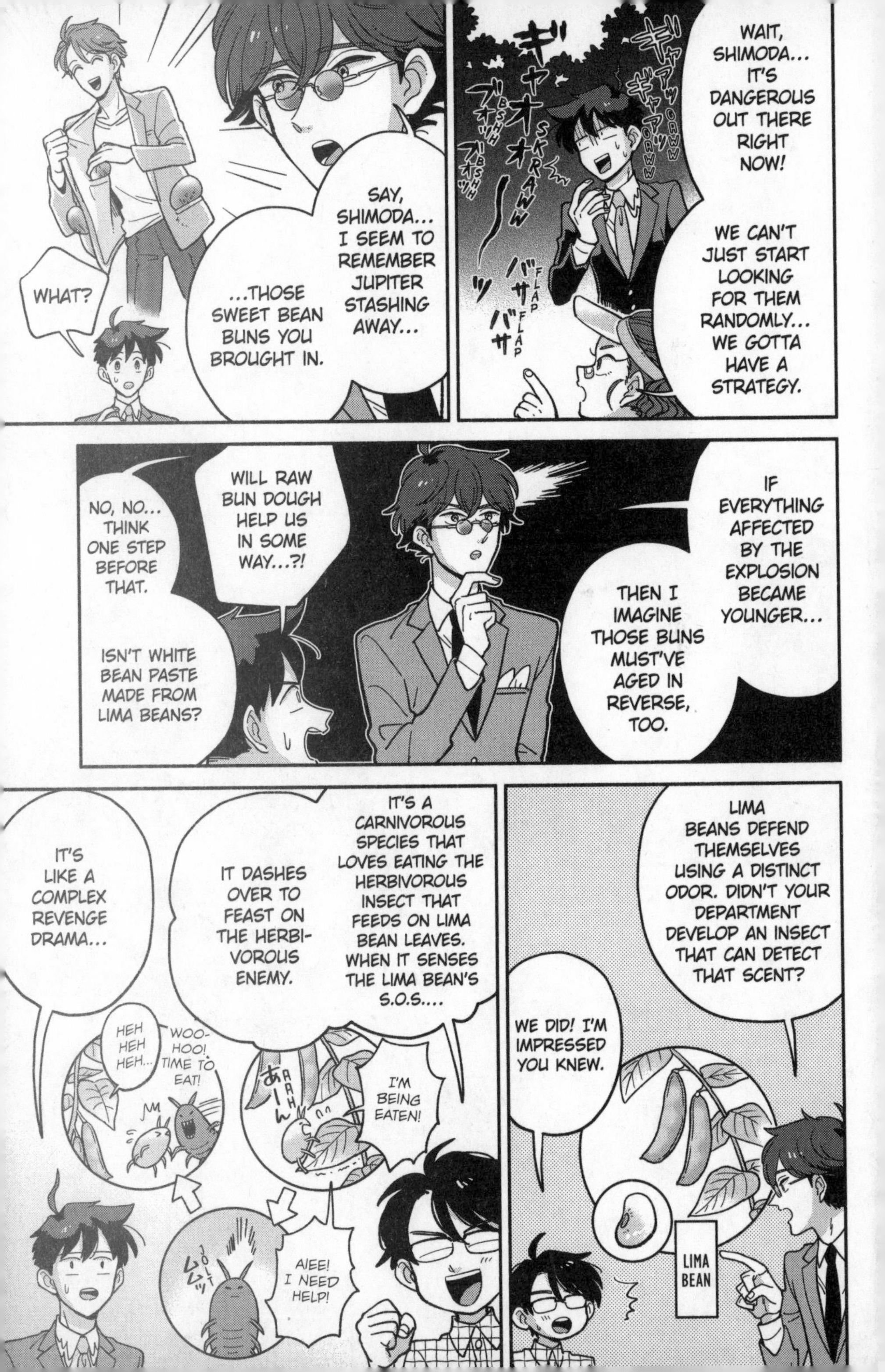
ギャアッ ギャアッ CAWW CAWW
ギャオオーッ SKRAWW
ブオッ BSHH ブオッ BSHH
バサ FLAP バサ FLAP
WAIT, SHIMODA... IT'S DANGEROUS OUT THERE RIGHT NOW!
WE CAN'T JUST START LOOKING FOR THEM RANDOMLY... WE GOTTA HAVE A STRATEGY.
SAY, SHIMODA... I SEEM TO REMEMBER JUPITER STASHING AWAY...
...THOSE SWEET BEAN BUNS YOU BROUGHT IN.
WHAT?
IF EVERYTHING AFFECTED BY THE EXPLOSION BECAME YOUNGER...
THEN I IMAGINE THOSE BUNS MUST'VE AGED IN REVERSE, TOO.
WILL RAW BUN DOUGH HELP US IN SOME WAY...?!
NO, NO... THINK ONE STEP BEFORE THAT.
ISN'T WHITE BEAN PASTE MADE FROM LIMA BEANS?
LIMA BEANS DEFEND THEMSELVES USING A DISTINCT ODOR. DIDN'T YOUR DEPARTMENT DEVELOP AN INSECT THAT CAN DETECT THAT SCENT?
WE DID! I'M IMPRESSED YOU KNEW.
LIMA BEAN
IT'S A CARNIVOROUS SPECIES THAT LOVES EATING THE HERBIVOROUS INSECT THAT FEEDS ON LIMA BEAN LEAVES. WHEN IT SENSES THE LIMA BEAN'S S.O.S....
IT DASHES OVER TO FEAST ON THE HERBI- VOROUS ENEMY.
IT'S LIKE A COMPLEX REVENGE DRAMA...
あーん AAH
I'M BEING EATEN!
HEH HEH HEH...
WOO- HOO! TIME TO EAT!
ムッ JOLT
AIEE! I NEED HELP!

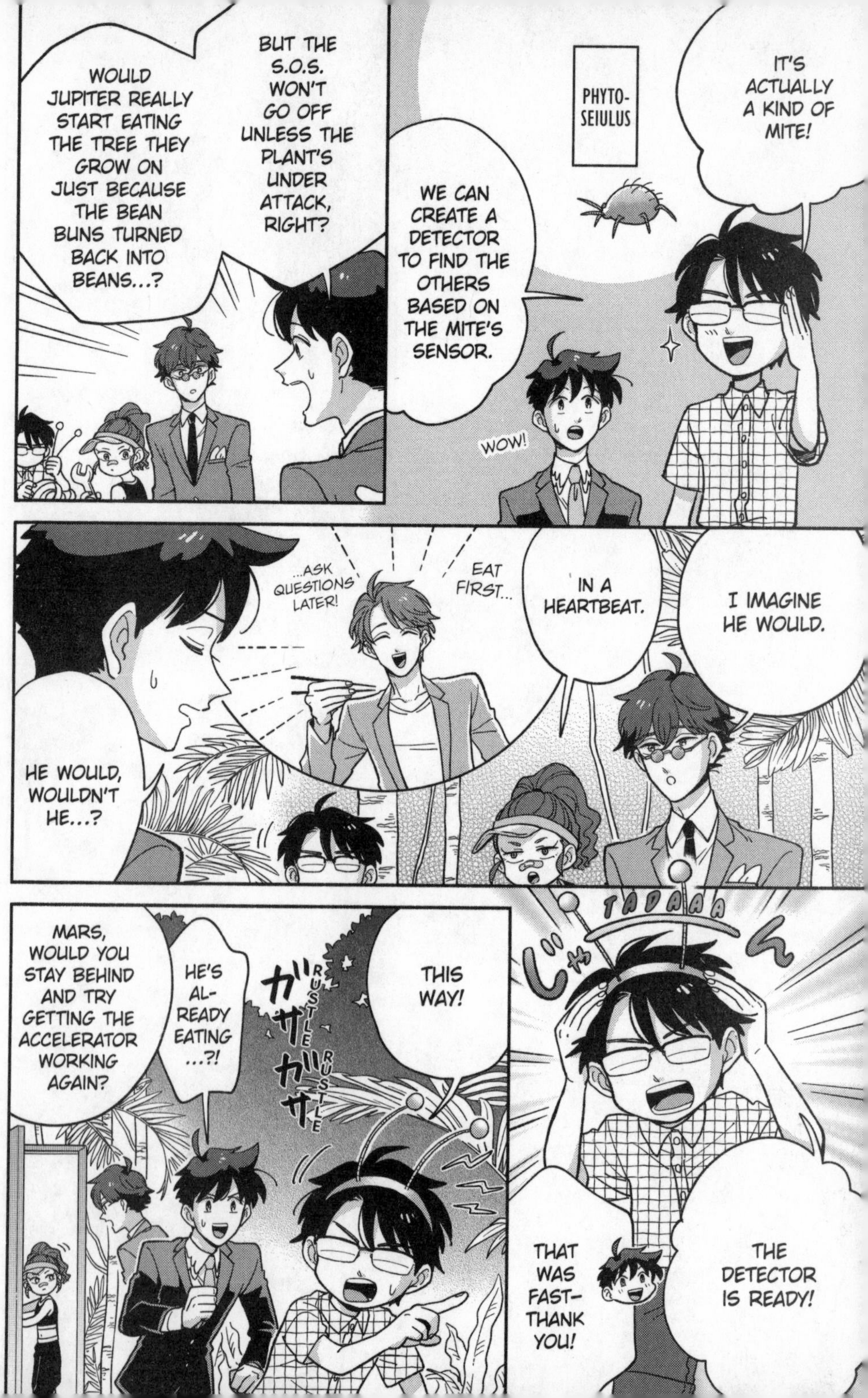
IT'S ACTUALLY A KIND OF MITE!
PHYTO-SEIULUS
WE CAN CREATE A DETECTOR TO FIND THE OTHERS BASED ON THE MITE'S SENSOR.
WOW!
BUT THE S.O.S. WON'T GO OFF UNLESS THE PLANT'S UNDER ATTACK, RIGHT?
WOULD JUPITER REALLY START EATING THE TREE THEY GROW ON JUST BECAUSE THE BEAN BUNS TURNED BACK INTO BEANS...?
I IMAGINE HE WOULD.
IN A HEARTBEAT.
EAT FIRST...
...ASK QUESTIONS LATER!
HE WOULD, WOULDN'T HE...?
じゃ〜ん
TADAAAA
THE DETECTOR IS READY!
THAT WAS FAST-THANK YOU!
THIS WAY!
ガサガサ
RUSTLE RUSTLE
HE'S AL-READY EATING...?!
MARS, WOULD YOU STAY BEHIND AND TRY GETTING THE ACCELERATOR WORKING AGAIN?

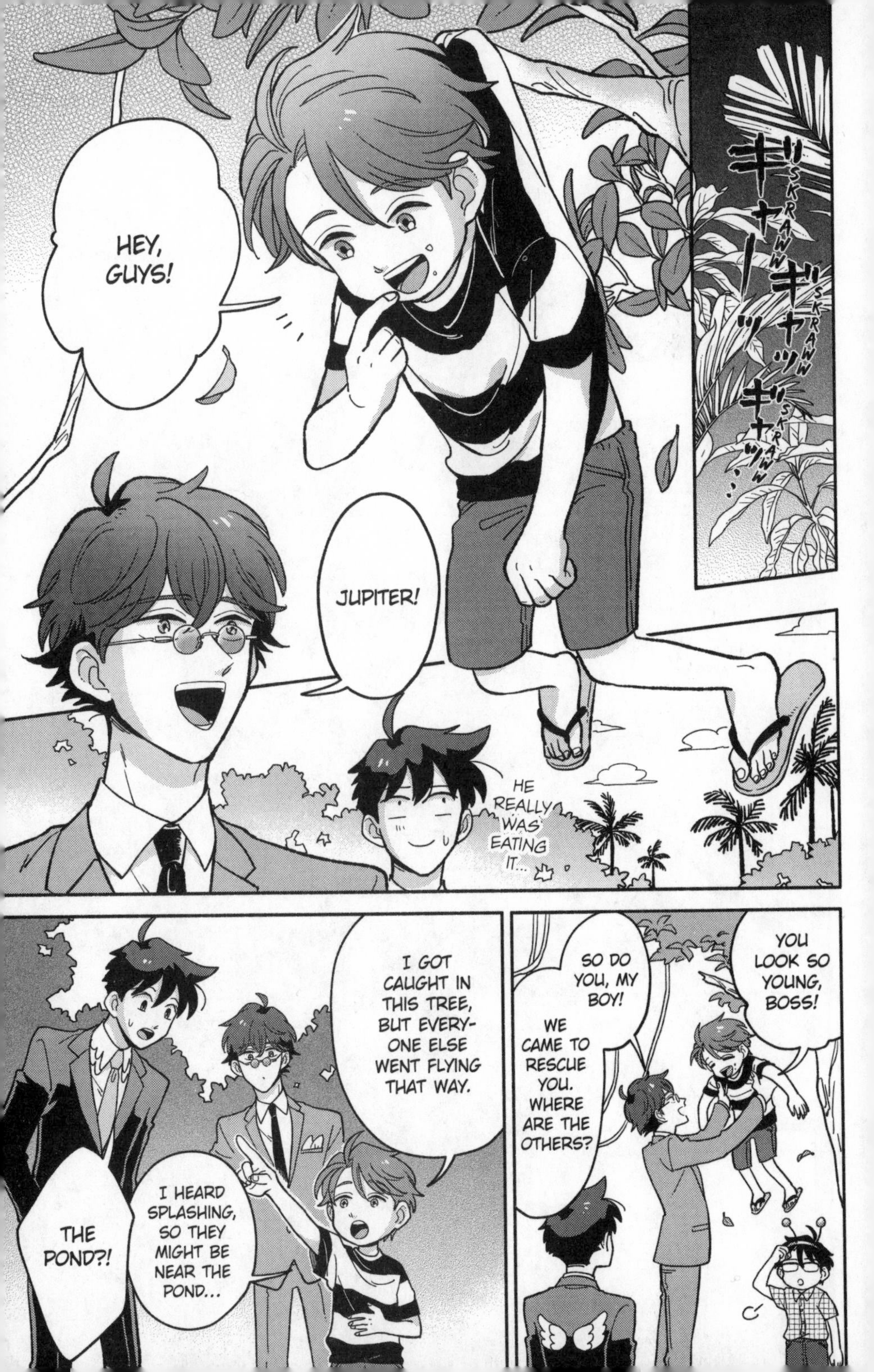
SKRAWW
SKRAWW
SKRAWW...
HEY, GUYS!
JUPITER!
HE REALLY WAS EATING IT...
YOU LOOK SO YOUNG, BOSS!
SO DO YOU, MY BOY!
WE CAME TO RESCUE YOU. WHERE ARE THE OTHERS?
I GOT CAUGHT IN THIS TREE, BUT EVERY-ONE ELSE WENT FLYING THAT WAY.
I HEARD SPLASHING, SO THEY MIGHT BE NEAR THE POND...
THE POND?!

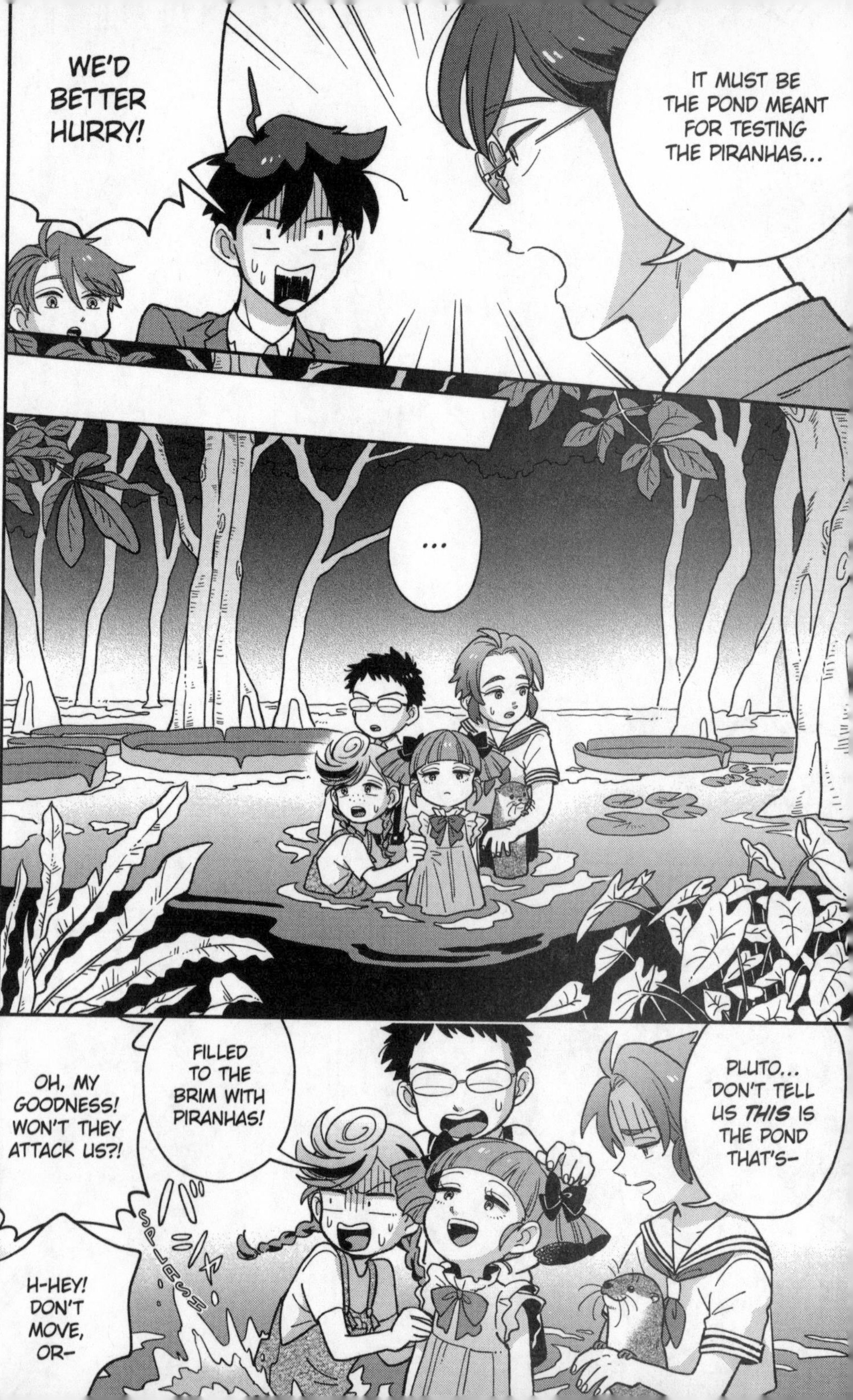
IT MUST BE THE POND MEANT FOR TESTING THE PIRANHAS...
WE'D BETTER HURRY!
...
PLUTO... DON'T TELL US *THIS* IS THE POND THAT'S–
FILLED TO THE BRIM WITH PIRANHAS!
OH, MY GOODNESS! WON'T THEY ATTACK US?!
SPLASH
H-HEY! DON'T MOVE, OR–

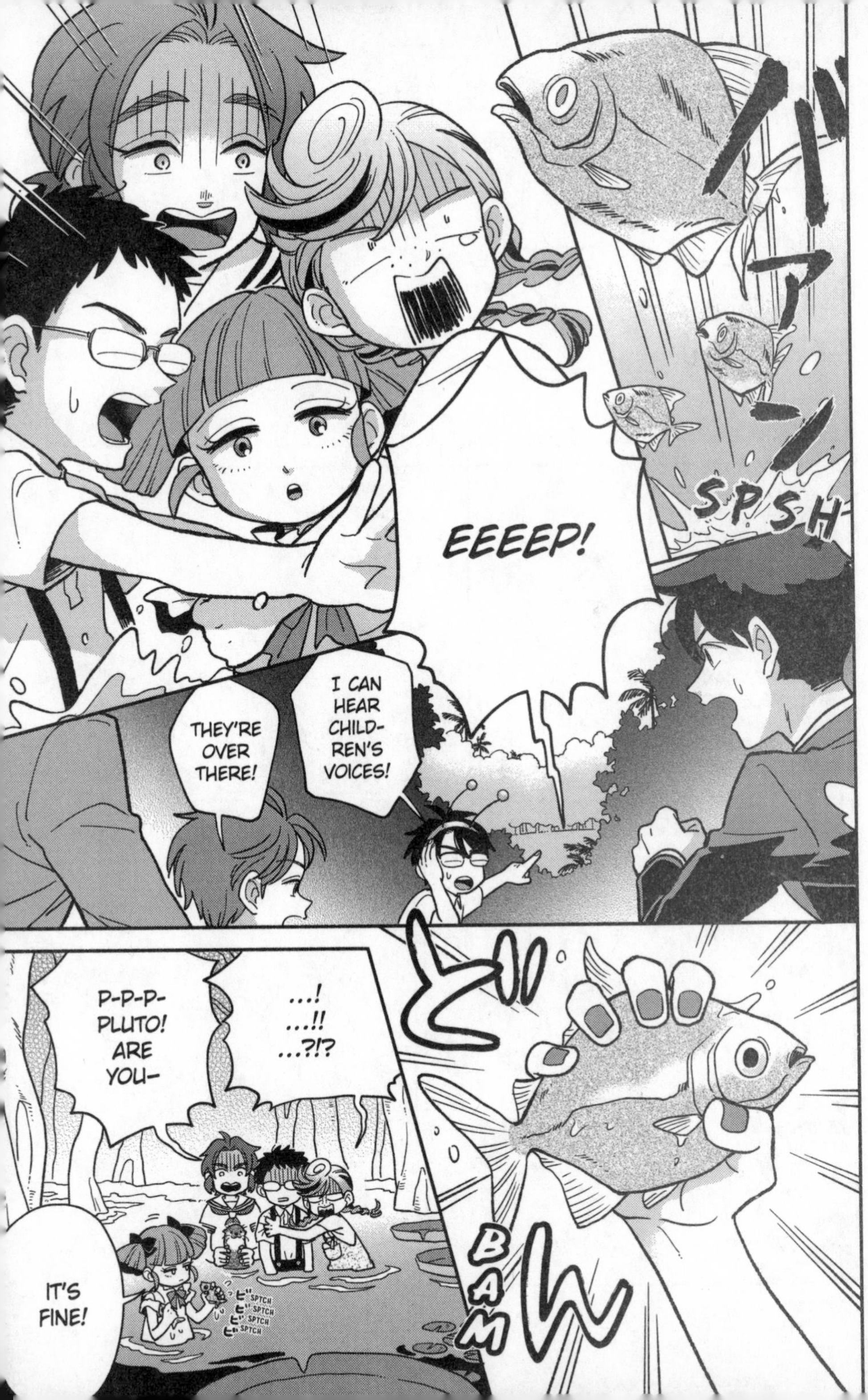
SPSH
EEEEP!
I CAN HEAR CHILD-REN'S VOICES!
THEY'RE OVER THERE!
BAM
...! ...!! ...?!?
P-P-P-PLUTO! ARE YOU-
SPTCH SPTCH SPTCH SPTCH
IT'S FINE!

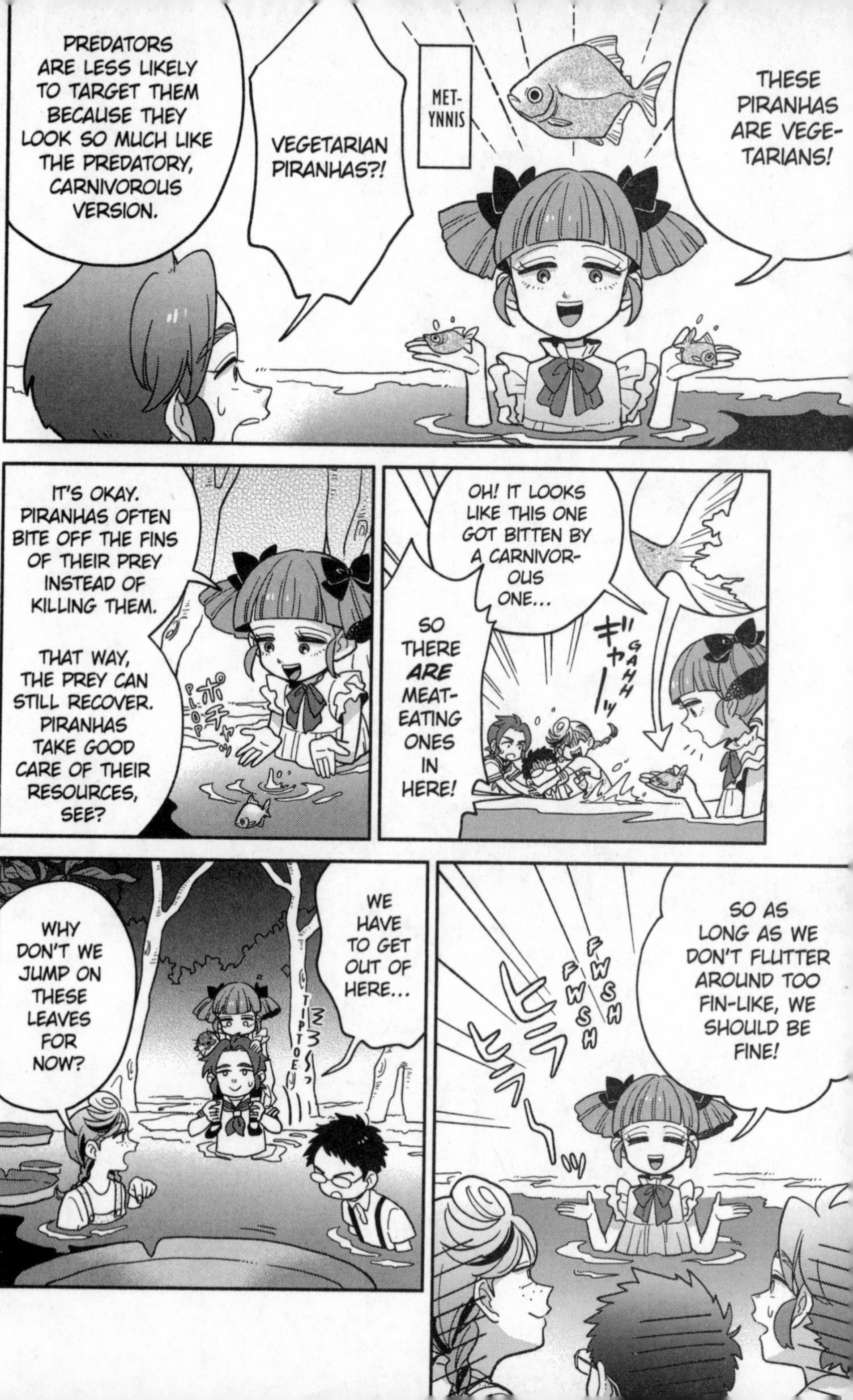
THESE PIRANHAS ARE VEGE-TARIANS!
MET-YNNIS
VEGETARIAN PIRANHAS?!
PREDATORS ARE LESS LIKELY TO TARGET THEM BECAUSE THEY LOOK SO MUCH LIKE THE PREDATORY, CARNIVOROUS VERSION.
OH! IT LOOKS LIKE THIS ONE GOT BITTEN BY A CARNIVOR-OUS ONE...
GAHH
SO THERE *ARE* MEAT-EATING ONES IN HERE!
IT'S OKAY. PIRANHAS OFTEN BITE OFF THE FINS OF THEIR PREY INSTEAD OF KILLING THEM.
THAT WAY, THE PREY CAN STILL RECOVER. PIRANHAS TAKE GOOD CARE OF THEIR RESOURCES, SEE?
PLOP
SO AS LONG AS WE DON'T FLUTTER AROUND TOO FIN-LIKE, WE SHOULD BE FINE!
FWSH
FWSH
WE HAVE TO GET OUT OF HERE...
TIPTOE
WHY DON'T WE JUMP ON THESE LEAVES FOR NOW?

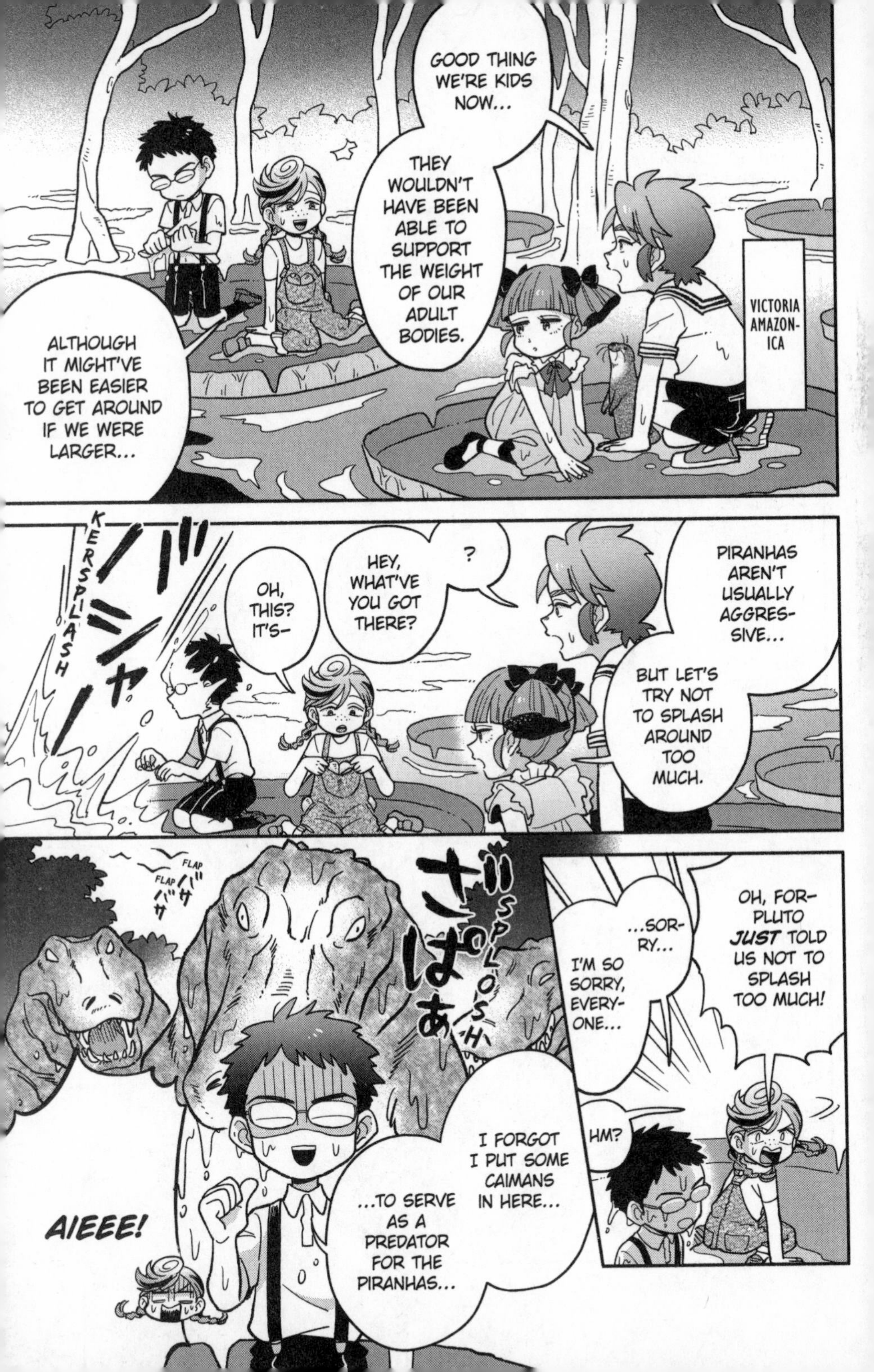
GOOD THING WE'RE KIDS NOW...
THEY WOULDN'T HAVE BEEN ABLE TO SUPPORT THE WEIGHT OF OUR ADULT BODIES.
VICTORIA AMAZON-ICA
ALTHOUGH IT MIGHT'VE BEEN EASIER TO GET AROUND IF WE WERE LARGER...
PIRANHAS AREN'T USUALLY AGGRES-SIVE...
BUT LET'S TRY NOT TO SPLASH AROUND TOO MUCH.
?
HEY, WHAT'VE YOU GOT THERE?
OH, THIS? IT'S-
KERSPLASH
OH, FOR-PLUTO *JUST* TOLD US NOT TO SPLASH TOO MUCH!
...SOR-RY...
I'M SO SORRY, EVERY-ONE...
HM?
SPLOOSH
FLAP
FLAP
I FORGOT I PUT SOME CAIMANS IN HERE...
...TO SERVE AS A PREDATOR FOR THE PIRANHAS...
AIEEE!

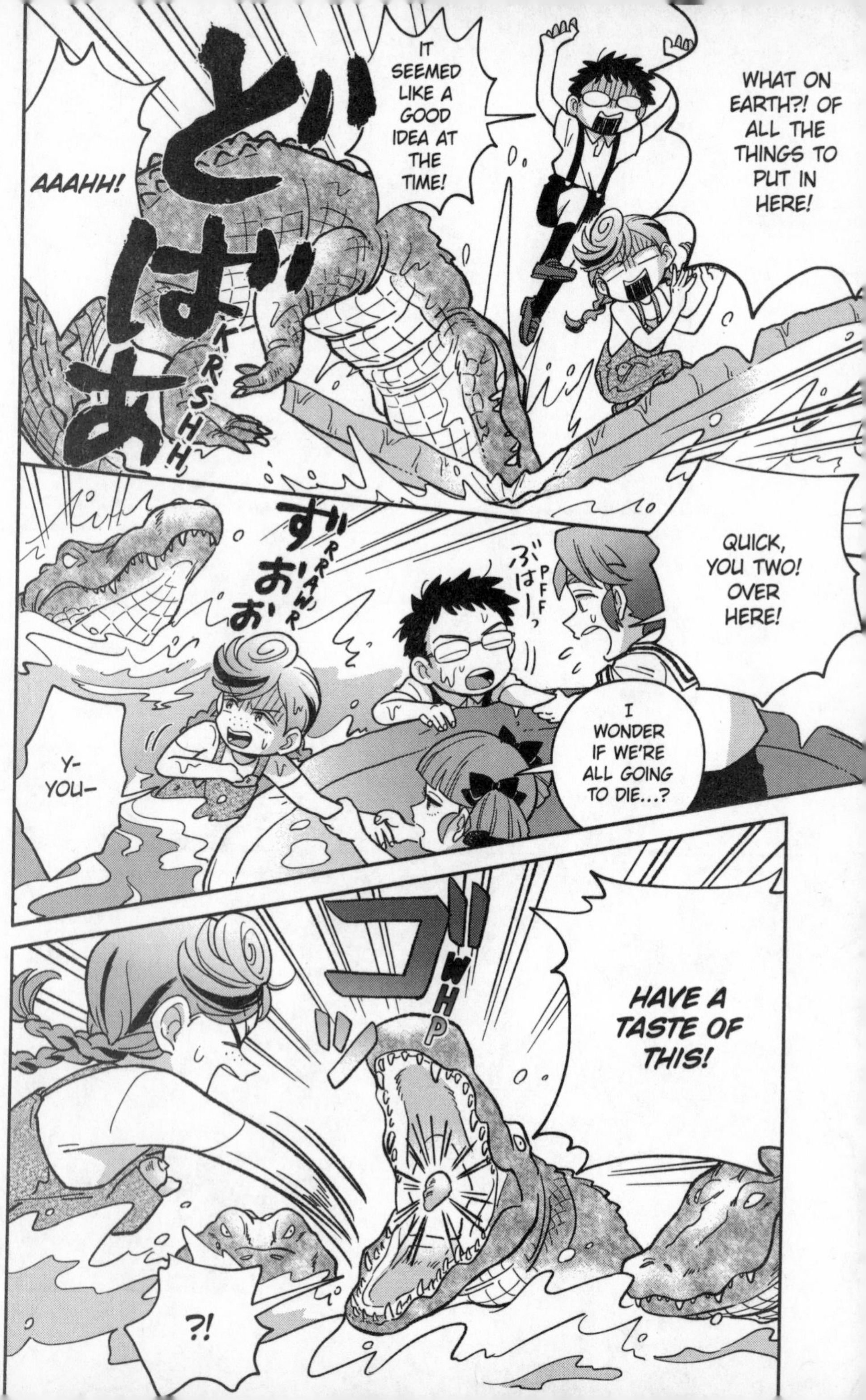
WHAT ON EARTH?! OF ALL THE THINGS TO PUT IN HERE!
IT SEEMED LIKE A GOOD IDEA AT THE TIME!
AAAHH!
どばあ
KRSHH
QUICK, YOU TWO! OVER HERE!
ぶはーっ
PFFF
RRAWR
I WONDER IF WE'RE ALL GOING TO DIE...?
Y-YOU—
HAVE A TASTE OF THIS!
WHP
?!

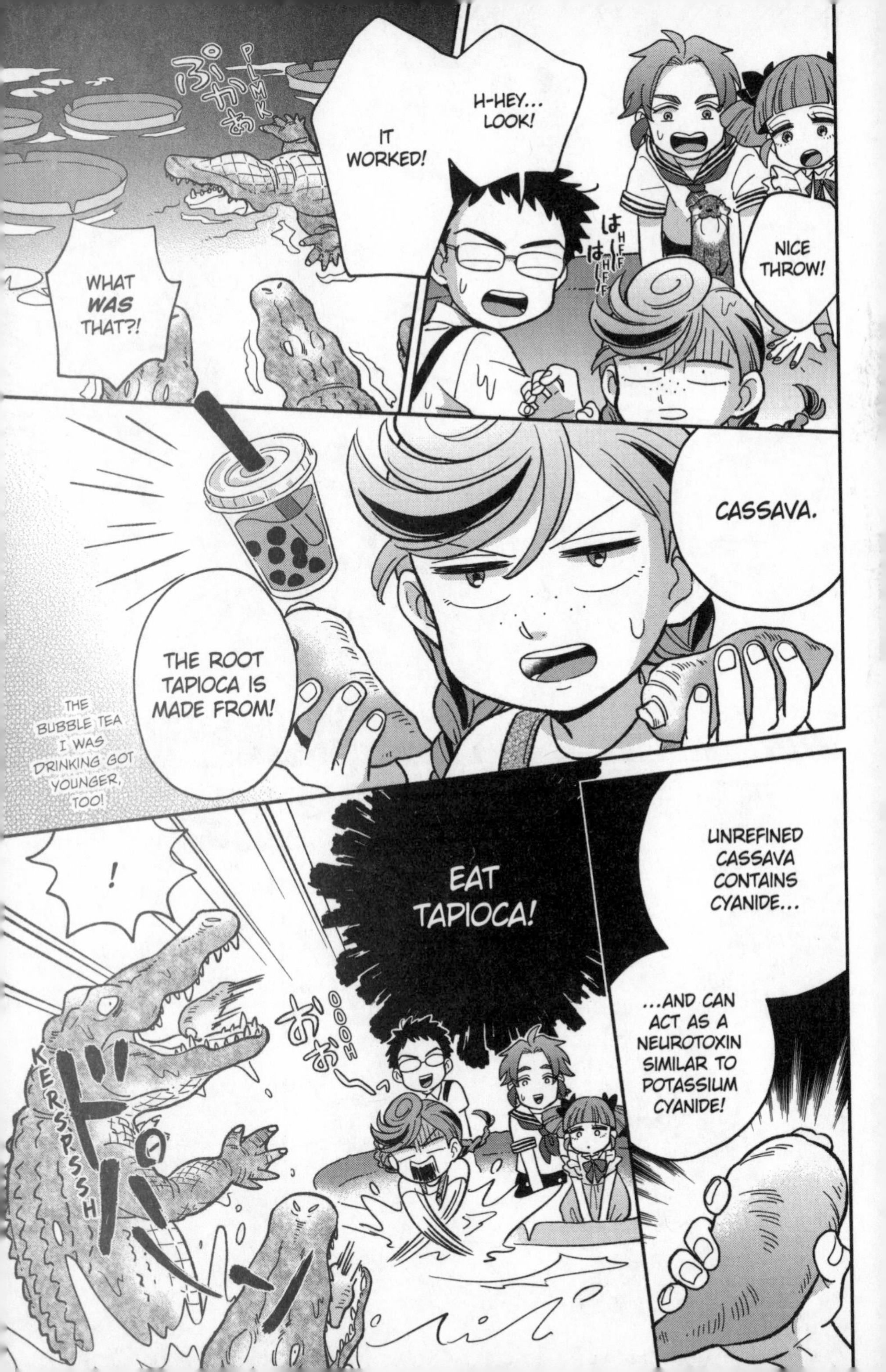
H-HEY... LOOK!
IT WORKED!
はは HFF HFF
NICE THROW!
ぷかぁ PLMK
WHAT WAS THAT?!
CASSAVA.
THE ROOT TAPIOCA IS MADE FROM!
THE BUBBLE TEA I WAS DRINKING GOT YOUNGER, TOO!
UNREFINED CASSAVA CONTAINS CYANIDE...
...AND CAN ACT AS A NEUROTOXIN SIMILAR TO POTASSIUM CYANIDE!
EAT TAPIOCA!
おお〜 OOOH
!
ドパッ KERSPSSH

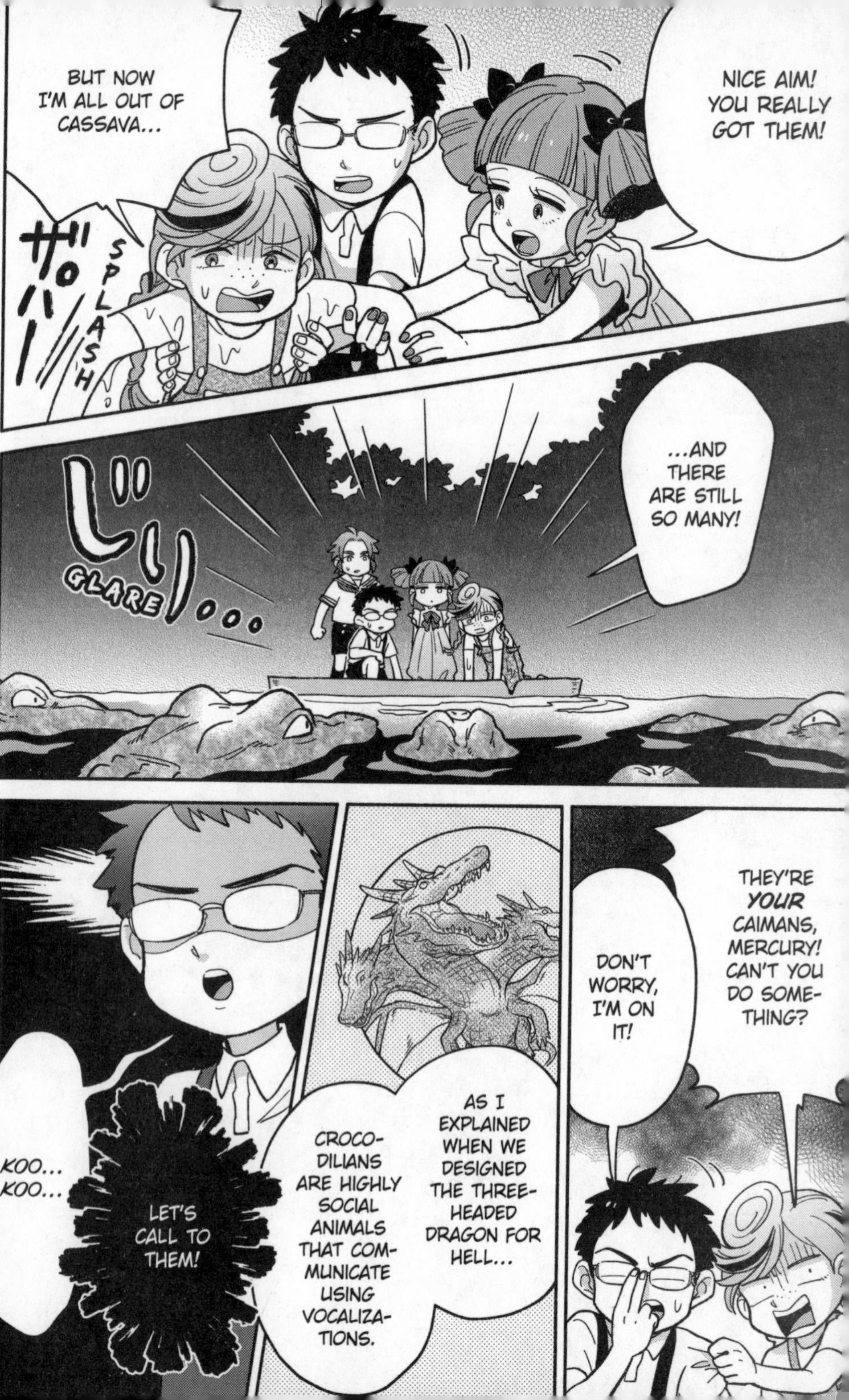
NICE AIM! YOU REALLY GOT THEM!
BUT NOW I'M ALL OUT OF CASSAVA...
SPLASH
...AND THERE ARE STILL SO MANY!
GLARE
THEY'RE *YOUR* CAIMANS, MERCURY! CAN'T YOU DO SOME-THING?
DON'T WORRY, I'M ON IT!
AS I EXPLAINED WHEN WE DESIGNED THE THREE-HEADED DRAGON FOR HELL...
CROCO-DILIANS ARE HIGHLY SOCIAL ANIMALS THAT COM-MUNICATE USING VOCALIZA-TIONS.
LET'S CALL TO THEM!
KOO... KOO...

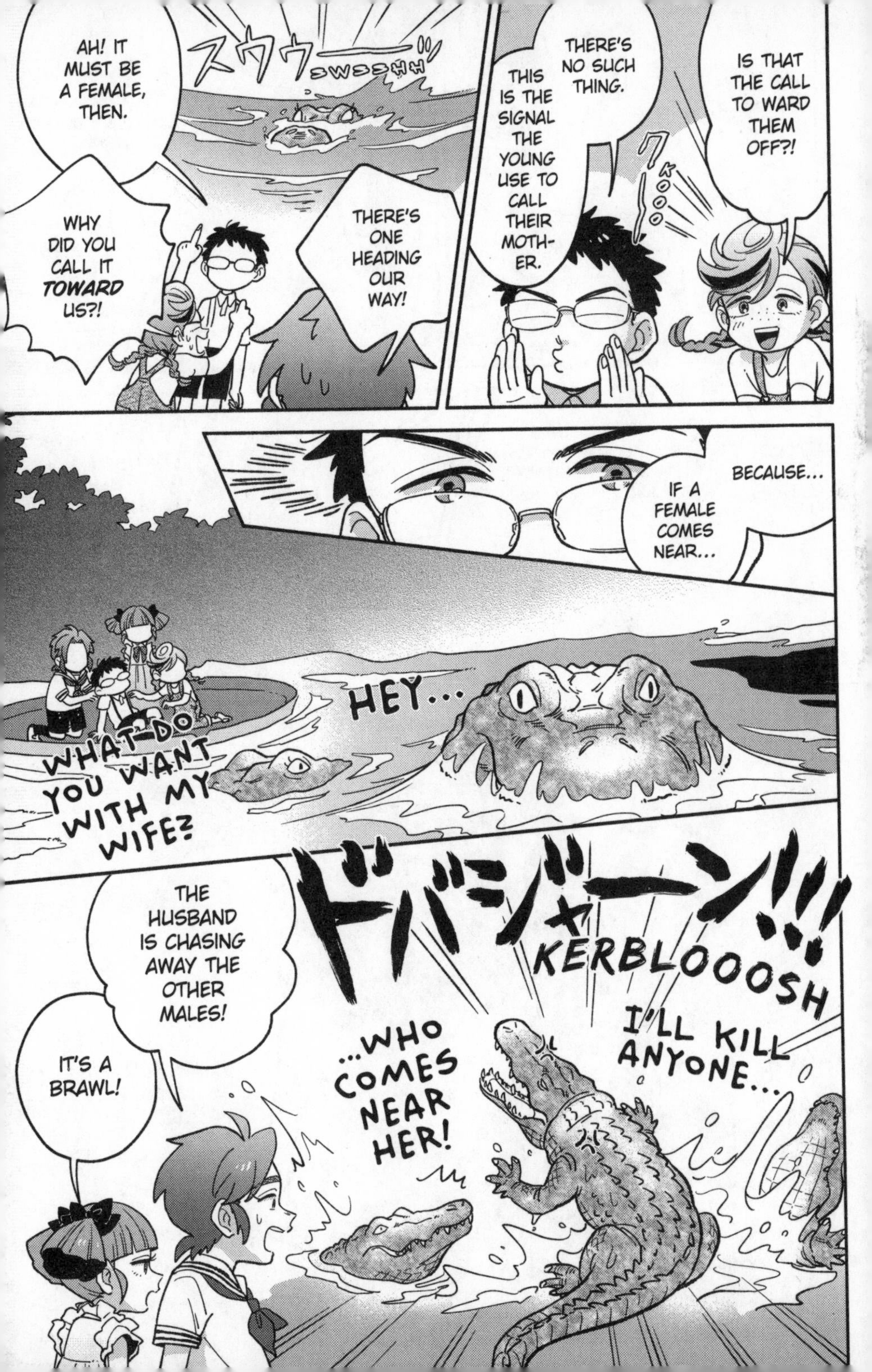

IS THAT THE CALL TO WARD THEM OFF?!
KOOO
THERE'S NO SUCH THING.
THIS IS THE SIGNAL THE YOUNG USE TO CALL THEIR MOTH-ER.
AH! IT MUST BE A FEMALE, THEN.
THERE'S ONE HEADING OUR WAY!
WHY DID YOU CALL IT *TOWARD* US?!
BECAUSE...
IF A FEMALE COMES NEAR...
HEY...
WHAT DO YOU WANT WITH MY WIFE?
KERBLOOOOSH
I'LL KILL ANYONE...
...WHO COMES NEAR HER!
THE HUSBAND IS CHASING AWAY THE OTHER MALES!
IT'S A BRAWL!

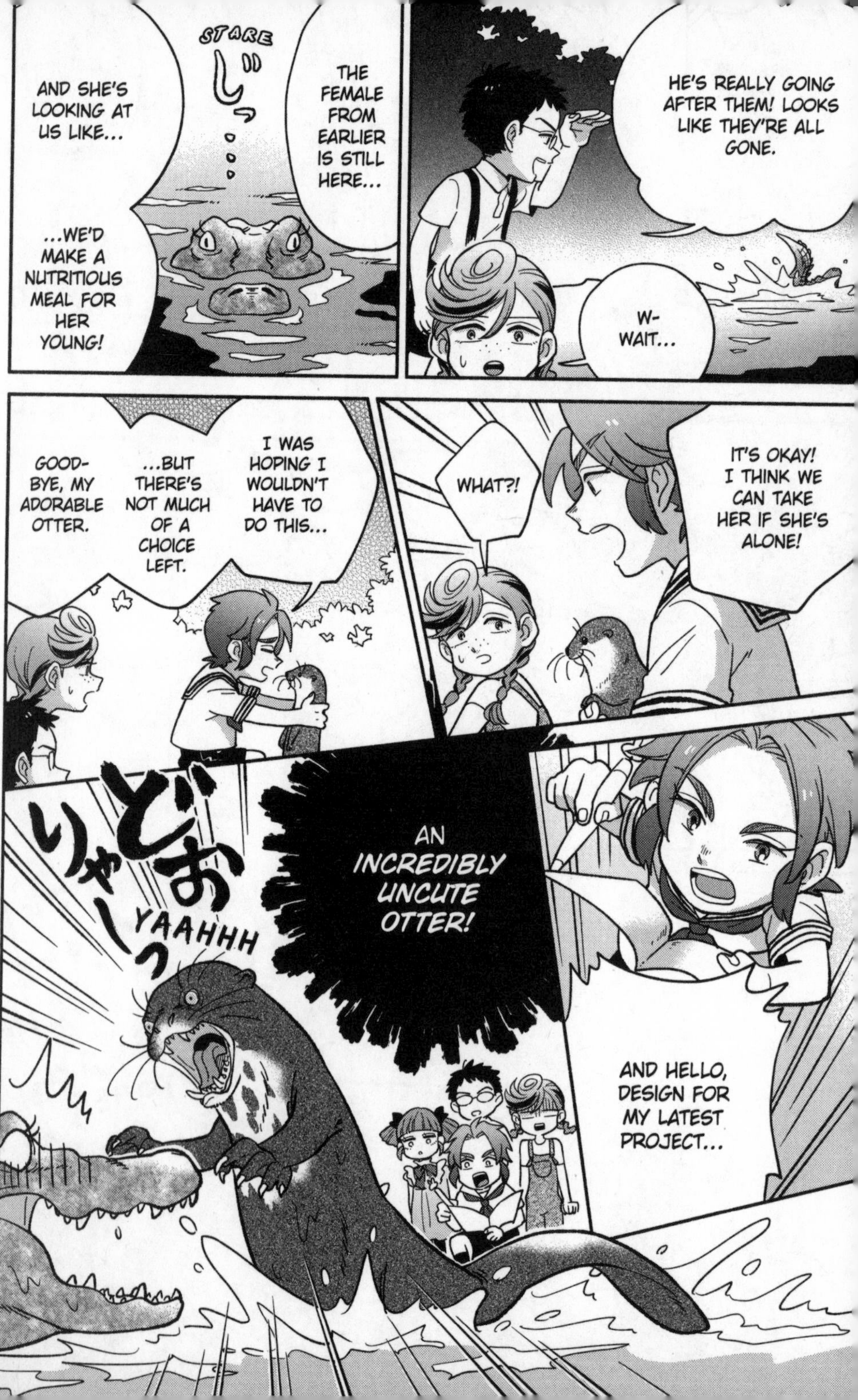

HE'S REALLY GOING AFTER THEM! LOOKS LIKE THEY'RE ALL GONE.
W-WAIT...
THE FEMALE FROM EARLIER IS STILL HERE...
STARE
じっ
AND SHE'S LOOKING AT US LIKE...
...WE'D MAKE A NUTRITIOUS MEAL FOR HER YOUNG!
IT'S OKAY! I THINK WE CAN TAKE HER IF SHE'S ALONE!
WHAT?!
I WAS HOPING I WOULDN'T HAVE TO DO THIS...
...BUT THERE'S NOT MUCH OF A CHOICE LEFT.
GOOD-BYE, MY ADORABLE OTTER.
AND HELLO, DESIGN FOR MY LATEST PROJECT...
AN INCREDIBLY UNCUTE OTTER!
どぉりゃーっ
YAAHHH

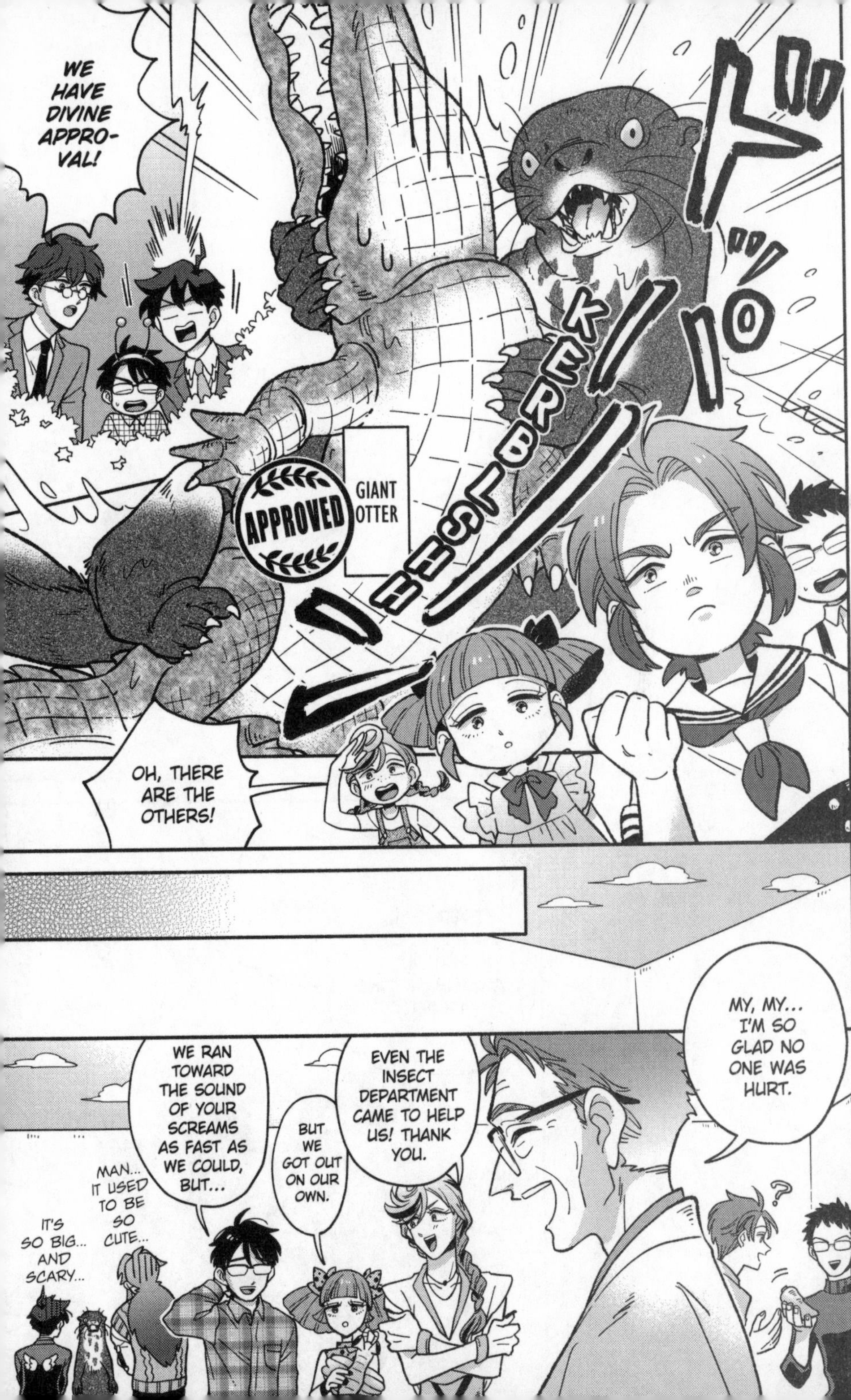
KERBLSHH
GIANT OTTER
APPROVED
WE HAVE DIVINE APPRO-VAL!
OH, THERE ARE THE OTHERS!
MY, MY... I'M SO GLAD NO ONE WAS HURT.
EVEN THE INSECT DEPARTMENT CAME TO HELP US! THANK YOU.
BUT WE GOT OUT ON OUR OWN.
WE RAN TOWARD THE SOUND OF YOUR SCREAMS AS FAST AS WE COULD, BUT...
MAN... IT USED TO BE SO CUTE...
IT'S SO BIG... AND SCARY...

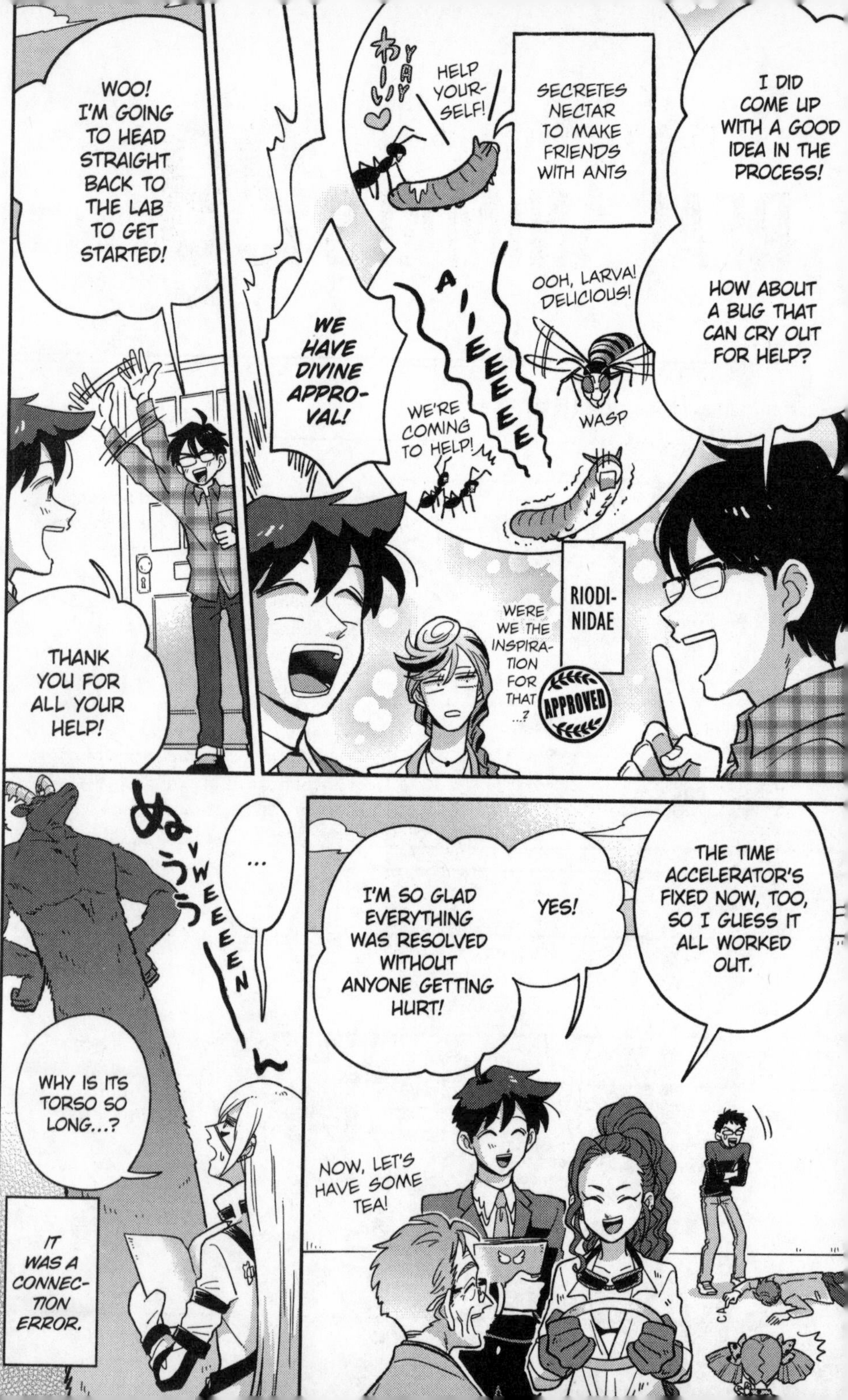
I DID COME UP WITH A GOOD IDEA IN THE PROCESS!
HOW ABOUT A BUG THAT CAN CRY OUT FOR HELP?
SECRETES NECTAR TO MAKE FRIENDS WITH ANTS
HELP YOURSELF!
わいわい YAY
OOH, LARVA! DELICIOUS!
WASP
AIEEEEEE
WE'RE COMING TO HELP!
RIODINIDAE
WERE WE THE INSPIRATION FOR THAT ...?
APPROVED
WE HAVE DIVINE APPROVAL!
WOO! I'M GOING TO HEAD STRAIGHT BACK TO THE LAB TO GET STARTED!
THANK YOU FOR ALL YOUR HELP!
THE TIME ACCELERATOR'S FIXED NOW, TOO, SO I GUESS IT ALL WORKED OUT.
YES!
I'M SO GLAD EVERYTHING WAS RESOLVED WITHOUT ANYONE GETTING HURT!
NOW, LET'S HAVE SOME TEA!
...
ぬうう WEEEEEN ん
WHY IS ITS TORSO SO LONG...?
IT WAS A CONNECTION ERROR.

THE ENCYCLOPEDIA OF REAL ANIMALS 29

ANIMAL 71 | PIRANHA

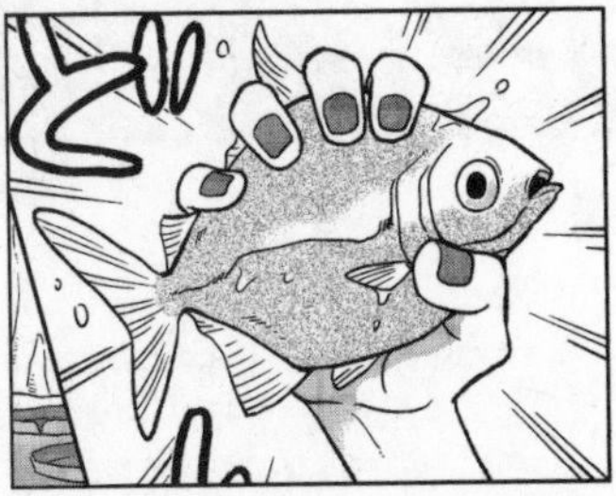

THE REAL THING

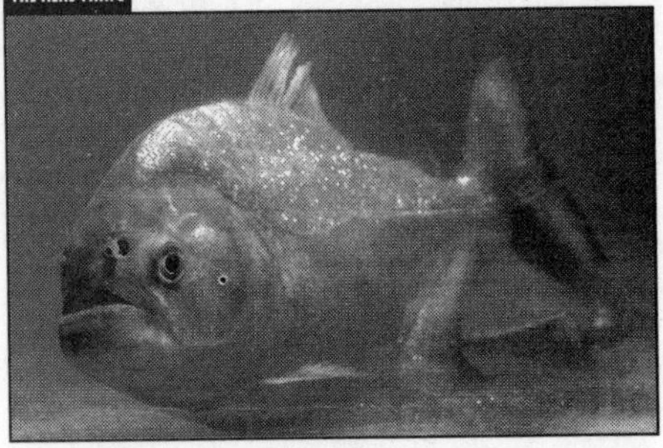

The illustration depicts an herbivorous metynnis, while the photo shows a carnivorous piranha.

Photo: Minden Pictures/Aflo

[Name]	Piranha
[Classification]	Class: Actinopterygii Order: Characiformes Family: Serrasalmidae
[Habitat]	Rivers of South America
[Length]	15-60 cm (6-24 in)

With its sharp teeth and powerful jaws, the piranha has earned a reputation as a fearsome predator and a role in horror films as "the man-eating fish of the Amazon." Contrary to its frightening image, the piranha is a generally timid and fearful fish. Rather than attacking large and healthy prey and leaving nothing but bones, the piranha often prefers to catch small prey from a hidden position or eat the fins and scales of other fish. It's wise to be careful, however, because it can be attracted by the scent of blood.

The "vegetarian piranha" introduced in this chapter is the metynnis, the piranha's close relative. The tribe's ancestor, the giant, omnivorous megapiranha, had a dentition similar to both the herbivorous metynnis and the carnivorous piranha. Some scientists believe the modern-day variety evolved from being herbivorous to omnivorous and then carnivorous over time.

ANIMAL 72

GIANT OTTER

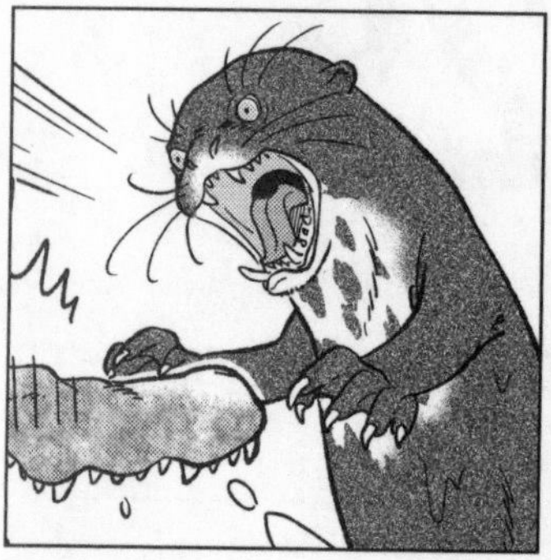

Contrary to its nickname "river wolf," the giant otter has a much scarier face than a wolf.

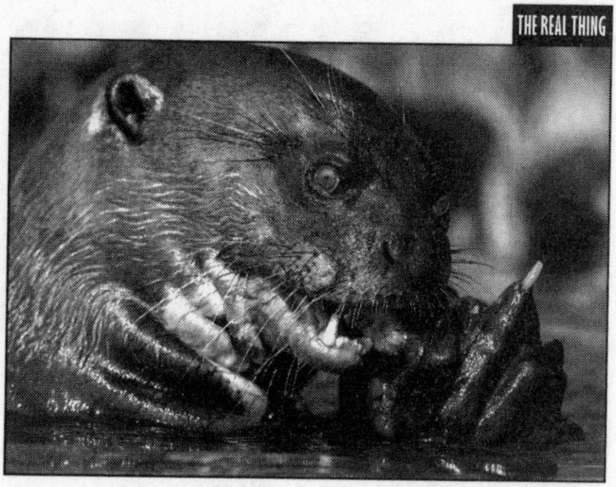
THE REAL THING

Photo: Minden Pictures/Aflo

The largest otter in the world, the giant otter was hunted to near-extinction for its fur, and its wild population is estimated to be in the low thousands. It swims gracefully in the rivers of South America using its webbed feat and wide, flat tail. The giant otter builds dens along the riverbed and among tree roots and gives birth to one to six pups at a time. It forms a family unit with a partner and the pair's pups, and remains in this group for life.

The species communicates via nine distinct vocalizations ranging from shrill screams to whistles. Its tendency to hunt in cooperative packs has earned it the nickname of "river wolf." A highly territorial animal, the giant otter will work together with its group members to mark the boundaries of its territory with their anal scent glands and patrol their area.

The giant otter has a varied diet, including fish, crustaceans, birds' eggs, snakes, small crocodilians, and aquatic mammals, and typically eats up to 3-4 kg (6.6-9 lbs) a day. Though it holds prey with its front paws, much like the other members of the Mustelidae family, it has none of its relatives' cuteness.

Its predators include large crocodilians and jaguars, which it combats with strongly cohesive social groups and the ability to maneuver with ease both on land and in water.

[Name]	*Pteronura brasiliensis*
[Classification]	Class: Mammalia Order: Carnivora Family: Mustelidae Genus: *Pteronura*
[Habitat]	Rivers of South America
[Length]	100-150 cm (3.3-5 ft)

HEAVEN'S DESIGN TEAM

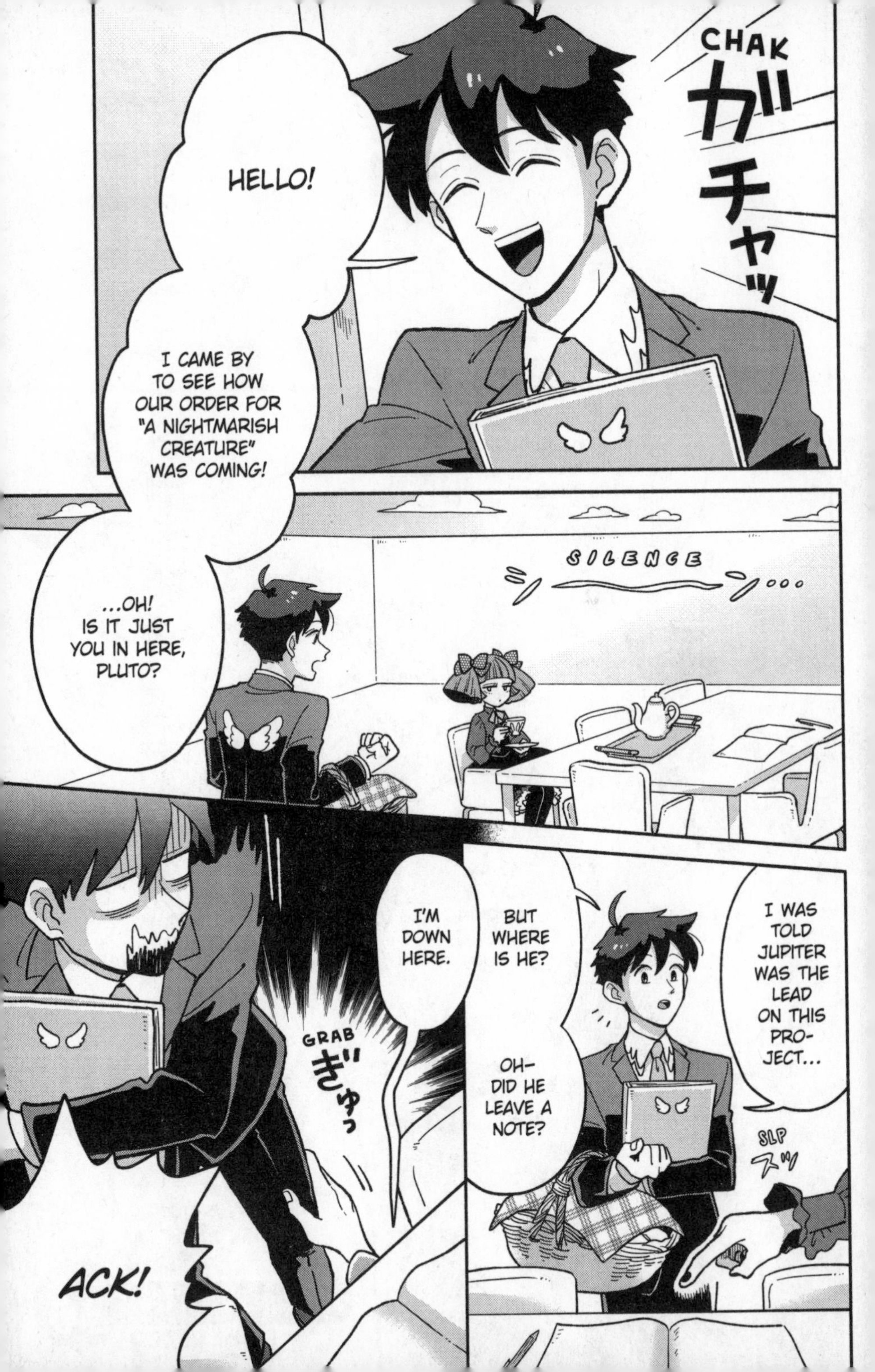
CHAK
ガチャッ
HELLO!
I CAME BY TO SEE HOW OUR ORDER FOR "A NIGHTMARISH CREATURE" WAS COMING!
SILENCE
...OH! IS IT JUST YOU IN HERE, PLUTO?
I WAS TOLD JUPITER WAS THE LEAD ON THIS PRO-JECT...
BUT WHERE IS HE?
OH- DID HE LEAVE A NOTE?
SLP
スッ
I'M DOWN HERE.
GRAB
ぎゅっ
ACK!

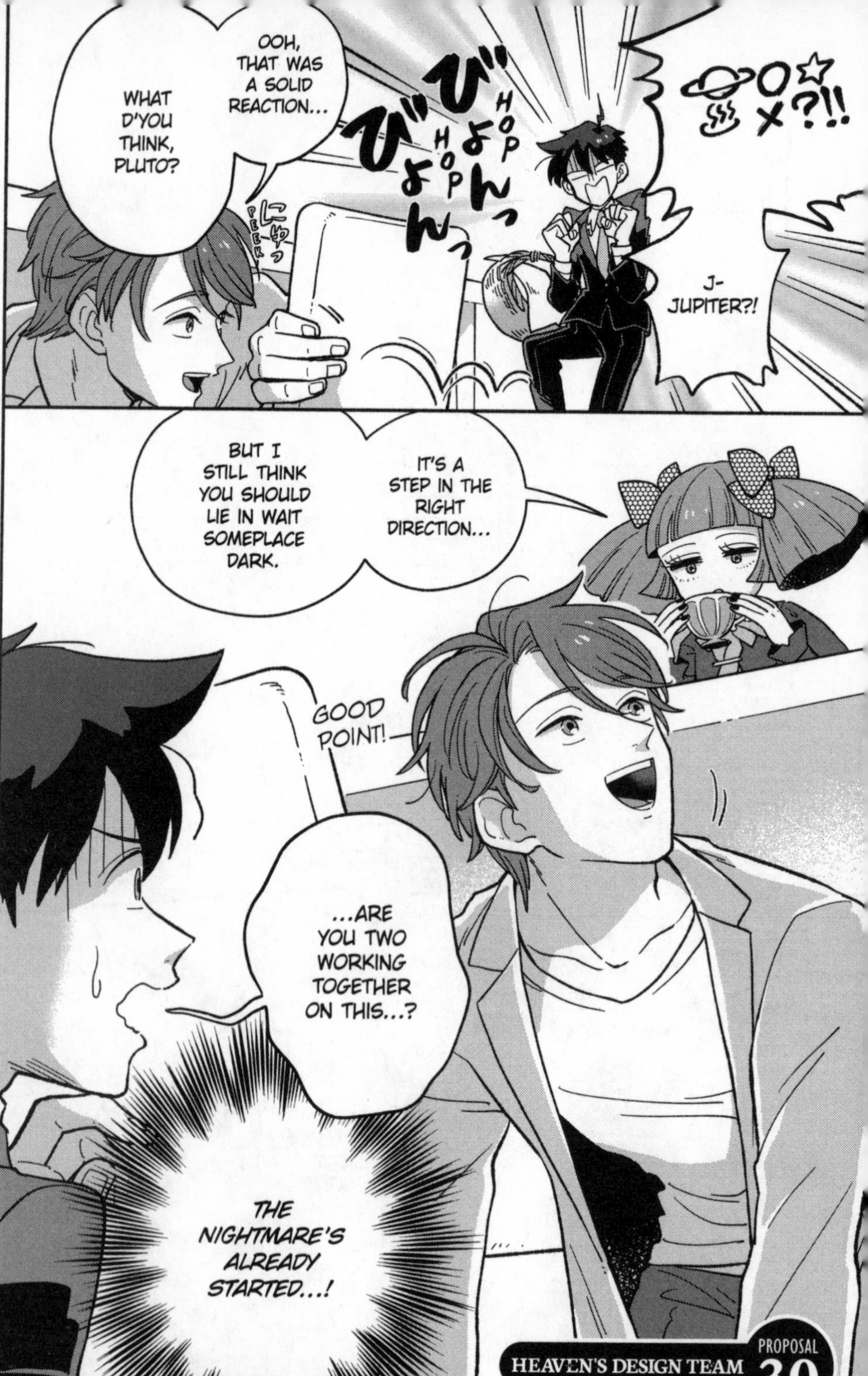

J-JUPITER?!
?!!
びよんっ HOP
びよんっ HOP
OOH, THAT WAS A SOLID REACTION...
WHAT D'YOU THINK, PLUTO?
にゅっ PEEK
IT'S A STEP IN THE RIGHT DIRECTION...
BUT I STILL THINK YOU SHOULD LIE IN WAIT SOMEPLACE DARK.
GOOD POINT!
...ARE YOU TWO WORKING TOGETHER ON THIS...?
THE NIGHTMARE'S ALREADY STARTED...!

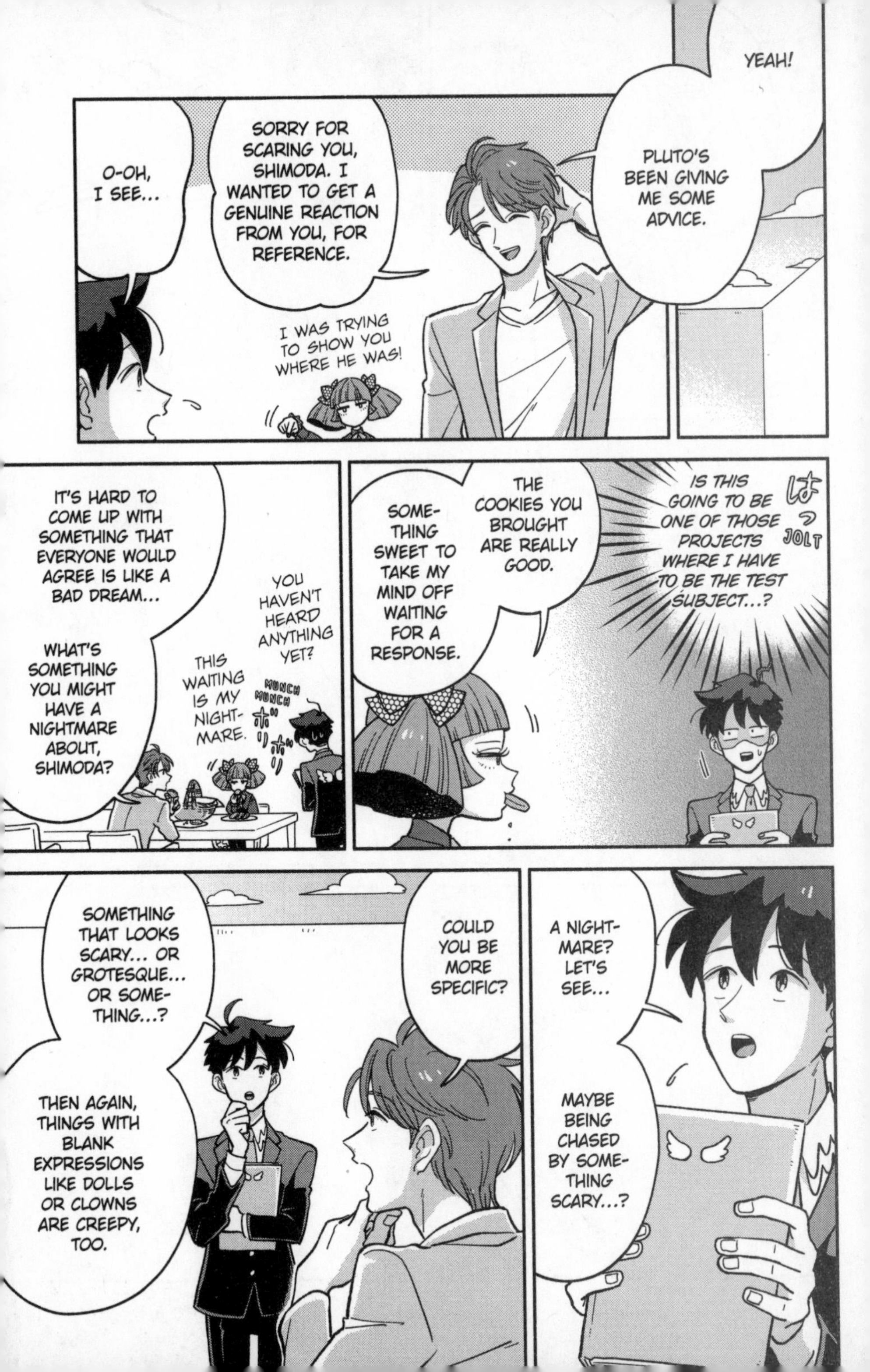
YEAH!
PLUTO'S BEEN GIVING ME SOME ADVICE.
SORRY FOR SCARING YOU, SHIMODA. I WANTED TO GET A GENUINE REACTION FROM YOU, FOR REFERENCE.
I WAS TRYING TO SHOW YOU WHERE HE WAS!
O-OH, I SEE...
はっ
JOLT
IS THIS GOING TO BE ONE OF THOSE PROJECTS WHERE I HAVE TO BE THE TEST SUBJECT...?
THE COOKIES YOU BROUGHT ARE REALLY GOOD.
SOME-THING SWEET TO TAKE MY MIND OFF WAITING FOR A RESPONSE.
IT'S HARD TO COME UP WITH SOMETHING THAT EVERYONE WOULD AGREE IS LIKE A BAD DREAM...
WHAT'S SOMETHING YOU MIGHT HAVE A NIGHTMARE ABOUT, SHIMODA?
YOU HAVEN'T HEARD ANYTHING YET?
THIS WAITING IS MY NIGHT-MARE.
MUNCH MUNCH
A NIGHT-MARE? LET'S SEE...
MAYBE BEING CHASED BY SOME-THING SCARY...?
COULD YOU BE MORE SPECIFIC?
SOMETHING THAT LOOKS SCARY... OR GROTESQUE... OR SOME-THING...?
THEN AGAIN, THINGS WITH BLANK EXPRESSIONS LIKE DOLLS OR CLOWNS ARE CREEPY, TOO.

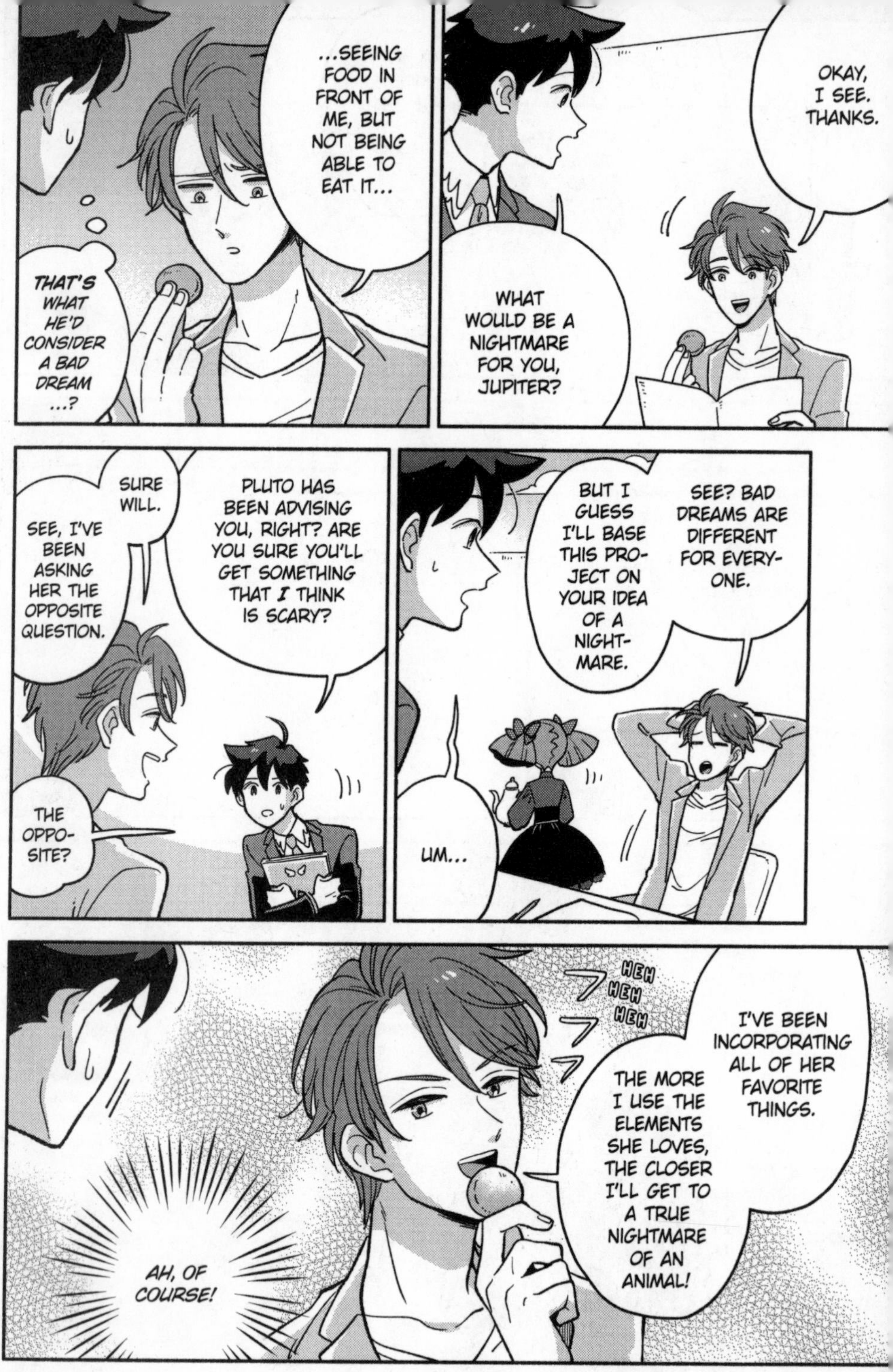
OKAY, I SEE. THANKS.
WHAT WOULD BE A NIGHTMARE FOR YOU, JUPITER?
...SEEING FOOD IN FRONT OF ME, BUT NOT BEING ABLE TO EAT IT...
THAT'S WHAT HE'D CONSIDER A BAD DREAM ...?
SEE? BAD DREAMS ARE DIFFERENT FOR EVERY-ONE.
BUT I GUESS I'LL BASE THIS PRO-JECT ON YOUR IDEA OF A NIGHT-MARE.
UM...
PLUTO HAS BEEN ADVISING YOU, RIGHT? ARE YOU SURE YOU'LL GET SOMETHING THAT I THINK IS SCARY?
SURE WILL.
SEE, I'VE BEEN ASKING HER THE OPPOSITE QUESTION.
THE OPPO-SITE?
I'VE BEEN INCORPORATING ALL OF HER FAVORITE THINGS.
HEH HEH HEH
THE MORE I USE THE ELEMENTS SHE LOVES, THE CLOSER I'LL GET TO A TRUE NIGHTMARE OF AN ANIMAL!
AH, OF COURSE!

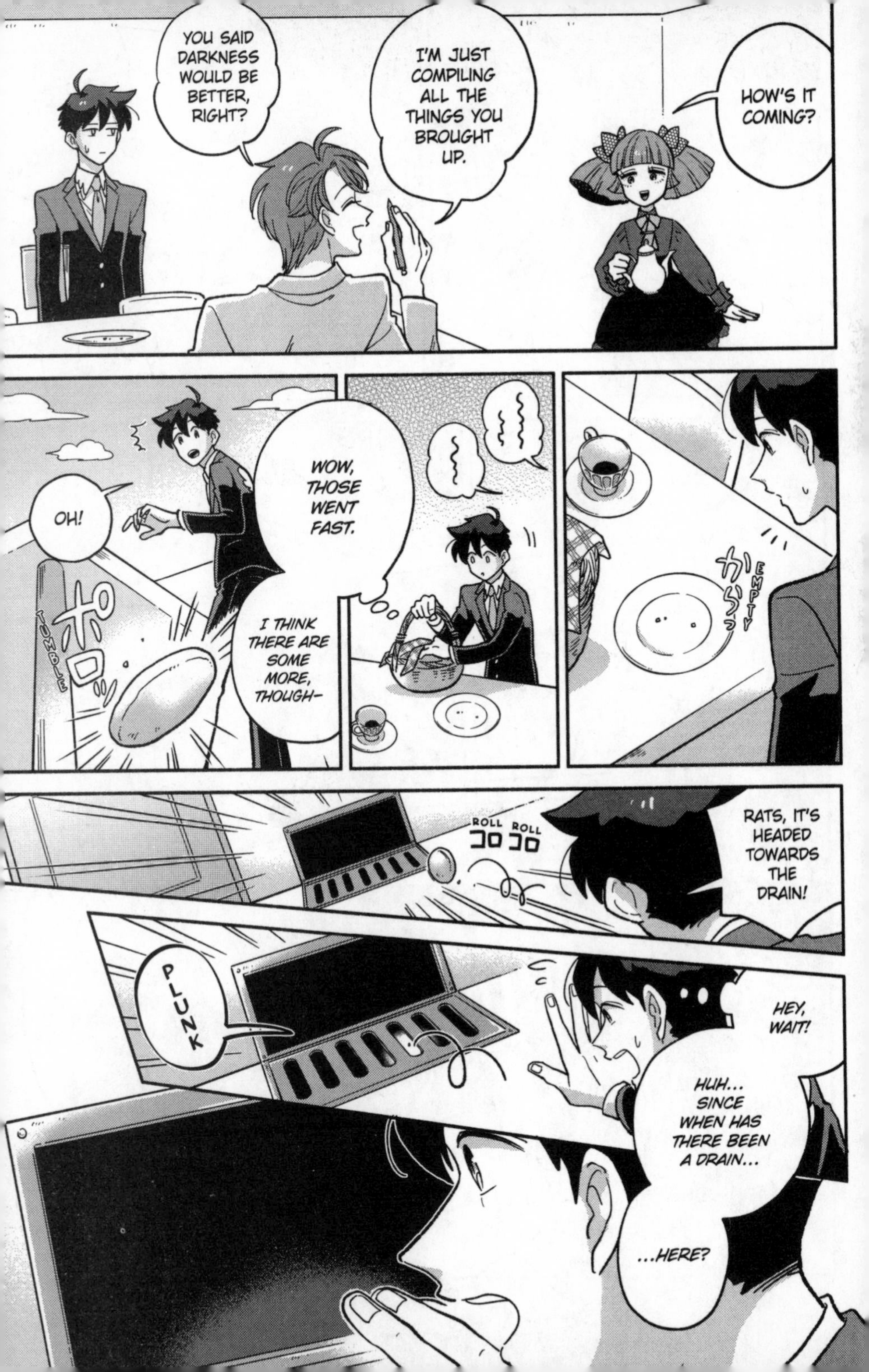
HOW'S IT COMING?
I'M JUST COMPILING ALL THE THINGS YOU BROUGHT UP.
YOU SAID DARKNESS WOULD BE BETTER, RIGHT?
EMPTY
からっ
WOW, THOSE WENT FAST.
I THINK THERE ARE SOME MORE, THOUGH-
OH!
TUMBLE
ポロ
RATS, IT'S HEADED TOWARDS THE DRAIN!
ROLL ROLL
コロコロ
HEY, WAIT!
PLUNK
HUH... SINCE WHEN HAS THERE BEEN A DRAIN...
...HERE?

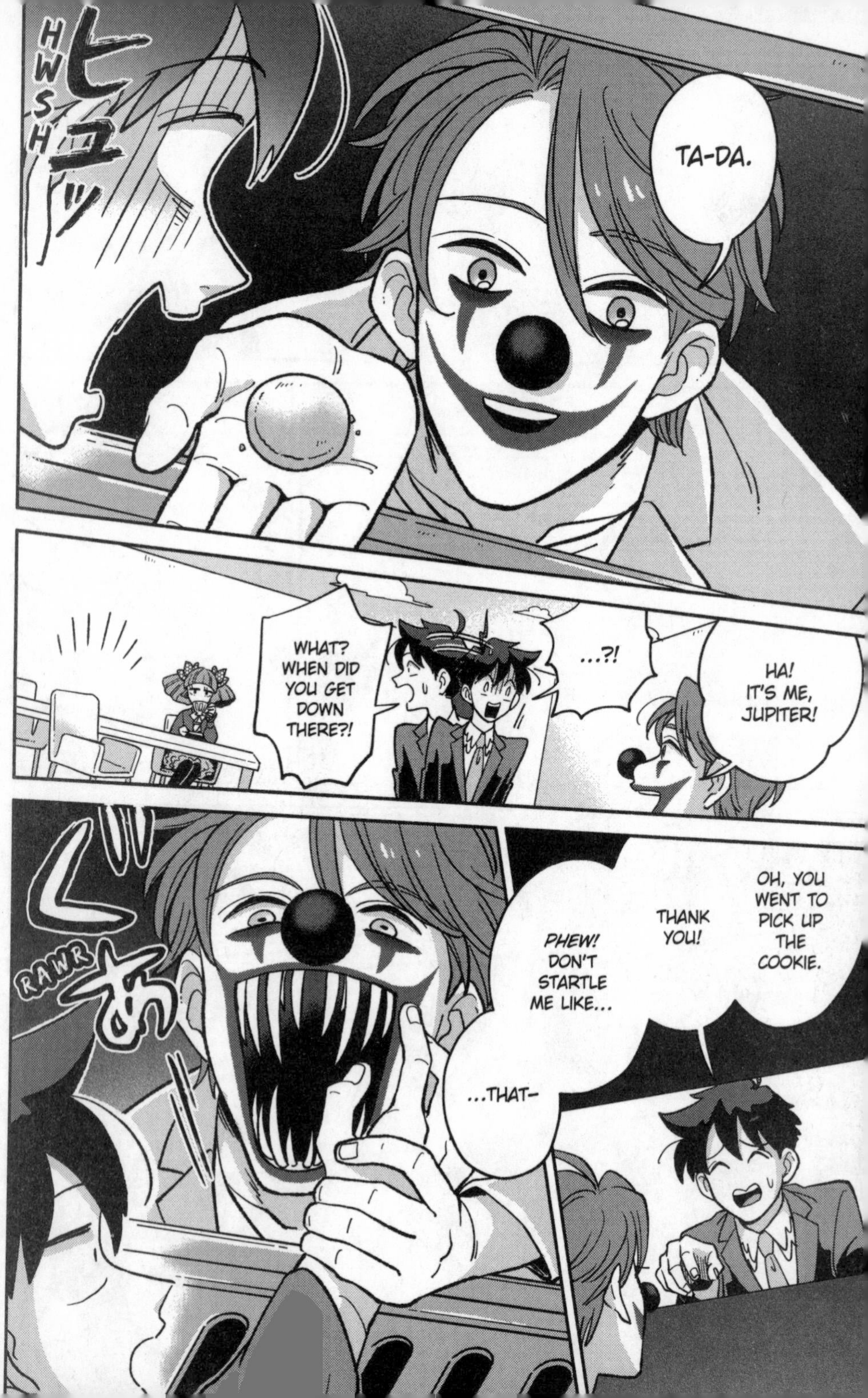
TA-DA.
HWSH
HA! IT'S ME, JUPITER!
...?!
WHAT? WHEN DID YOU GET DOWN THERE?!
OH, YOU WENT TO PICK UP THE COOKIE.
THANK YOU!
PHEW! DON'T STARTLE ME LIKE...
...THAT-
RAWR

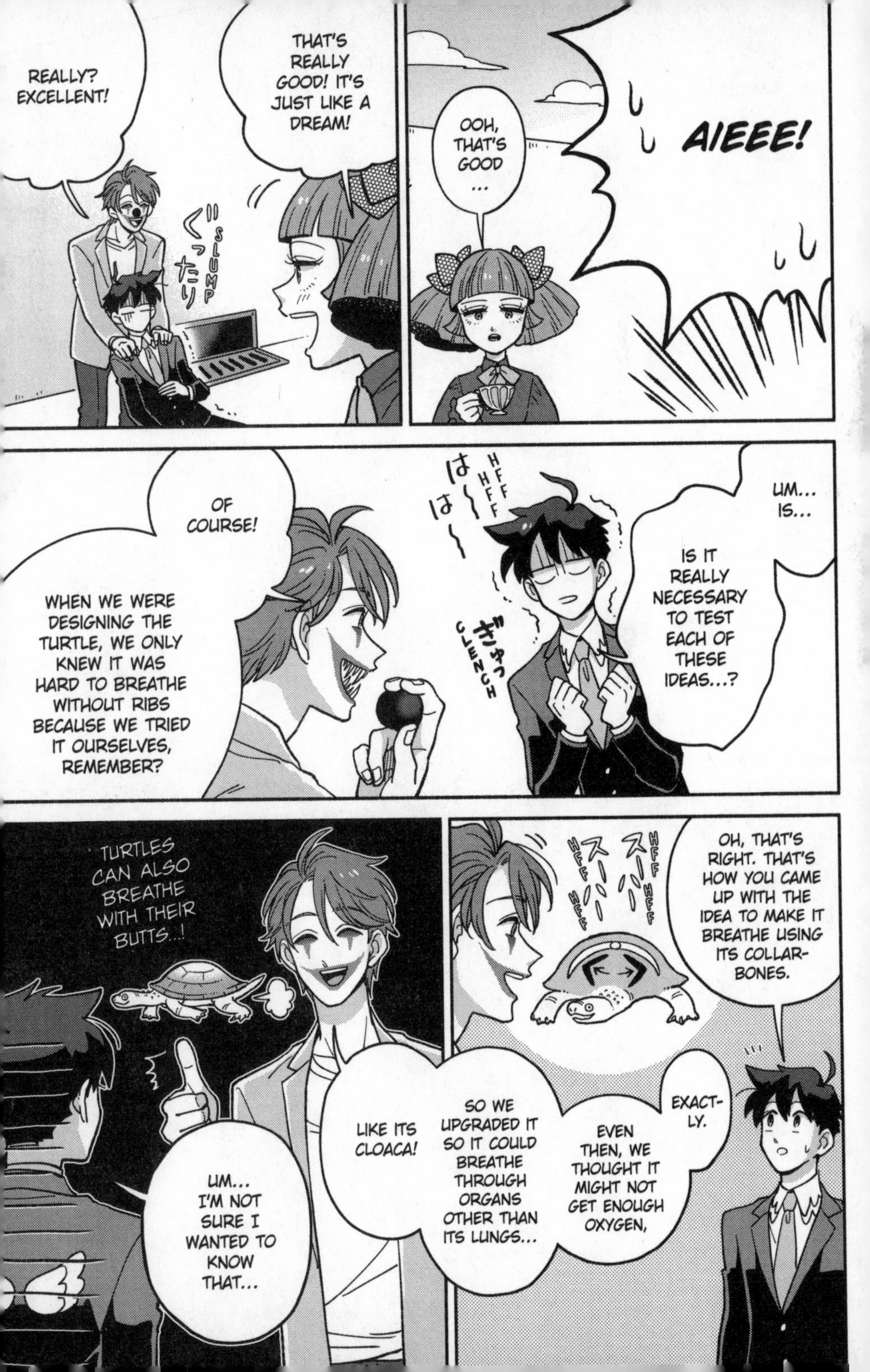
OOH, THAT'S GOOD ...
AIEEE!
THAT'S REALLY GOOD! IT'S JUST LIKE A DREAM!
REALLY? EXCELLENT!
くったり SLUMP
UM... IS...
IS IT REALLY NECESSARY TO TEST EACH OF THESE IDEAS...?
はー はー HFF HFF HFF
ぎゅっ CLENCH
OF COURSE!
WHEN WE WERE DESIGNING THE TURTLE, WE ONLY KNEW IT WAS HARD TO BREATHE WITHOUT RIBS BECAUSE WE TRIED IT OURSELVES, REMEMBER?
OH, THAT'S RIGHT. THAT'S HOW YOU CAME UP WITH THE IDEA TO MAKE IT BREATHE USING ITS COLLAR-BONES.
スーハー HFF HFF HFF HFF
EXACT-LY.
EVEN THEN, WE THOUGHT IT MIGHT NOT GET ENOUGH OXYGEN,
SO WE UPGRADED IT SO IT COULD BREATHE THROUGH ORGANS OTHER THAN ITS LUNGS...
LIKE ITS CLOACA!
TURTLES CAN ALSO BREATHE WITH THEIR BUTTS...!
UM... I'M NOT SURE I WANTED TO KNOW THAT...

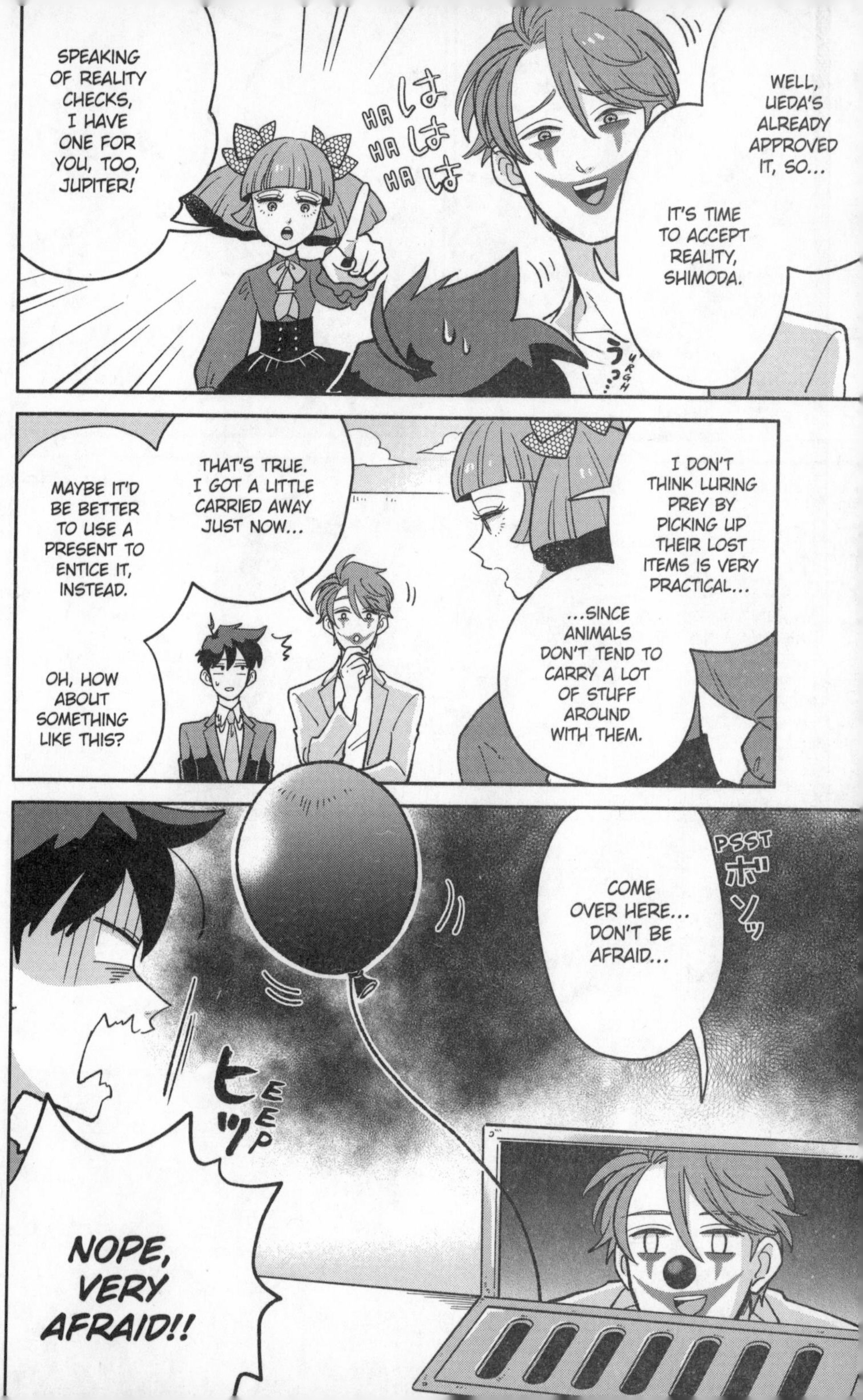
WELL, UEDA'S ALREADY APPROVED IT, SO...
IT'S TIME TO ACCEPT REALITY, SHIMODA.
う… URGH
ははは HA HA HA
SPEAKING OF REALITY CHECKS, I HAVE ONE FOR YOU, TOO, JUPITER!
I DON'T THINK LURING PREY BY PICKING UP THEIR LOST ITEMS IS VERY PRACTICAL...
...SINCE ANIMALS DON'T TEND TO CARRY A LOT OF STUFF AROUND WITH THEM.
THAT'S TRUE. I GOT A LITTLE CARRIED AWAY JUST NOW...
MAYBE IT'D BE BETTER TO USE A PRESENT TO ENTICE IT, INSTEAD.
OH, HOW ABOUT SOMETHING LIKE THIS?
ボソッ PSST
COME OVER HERE... DON'T BE AFRAID...
ヒッ EEEP
NOPE, VERY AFRAID!!

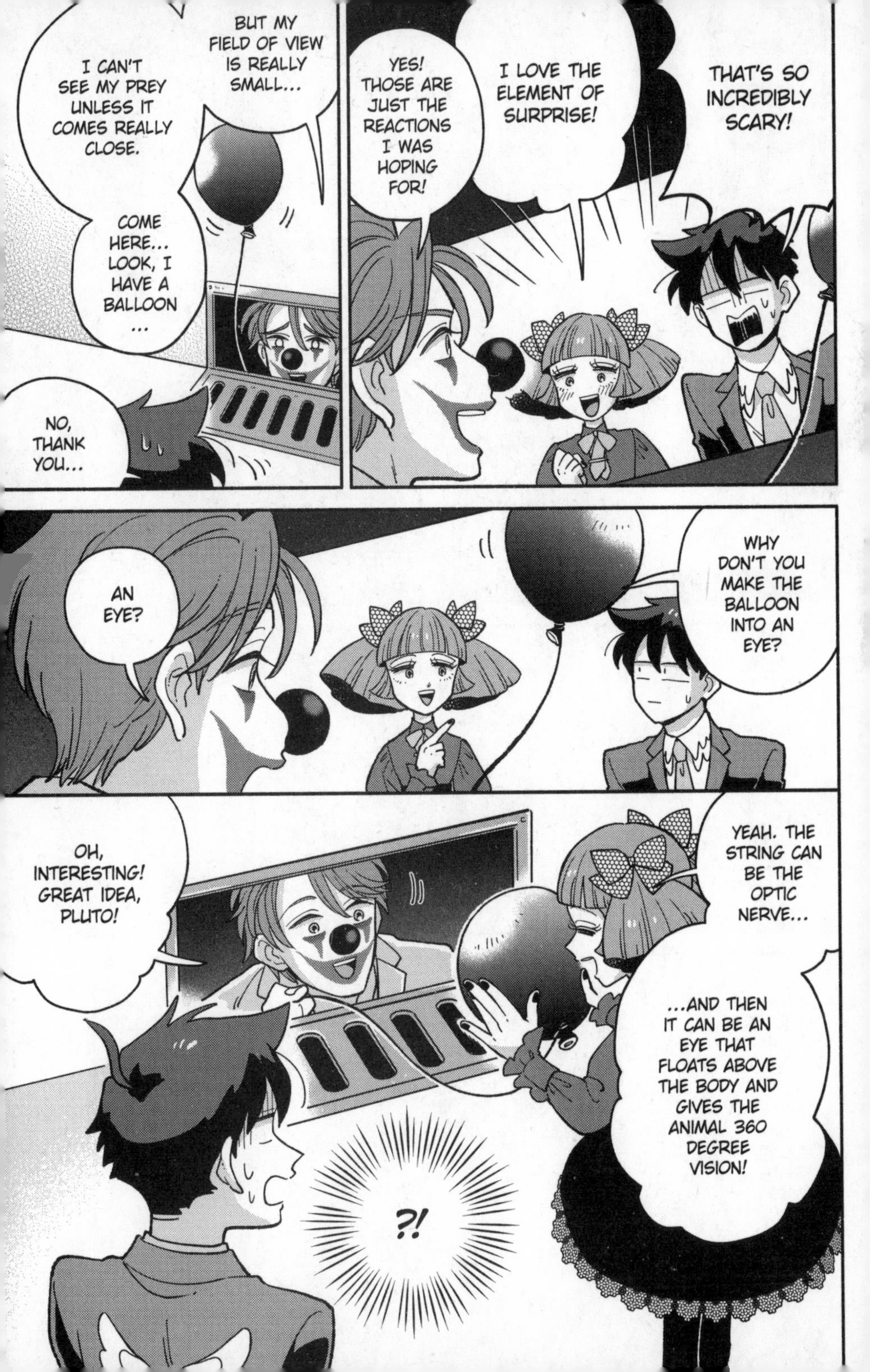
THAT'S SO INCREDIBLY SCARY!
I LOVE THE ELEMENT OF SURPRISE!
YES! THOSE ARE JUST THE REACTIONS I WAS HOPING FOR!
BUT MY FIELD OF VIEW IS REALLY SMALL...
I CAN'T SEE MY PREY UNLESS IT COMES REALLY CLOSE.
COME HERE... LOOK, I HAVE A BALLOON ...
NO, THANK YOU...
WHY DON'T YOU MAKE THE BALLOON INTO AN EYE?
AN EYE?
YEAH. THE STRING CAN BE THE OPTIC NERVE...
...AND THEN IT CAN BE AN EYE THAT FLOATS ABOVE THE BODY AND GIVES THE ANIMAL 360 DEGREE VISION!
OH, INTERESTING! GREAT IDEA, PLUTO!
?!

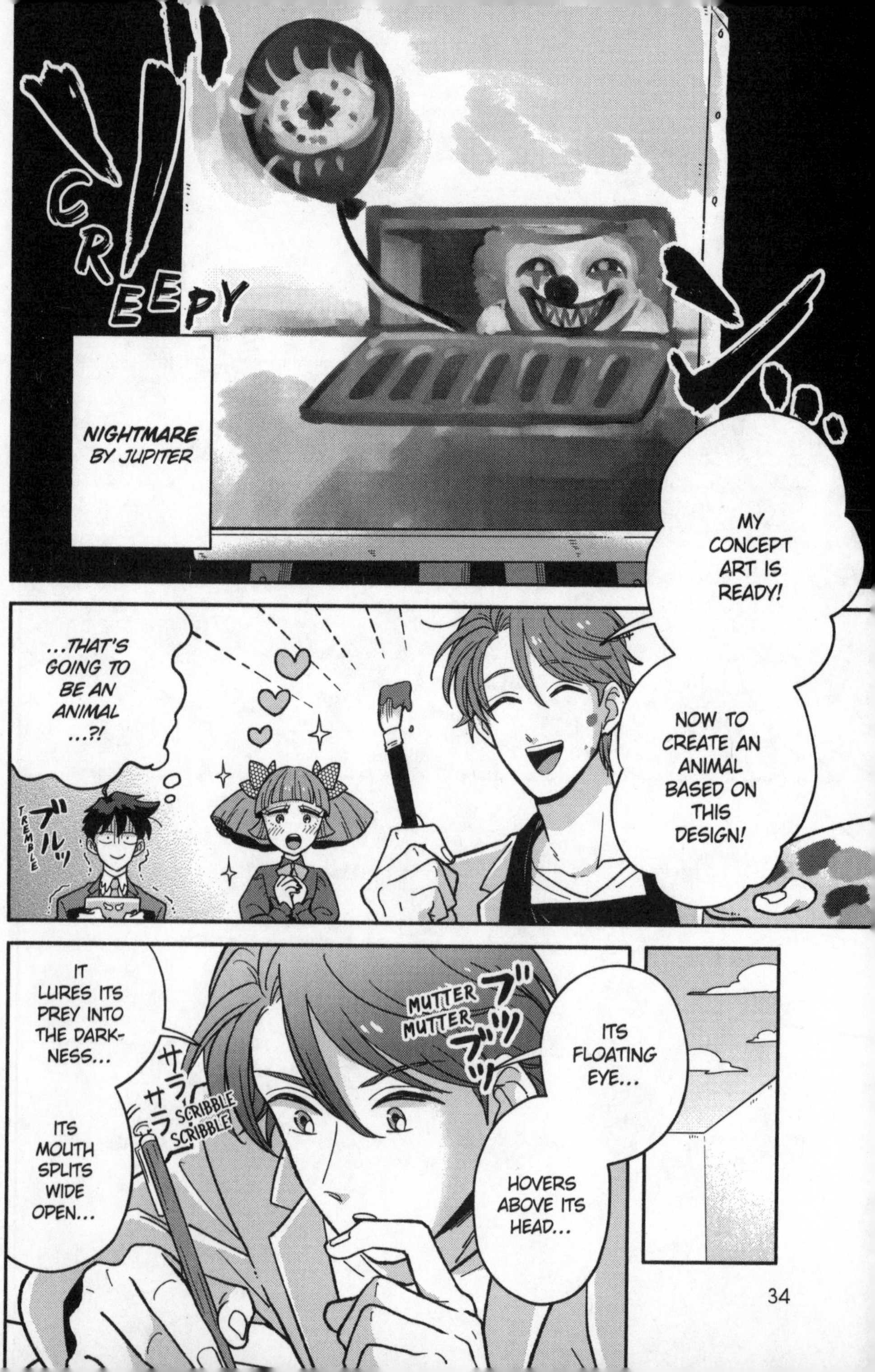
CREEPY
NIGHTMARE BY JUPITER
MY CONCEPT ART IS READY!
NOW TO CREATE AN ANIMAL BASED ON THIS DESIGN!
...THAT'S GOING TO BE AN ANIMAL ...?!
TREMBLE ブルッ
ITS FLOATING EYE...
HOVERS ABOVE ITS HEAD...
MUTTER MUTTER ブツブツ
IT LURES ITS PREY INTO THE DARK-NESS...
ITS MOUTH SPLITS WIDE OPEN...
SCRIBBLE SCRIBBLE サラサラ

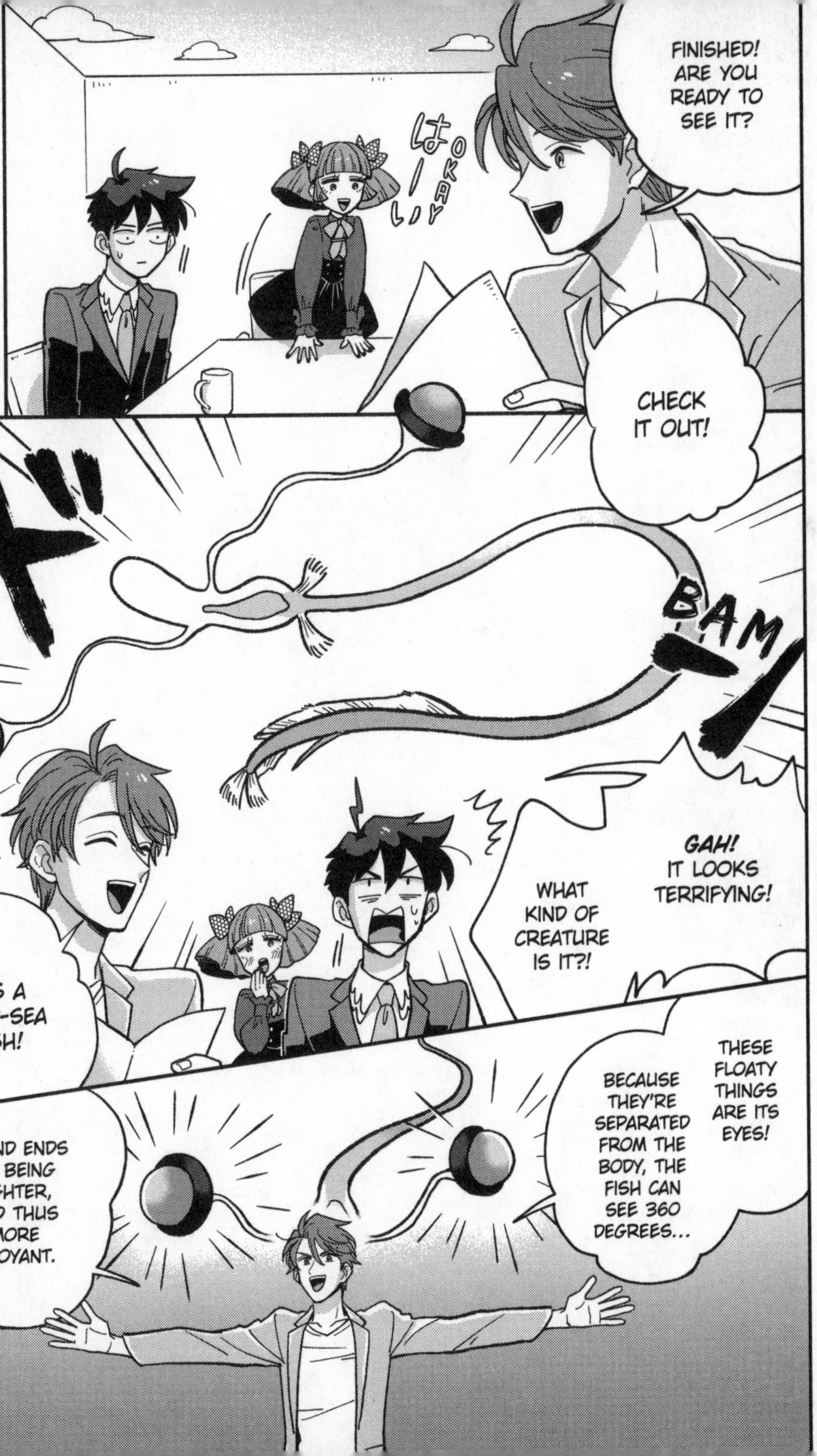
FINISHED! ARE YOU READY TO SEE IT?
はーい OKAY
CHECK IT OUT!
ド
BAM
GAH! IT LOOKS TERRIFYING!
WHAT KIND OF CREATURE IS IT?!
IT'S A DEEP-SEA FISH!
THESE FLOATY THINGS ARE ITS EYES!
BECAUSE THEY'RE SEPARATED FROM THE BODY, THE FISH CAN SEE 360 DEGREES...
...AND ENDS UP BEING LIGHTER, AND THUS MORE BUOYANT.

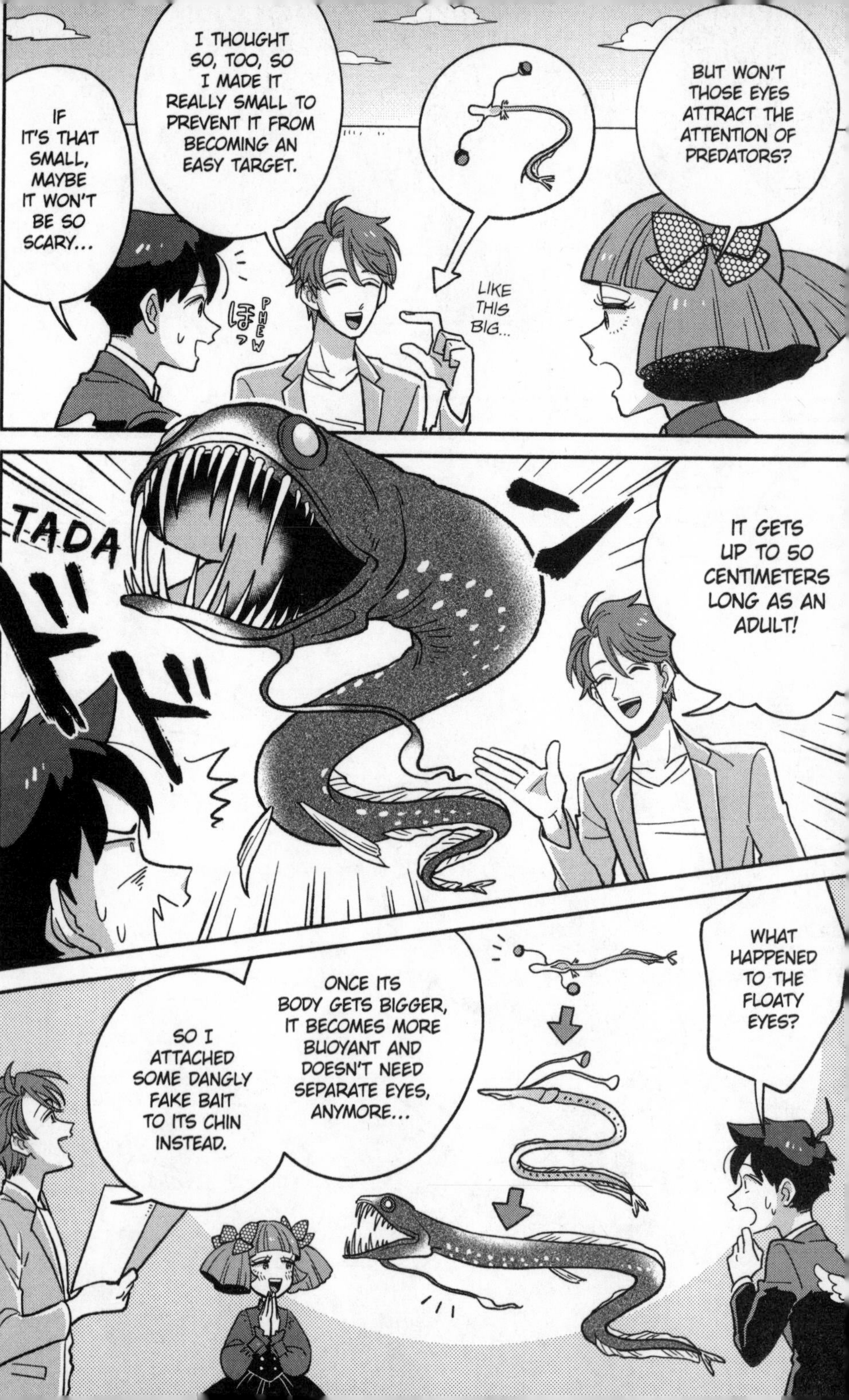
BUT WON'T THOSE EYES ATTRACT THE ATTENTION OF PREDATORS?
I THOUGHT SO, TOO, SO I MADE IT REALLY SMALL TO PREVENT IT FROM BECOMING AN EASY TARGET.
LIKE THIS BIG...
IF IT'S THAT SMALL, MAYBE IT WON'T BE SO SCARY...
ほっ PHEW
IT GETS UP TO 50 CENTIMETERS LONG AS AN ADULT!
TADA
ドド
WHAT HAPPENED TO THE FLOATY EYES?
ONCE ITS BODY GETS BIGGER, IT BECOMES MORE BUOYANT AND DOESN'T NEED SEPARATE EYES, ANYMORE...
SO I ATTACHED SOME DANGLY FAKE BAIT TO ITS CHIN INSTEAD.

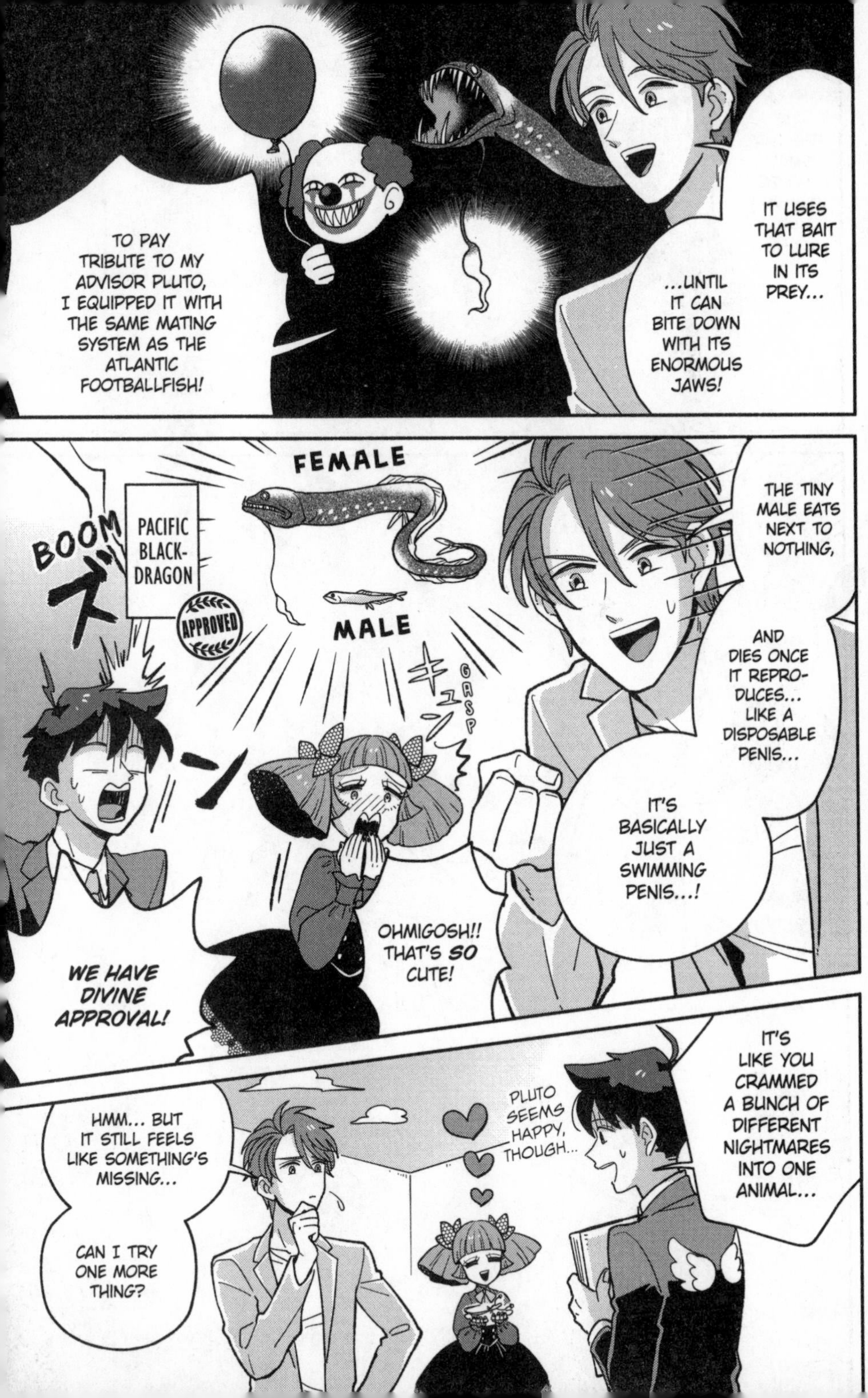
IT USES THAT BAIT TO LURE IN ITS PREY...
...UNTIL IT CAN BITE DOWN WITH ITS ENORMOUS JAWS!
TO PAY TRIBUTE TO MY ADVISOR PLUTO, I EQUIPPED IT WITH THE SAME MATING SYSTEM AS THE ATLANTIC FOOTBALLFISH!
THE TINY MALE EATS NEXT TO NOTHING,
AND DIES ONCE IT REPRODUCES... LIKE A DISPOSABLE PENIS...
IT'S BASICALLY JUST A SWIMMING PENIS...!
FEMALE
MALE
GASP
OHMIGOSH!! THAT'S *SO* CUTE!
PACIFIC BLACK-DRAGON
APPROVED
BOOM
WE HAVE DIVINE APPROVAL!
IT'S LIKE YOU CRAMMED A BUNCH OF DIFFERENT NIGHTMARES INTO ONE ANIMAL...
PLUTO SEEMS HAPPY, THOUGH...
HMM... BUT IT STILL FEELS LIKE SOMETHING'S MISSING...
CAN I TRY ONE MORE THING?

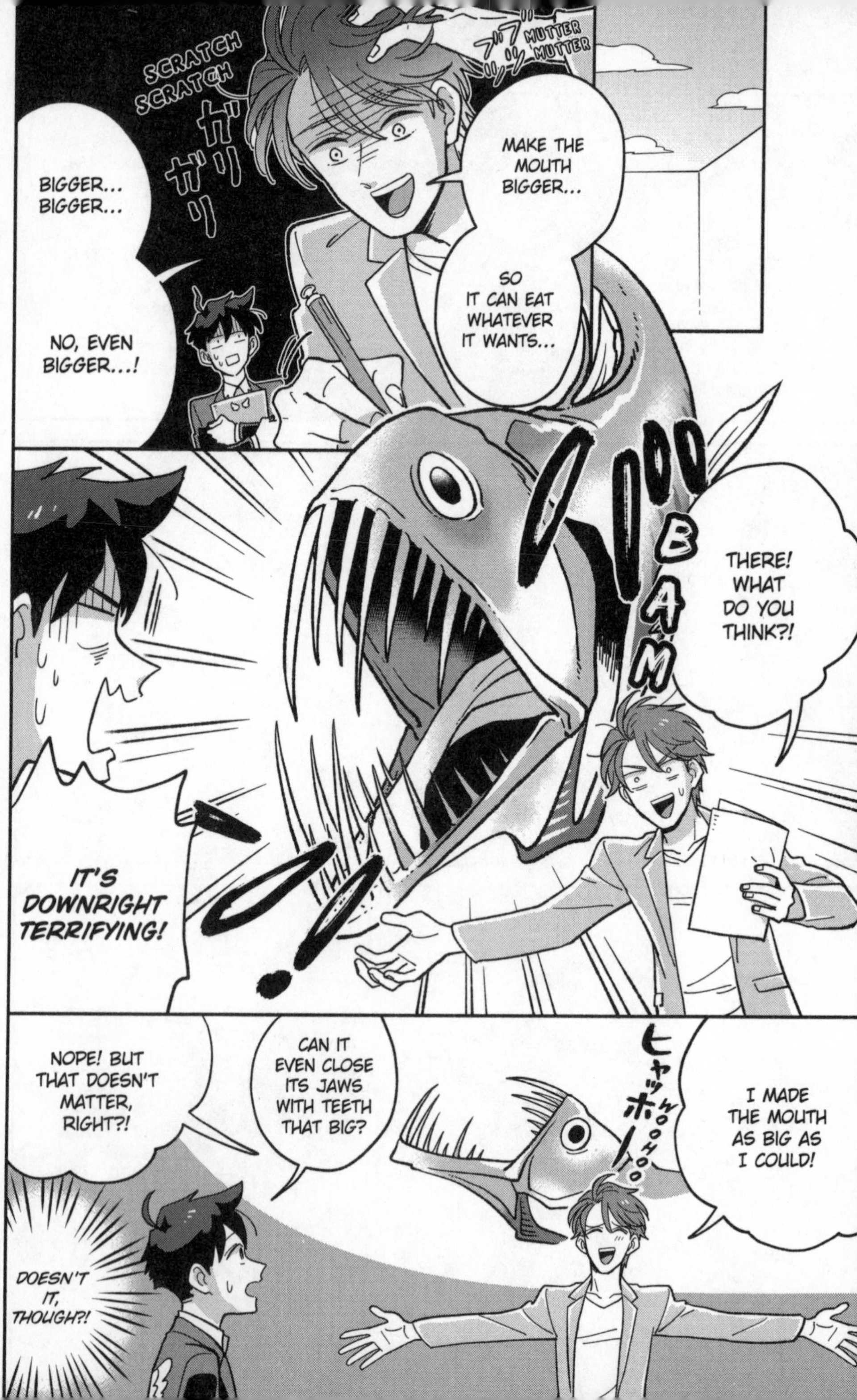
ブツブツ
MUTTER MUTTER
MAKE THE MOUTH BIGGER...
SO IT CAN EAT WHATEVER IT WANTS...
SCRATCH SCRATCH
ガリガリ
BIGGER... BIGGER...
NO, EVEN BIGGER...!
THERE! WHAT DO YOU THINK?!
BAM
IT'S DOWNRIGHT TERRIFYING!
I MADE THE MOUTH AS BIG AS I COULD!
ヒャッホー
WOOHOO
CAN IT EVEN CLOSE ITS JAWS WITH TEETH THAT BIG?
NOPE! BUT THAT DOESN'T MATTER, RIGHT?!
DOESN'T IT, THOUGH?!

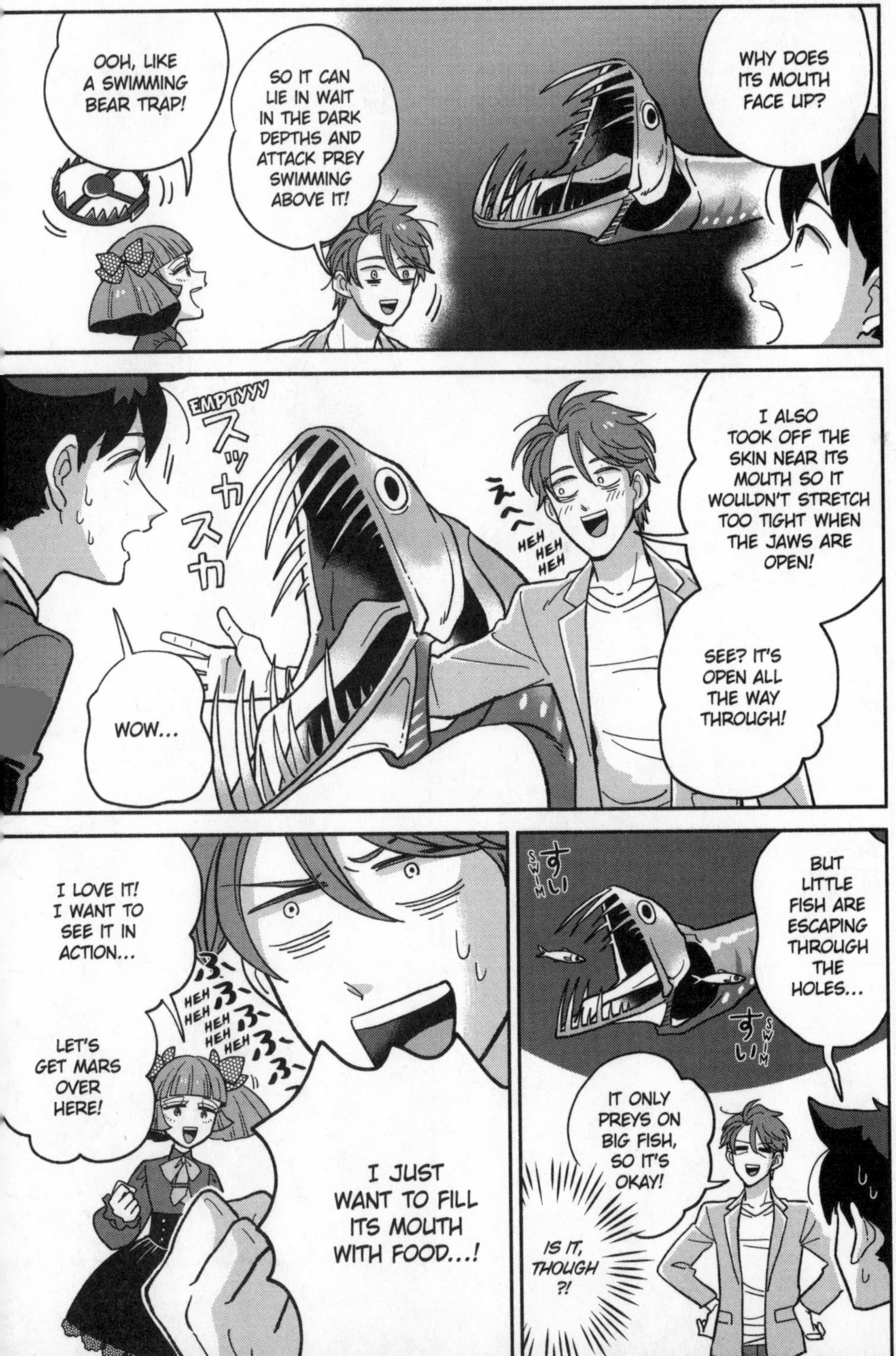

WHY DOES ITS MOUTH FACE UP?
SO IT CAN LIE IN WAIT IN THE DARK DEPTHS AND ATTACK PREY SWIMMING ABOVE IT!
OOH, LIKE A SWIMMING BEAR TRAP!
I ALSO TOOK OFF THE SKIN NEAR ITS MOUTH SO IT WOULDN'T STRETCH TOO TIGHT WHEN THE JAWS ARE OPEN!
SEE? IT'S OPEN ALL THE WAY THROUGH!
えへへ HEH HEH HEH
EMPTYYY スッカスカ
WOW...
BUT LITTLE FISH ARE ESCAPING THROUGH THE HOLES...
すい SWIM
すい SWIM
IT ONLY PREYS ON BIG FISH, SO IT'S OKAY!
IS IT, THOUGH ?!
I LOVE IT! I WANT TO SEE IT IN ACTION...
ふふふふ HEH HEH HEH HEH HEH
LET'S GET MARS OVER HERE!
I JUST WANT TO FILL ITS MOUTH WITH FOOD...!

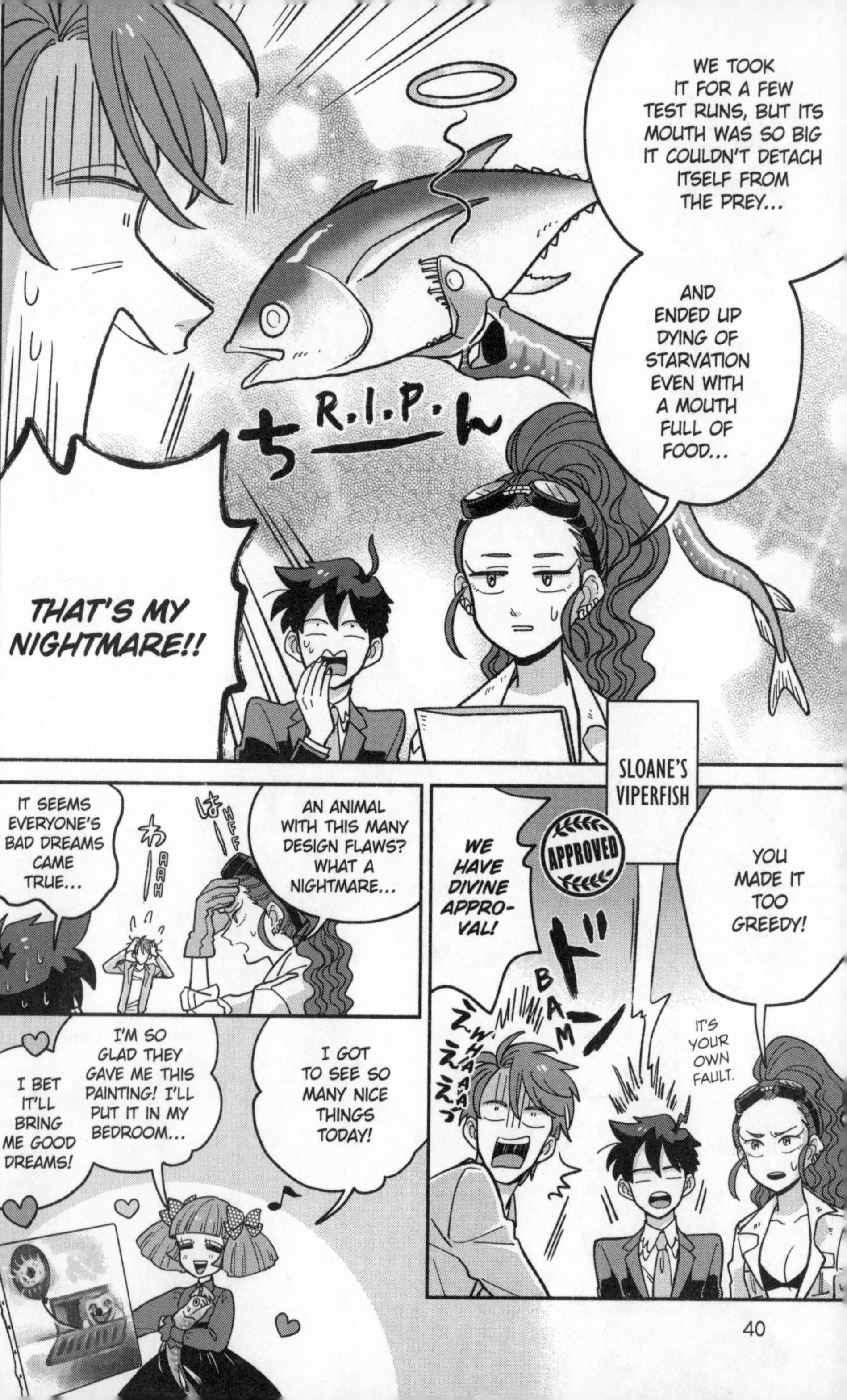
WE TOOK IT FOR A FEW TEST RUNS, BUT ITS MOUTH WAS SO BIG IT COULDN'T DETACH ITSELF FROM THE PREY...
AND ENDED UP DYING OF STARVATION EVEN WITH A MOUTH FULL OF FOOD...
R.I.P.
THAT'S MY NIGHTMARE!!
SLOANE'S VIPERFISH
YOU MADE IT TOO GREEDY!
APPROVED
WE HAVE DIVINE APPROVAL!
BAM
IT'S YOUR OWN FAULT.
WHAAAA
AN ANIMAL WITH THIS MANY DESIGN FLAWS? WHAT A NIGHTMARE...
HFF
AAAH
IT SEEMS EVERYONE'S BAD DREAMS CAME TRUE...
I GOT TO SEE SO MANY NICE THINGS TODAY!
I'M SO GLAD THEY GAVE ME THIS PAINTING! I'LL PUT IT IN MY BEDROOM...
I BET IT'LL BRING ME GOOD DREAMS!

THE ENCYCLOPEDIA OF
REAL ANIMALS 30

| ANIMAL 73 | SLOANE'S VIPERFISH |

THE REAL THING

Photophores line the sides of Sloane's viperfish like an electric signboard.

Photo: Minden Pictures/Aflo

Sloane's viperfish swings its elongated dorsal spine like a fishing rod and uses the photophore attached to the end to attract prey. Its hunting technique involves more than simply opening its massive jaws, however. When prey gets close enough, *C. sloani* throws back its head and shoves its lower jaw forward, thrusting its long fangs to impale its victim. The second it secures its target, it returns its head to its original position, which crams the prey into its mouth. Thanks to this unusual action, Sloane's viperfish can swallow prey much larger than itself.

In order to make head movement easier, *C. sloani*'s spine is atrophied near its head, and when its mouth is fully open, its lower jawbone detaches. Some stories describe Sloane's viperfish catching prey too big to swallow and dying of starvation while its meal is still in its jaws.

[Name]	*Chauliodus sloani*
[Classification]	Class: Actinopterygii
	Order: Stomiiformes
	Family: Stomiidae
	Genus: *Chauliodus*
[Habitat]	Deep seas at depths of 500-2,800 m (1,640-9,186 ft)
[Length]	Approximately 35 cm (14 in)

| # PACIFIC BLACKDRAGON

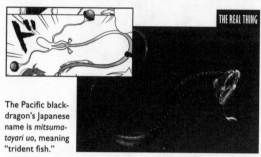

THE REAL THING

The Pacific black-dragon's Japanese name is *mitsuma-tayari uo*, meaning "trident fish."

Photo: Minden Pictures/Aflo

[Name]	*Idiacanthus antrostomus*
[Classification]	Class: Actinopterygii
	Order: Stomiiformes
	Family: Stomiidae
	Genus: *Idiacanthus*
[Habitat]	Deep seas at depths of 500-2,800 m (1,640-9,186 ft)
[Length]	4-50 cm (1.6-20 in)

In its larval stage, the Pacific blackdragon's eyes dangle at the end of long stalks, giving it a distinctive appearance. When it reaches adulthood, the stalks shrink and the eyes assume a fixed position; then, the mouth develops to an abnormal size. This deep sea fish almost resembles a shapeshifting monster.

Its scale-less skin is dark black all over, and it uses the photophore at the end of its chin barbel to lure prey. Females can grow up to 50 cm (20 in), while the males only reach a maximum length of 5 cm (2 in).

SPECIAL FEATURE | BUTT-BREATHING TURTLES

A turtle's shell is an adaptation of its ribs. While the hard shell offers protection for its body, it sacrifices the ability to inflate and deflate the lungs for breathing. As a result of this, some species have developed specialized techniques to breathe. Certain turtles that live primarily in water, for example, can breathe not only using their lungs, but also through their skin, or a posterior orifice. This all-purpose hole, called a "cloaca," can contain their digestive and reproductive tracts. Turtles with this adaptation pull water through their cloacas and into pouch-like organs, which absorb oxygen from the water.

TURTLES CAN ALSO BREATHE WITH THEIR BUTTS...!

The Fitzroy River turtle pictured above has an unusually large cloaca and is a highly adept cloacal breather.

HEAVEN'S DESIGN TEAM

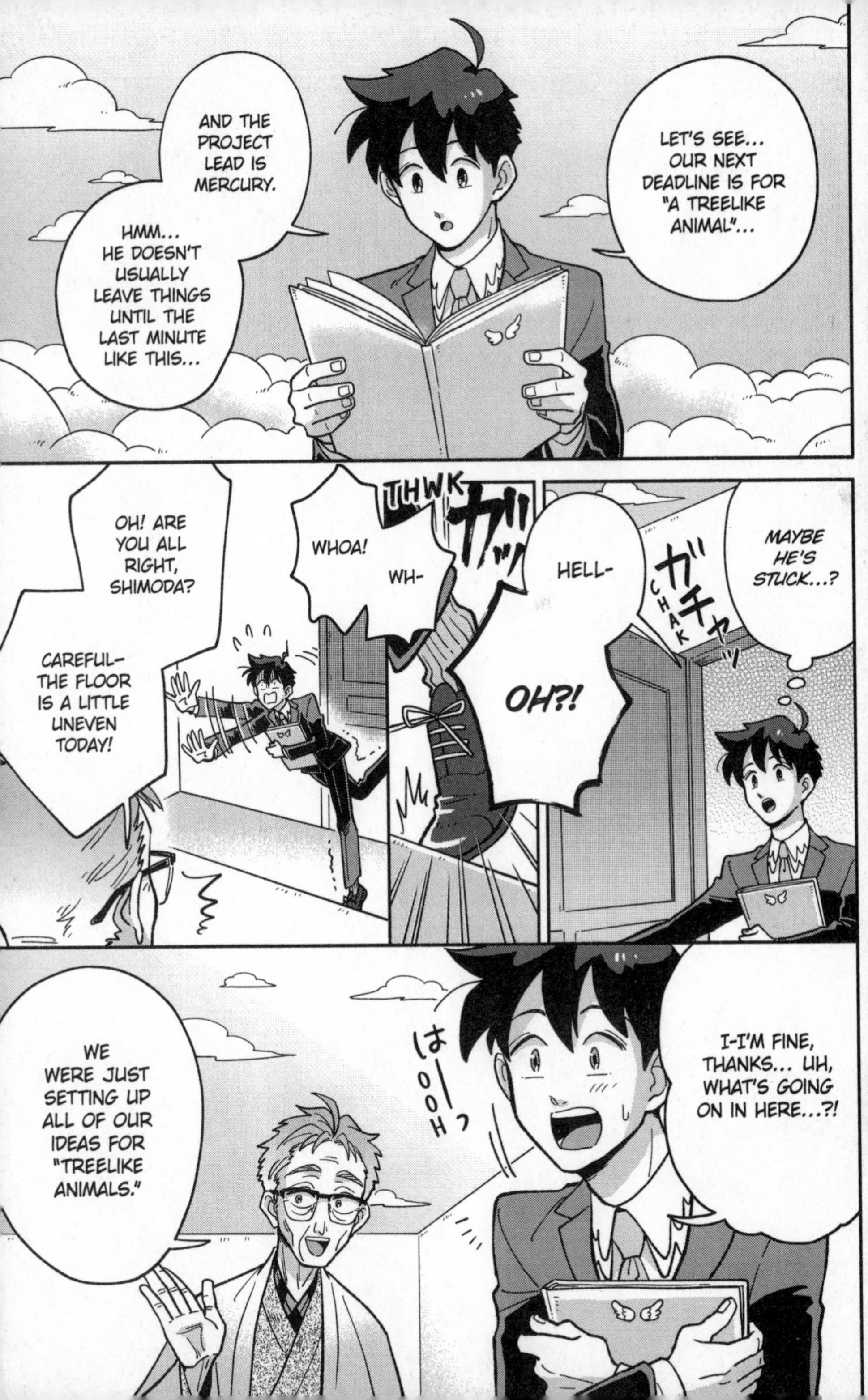
LET'S SEE… OUR NEXT DEADLINE IS FOR "A TREELIKE ANIMAL"…
AND THE PROJECT LEAD IS MERCURY.
HMM… HE DOESN'T USUALLY LEAVE THINGS UNTIL THE LAST MINUTE LIKE THIS…
MAYBE HE'S STUCK…?
CHAK ガチャッ
HELL-
OH?!
THWK ガッ
WHOA!
WH-
OH! ARE YOU ALL RIGHT, SHIMODA?
CAREFUL- THE FLOOR IS A LITTLE UNEVEN TODAY!
I-I'M FINE, THANKS… UH, WHAT'S GOING ON IN HERE…?!
HOOH はーっ
WE WERE JUST SETTING UP ALL OF OUR IDEAS FOR "TREELIKE ANIMALS."

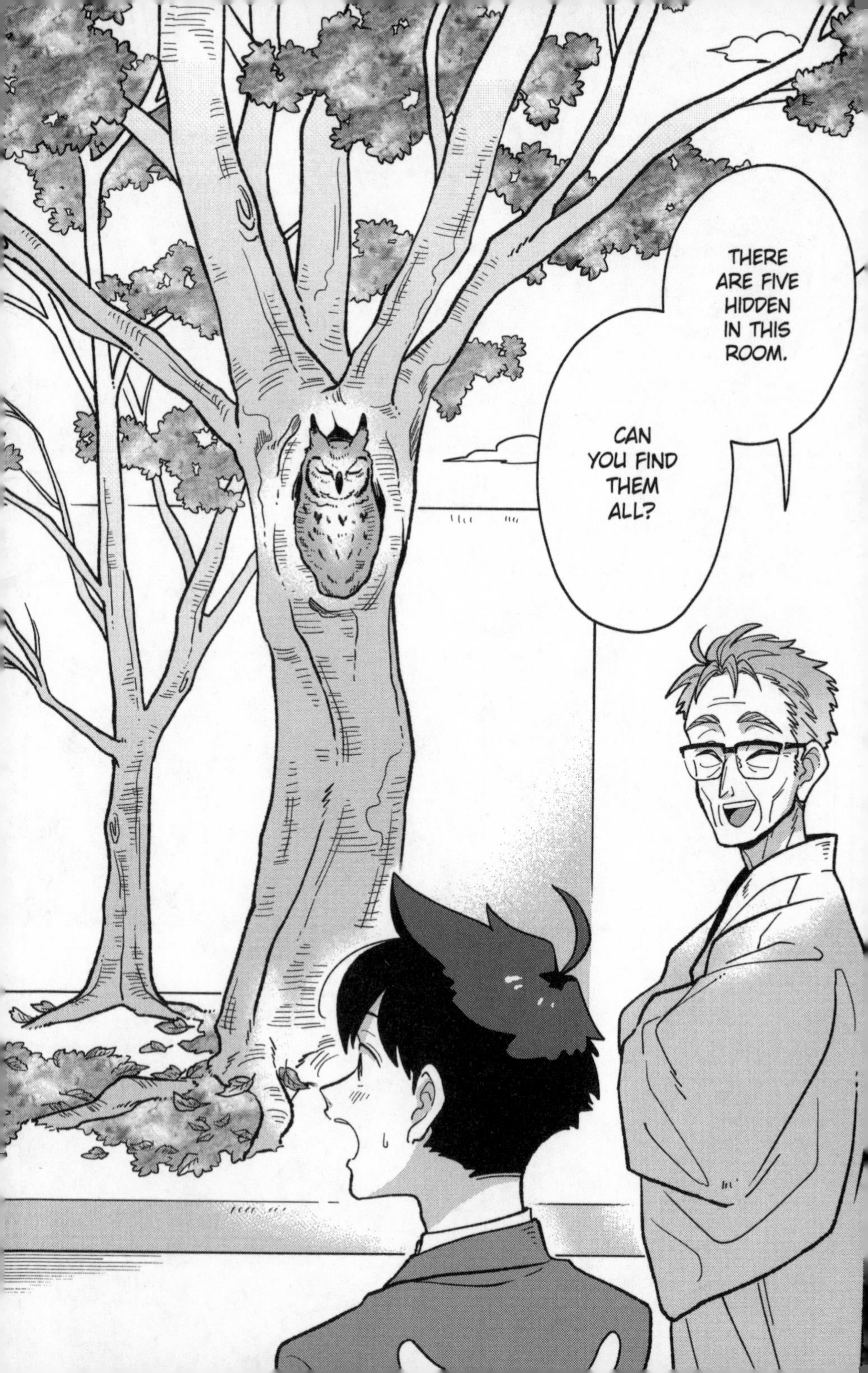
THERE ARE FIVE HIDDEN IN THIS ROOM.
CAN YOU FIND THEM ALL?

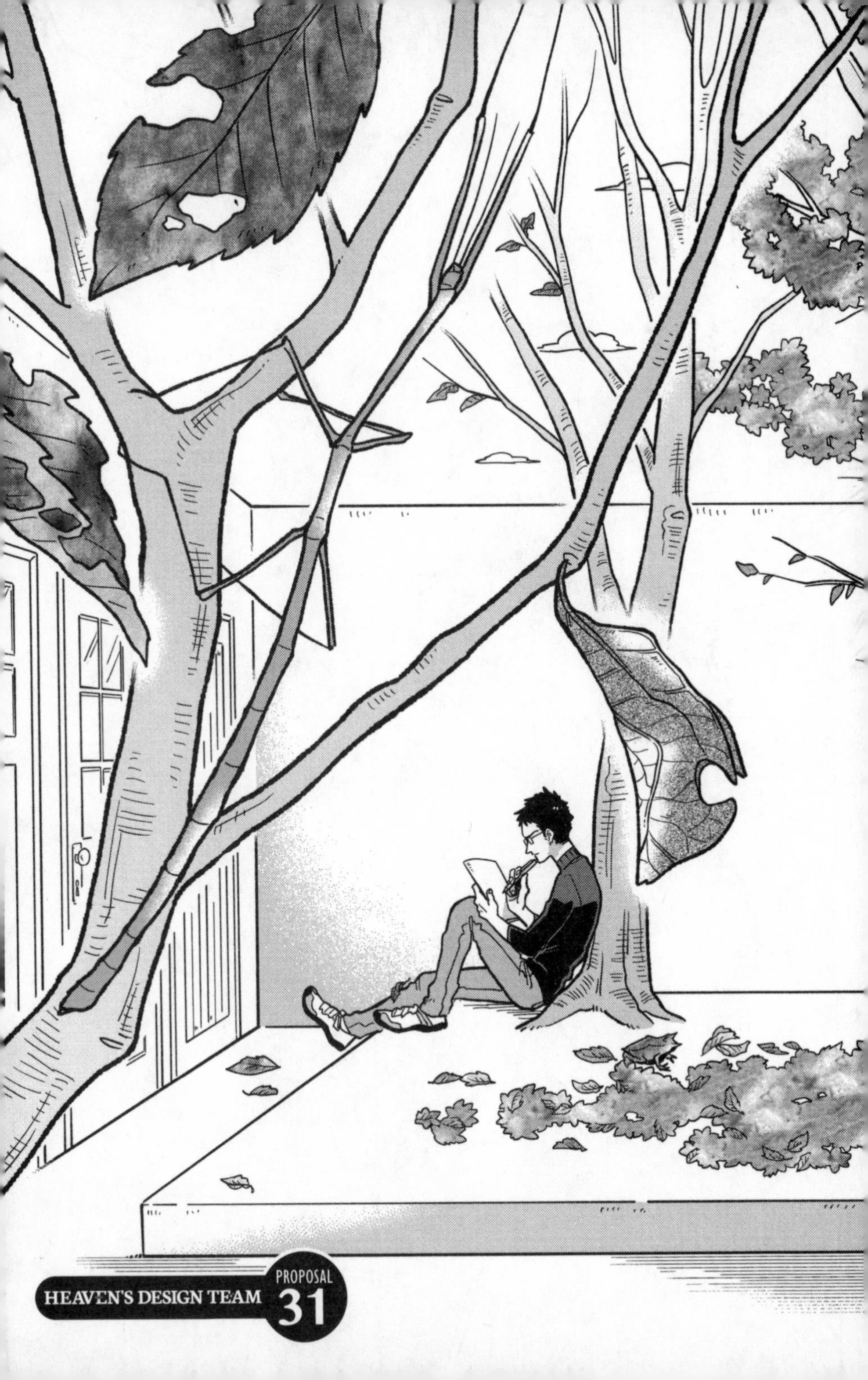
HEAVEN'S DESIGN TEAM
PROPOSAL
31

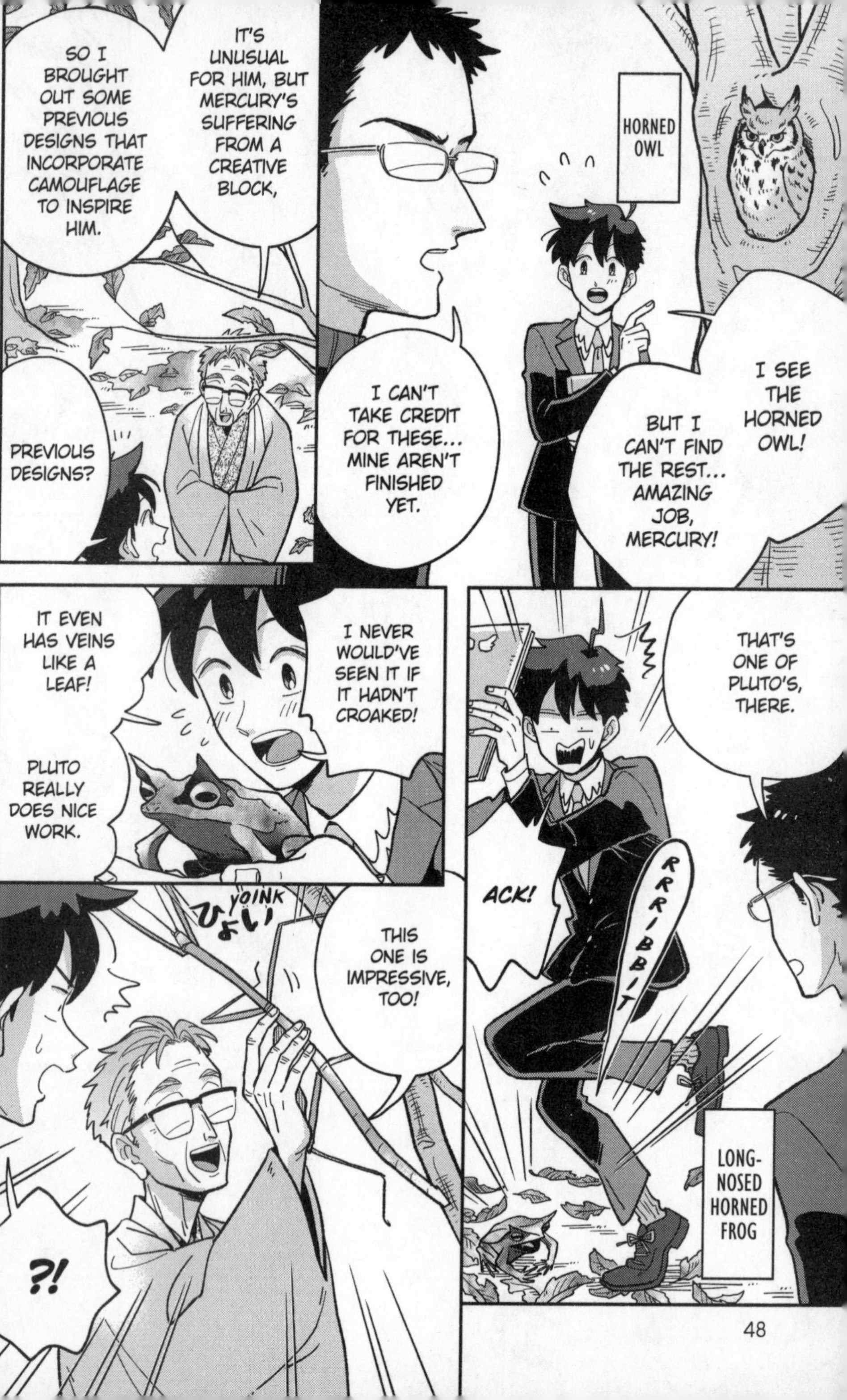
HORNED OWL
I SEE THE HORNED OWL!
BUT I CAN'T FIND THE REST... AMAZING JOB, MERCURY!
I CAN'T TAKE CREDIT FOR THESE... MINE AREN'T FINISHED YET.
IT'S UNUSUAL FOR HIM, BUT MERCURY'S SUFFERING FROM A CREATIVE BLOCK,
SO I BROUGHT OUT SOME PREVIOUS DESIGNS THAT INCORPORATE CAMOUFLAGE TO INSPIRE HIM.
PREVIOUS DESIGNS?
THAT'S ONE OF PLUTO'S, THERE.
ACK!
RRRIBBIT
LONG-NOSED HORNED FROG
I NEVER WOULD'VE SEEN IT IF IT HADN'T CROAKED!
IT EVEN HAS VEINS LIKE A LEAF!
PLUTO REALLY DOES NICE WORK.
THIS ONE IS IMPRESSIVE, TOO!
YOINK
ひょい
?!

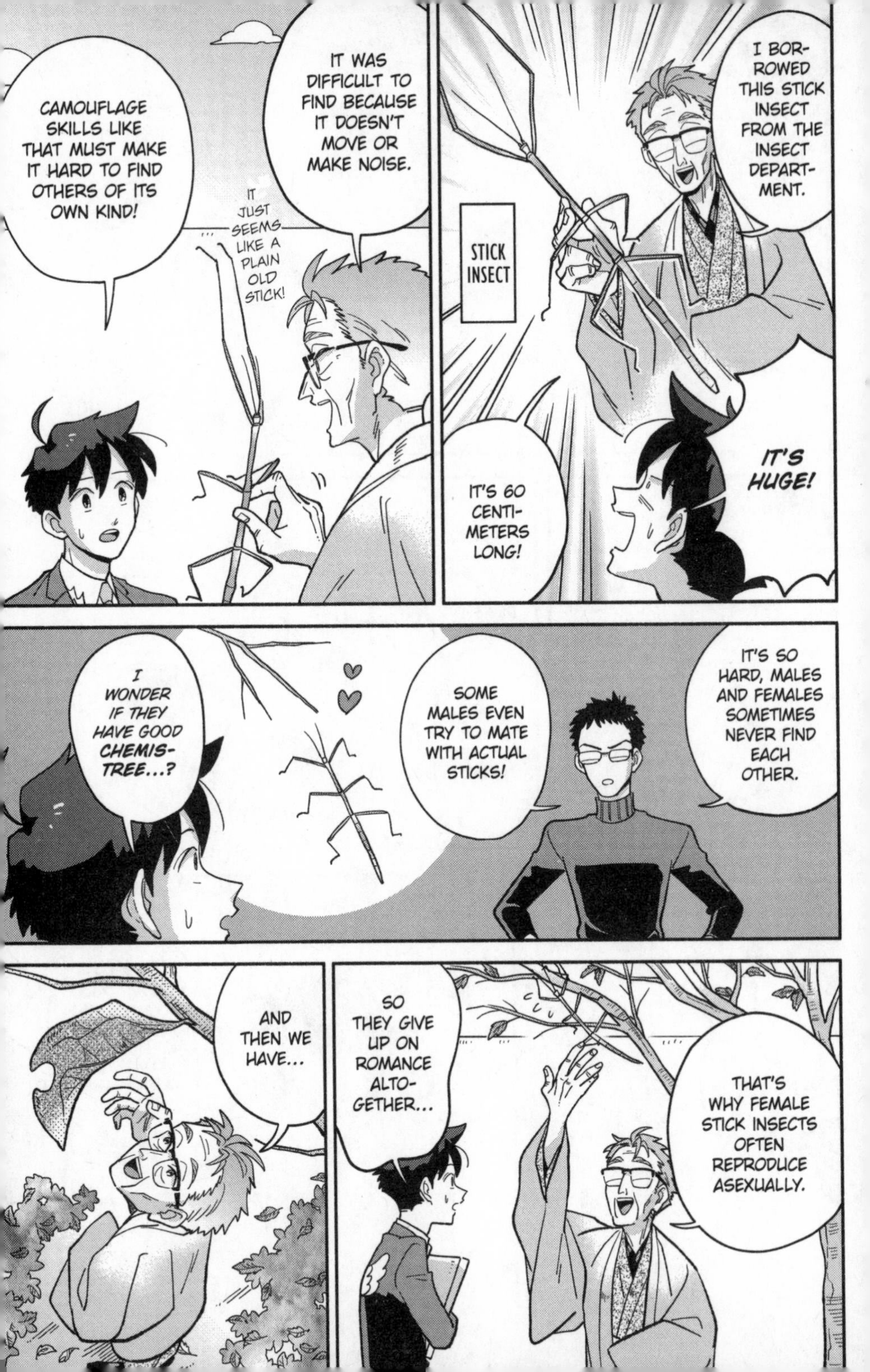
I BORROWED THIS STICK INSECT FROM THE INSECT DEPARTMENT.
STICK INSECT
IT'S HUGE!
IT'S 60 CENTIMETERS LONG!
IT WAS DIFFICULT TO FIND BECAUSE IT DOESN'T MOVE OR MAKE NOISE.
IT JUST SEEMS LIKE A PLAIN OLD STICK!
CAMOUFLAGE SKILLS LIKE THAT MUST MAKE IT HARD TO FIND OTHERS OF ITS OWN KIND!
IT'S SO HARD, MALES AND FEMALES SOMETIMES NEVER FIND EACH OTHER.
SOME MALES EVEN TRY TO MATE WITH ACTUAL STICKS!
I WONDER IF THEY HAVE GOOD CHEMISTREE...?
THAT'S WHY FEMALE STICK INSECTS OFTEN REPRODUCE ASEXUALLY.
SO THEY GIVE UP ON ROMANCE ALTOGETHER...
AND THEN WE HAVE...

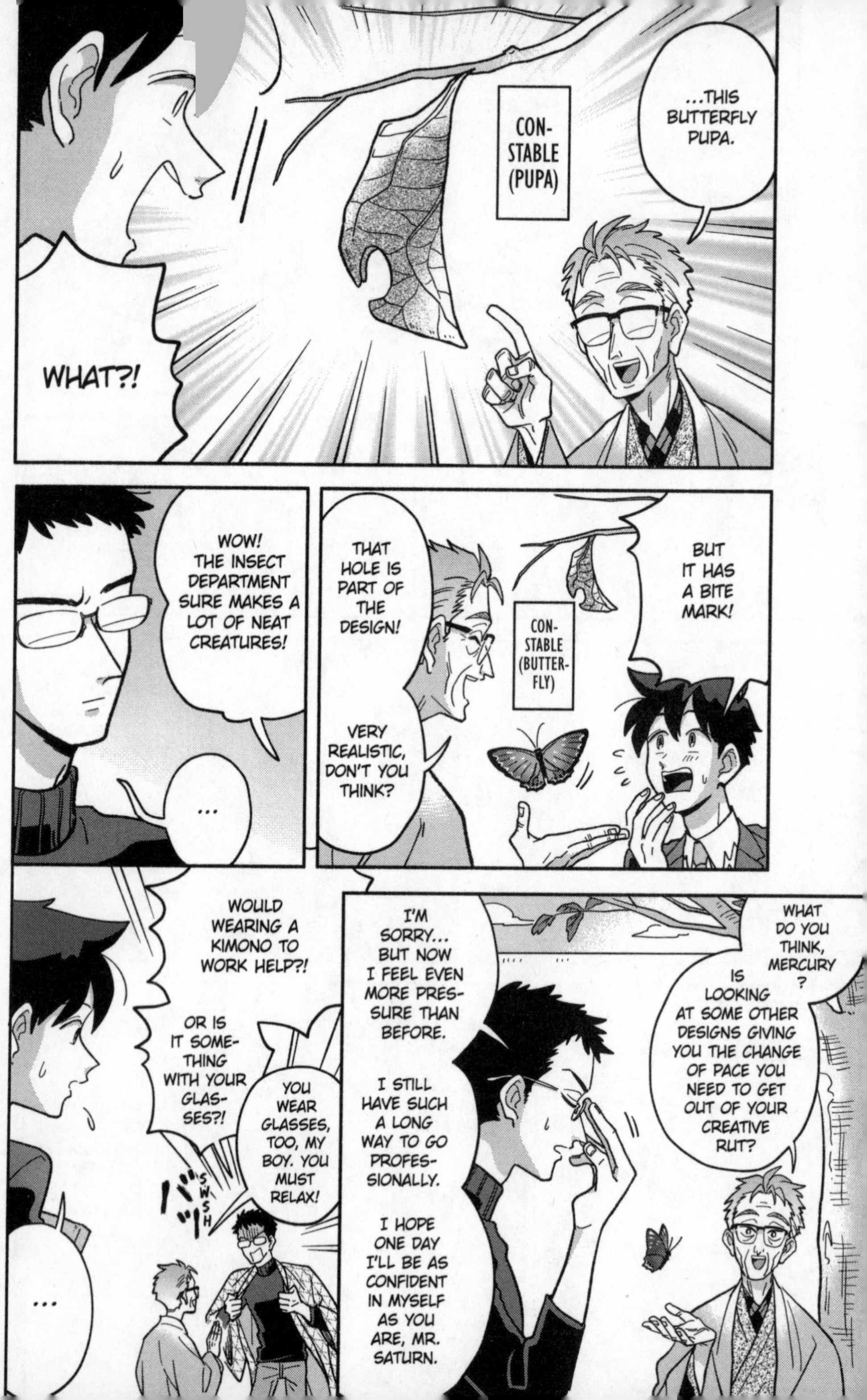
...THIS BUTTERFLY PUPA.
CON-STABLE (PUPA)
WHAT?!
BUT IT HAS A BITE MARK!
CON-STABLE (BUTTER-FLY)
THAT HOLE IS PART OF THE DESIGN!
VERY REALISTIC, DON'T YOU THINK?
WOW! THE INSECT DEPARTMENT SURE MAKES A LOT OF NEAT CREATURES!
...
WHAT DO YOU THINK, MERCURY?
IS LOOKING AT SOME OTHER DESIGNS GIVING YOU THE CHANGE OF PACE YOU NEED TO GET OUT OF YOUR CREATIVE RUT?
I'M SORRY... BUT NOW I FEEL EVEN MORE PRES-SURE THAN BEFORE.
I STILL HAVE SUCH A LONG WAY TO GO PROFES-SIONALLY.
I HOPE ONE DAY I'LL BE AS CONFIDENT IN MYSELF AS YOU ARE, MR. SATURN.
WOULD WEARING A KIMONO TO WORK HELP?!
OR IS IT SOME-THING WITH YOUR GLAS-SES?!
YOU WEAR GLASSES, TOO, MY BOY. YOU MUST RELAX!
SWSH
...

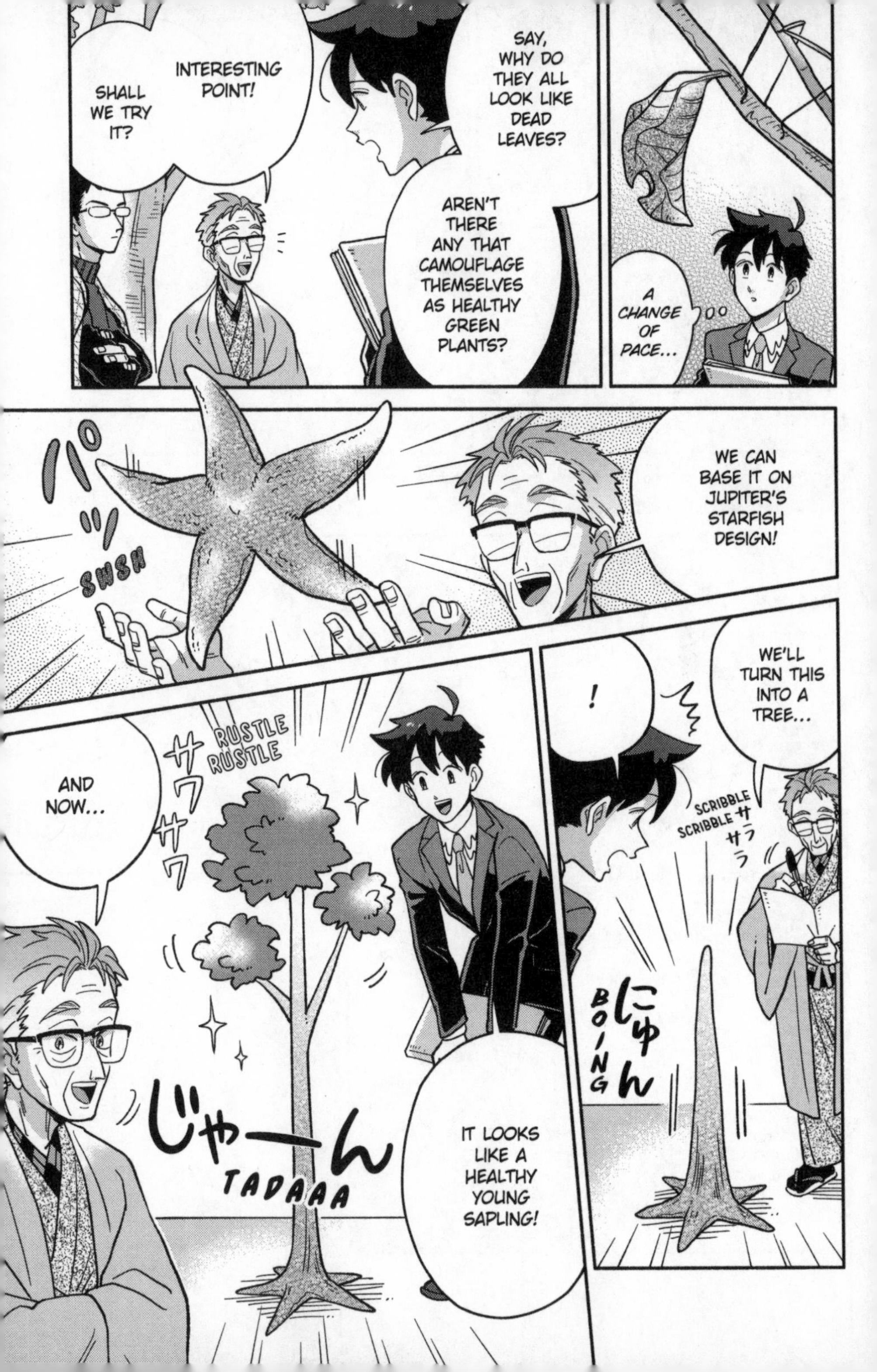
A CHANGE OF PACE...
SAY, WHY DO THEY ALL LOOK LIKE DEAD LEAVES?
AREN'T THERE ANY THAT CAMOUFLAGE THEMSELVES AS HEALTHY GREEN PLANTS?
INTERESTING POINT!
SHALL WE TRY IT?
WE CAN BASE IT ON JUPITER'S STARFISH DESIGN!
パッ
SWSH
WE'LL TURN THIS INTO A TREE...
!
サラサラ
SCRIBBLE SCRIBBLE
にゅん
BOING
AND NOW...
サワサワ
RUSTLE RUSTLE
じゃーん
TADAAA
IT LOOKS LIKE A HEALTHY YOUNG SAPLING!

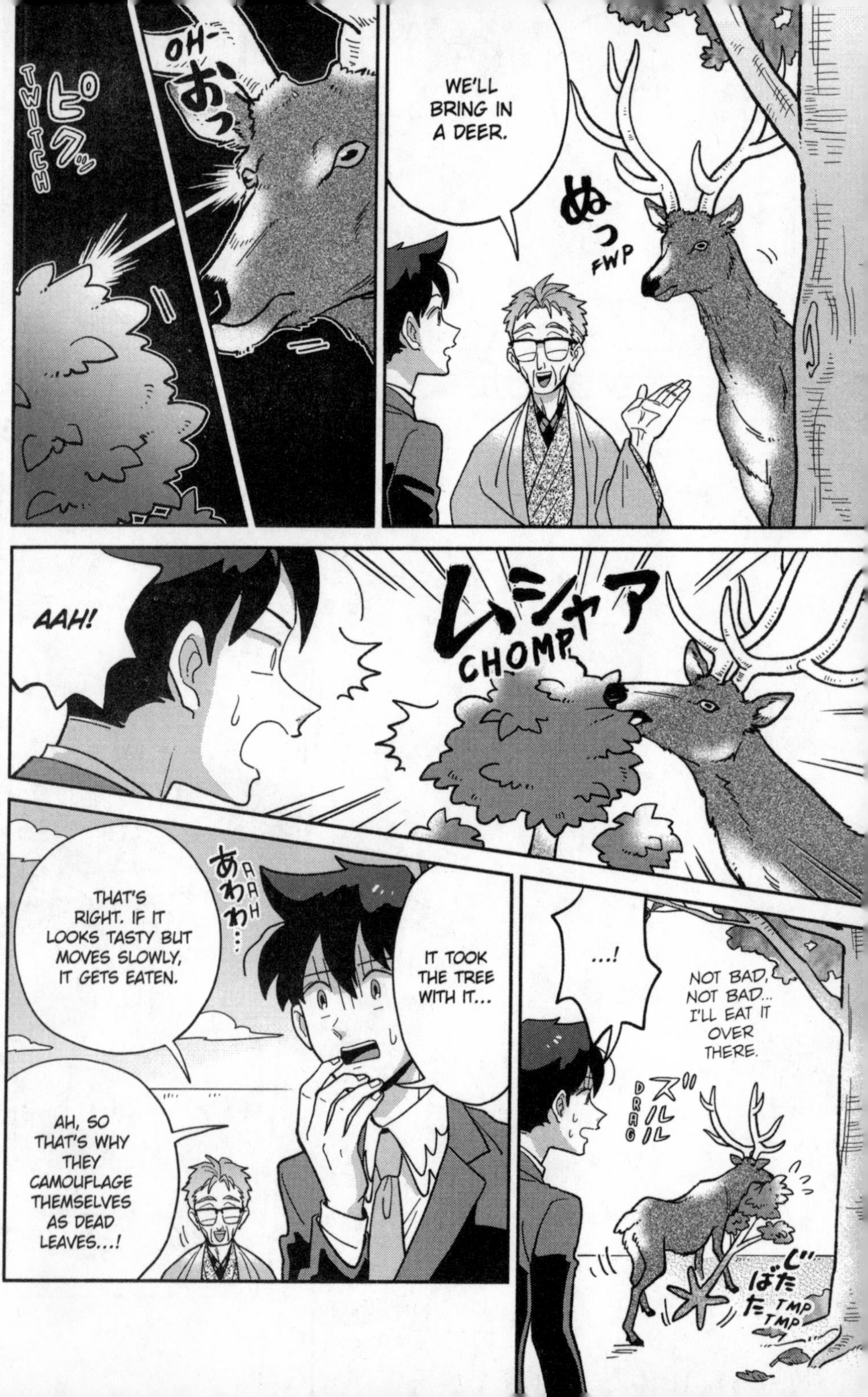
WE'LL BRING IN A DEER.
ぬっ
FWP
OH-
あっ
ピクッ
TWITCH
ムシャア
CHOMP
AAH!
...!
NOT BAD, NOT BAD... I'LL EAT IT OVER THERE.
ズルル
DRAG
じたばた
TMP TMP
IT TOOK THE TREE WITH IT...
あわわ...
AAAH
THAT'S RIGHT. IF IT LOOKS TASTY BUT MOVES SLOWLY, IT GETS EATEN.
AH, SO THAT'S WHY THEY CAMOUFLAGE THEMSELVES AS DEAD LEAVES...!

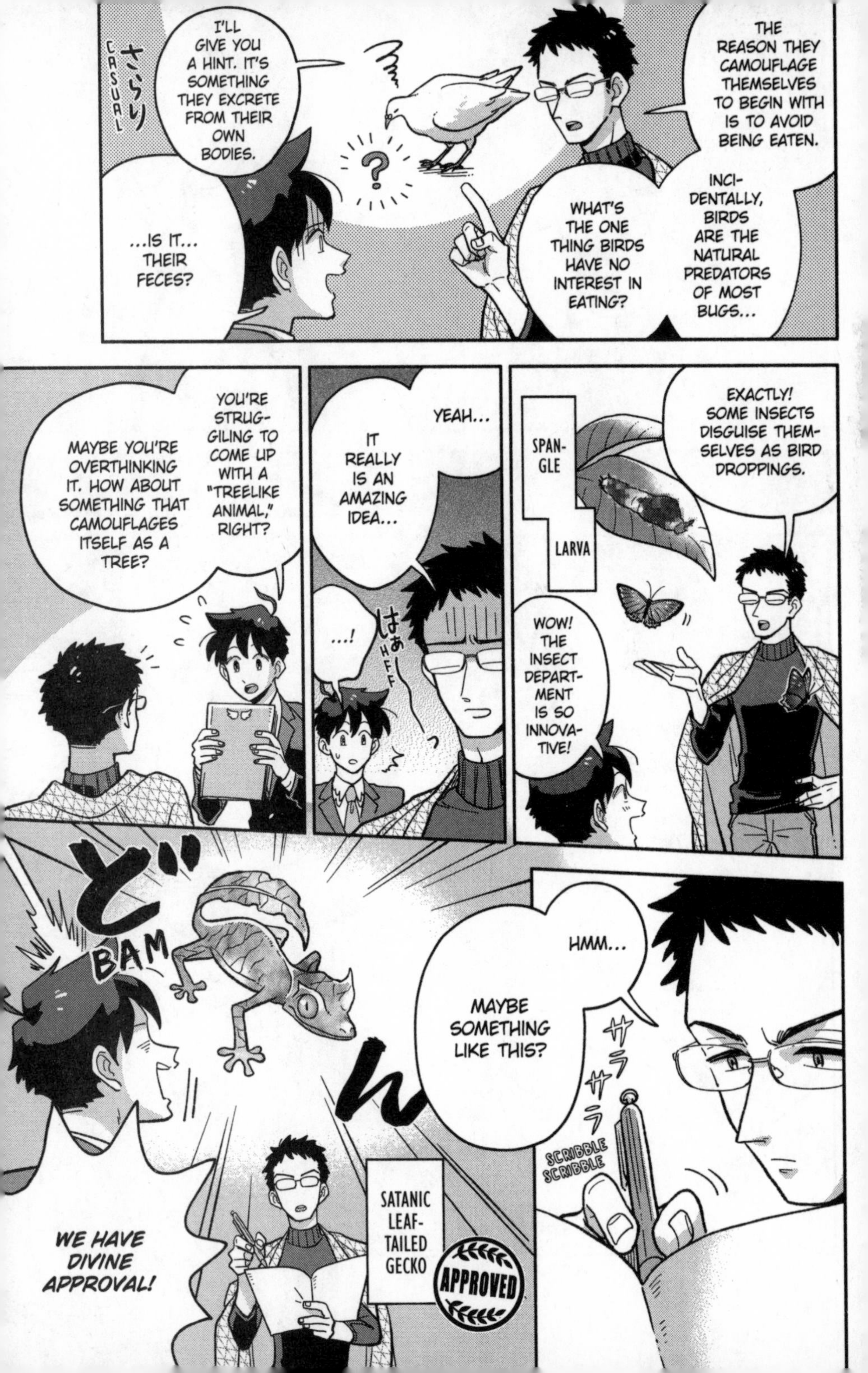
THE REASON THEY CAMOUFLAGE THEMSELVES TO BEGIN WITH IS TO AVOID BEING EATEN.
INCIDENTALLY, BIRDS ARE THE NATURAL PREDATORS OF MOST BUGS...
WHAT'S THE ONE THING BIRDS HAVE NO INTEREST IN EATING?
I'LL GIVE YOU A HINT. IT'S SOMETHING THEY EXCRETE FROM THEIR OWN BODIES.
さらり
CASUAL
?
...IS IT... THEIR FECES?
EXACTLY! SOME INSECTS DISGUISE THEMSELVES AS BIRD DROPPINGS.
SPANGLE
LARVA
WOW! THE INSECT DEPARTMENT IS SO INNOVATIVE!
YEAH...
IT REALLY IS AN AMAZING IDEA...
はぁ
HFF
...!
YOU'RE STRUGGILING TO COME UP WITH A "TREELIKE ANIMAL," RIGHT?
MAYBE YOU'RE OVERTHINKING IT. HOW ABOUT SOMETHING THAT CAMOUFLAGES ITSELF AS A TREE?
HMM...
MAYBE SOMETHING LIKE THIS?
サラサラ
SCRIBBLE SCRIBBLE
どん
BAM
SATANIC LEAF-TAILED GECKO
APPROVED
WE HAVE DIVINE APPROVAL!

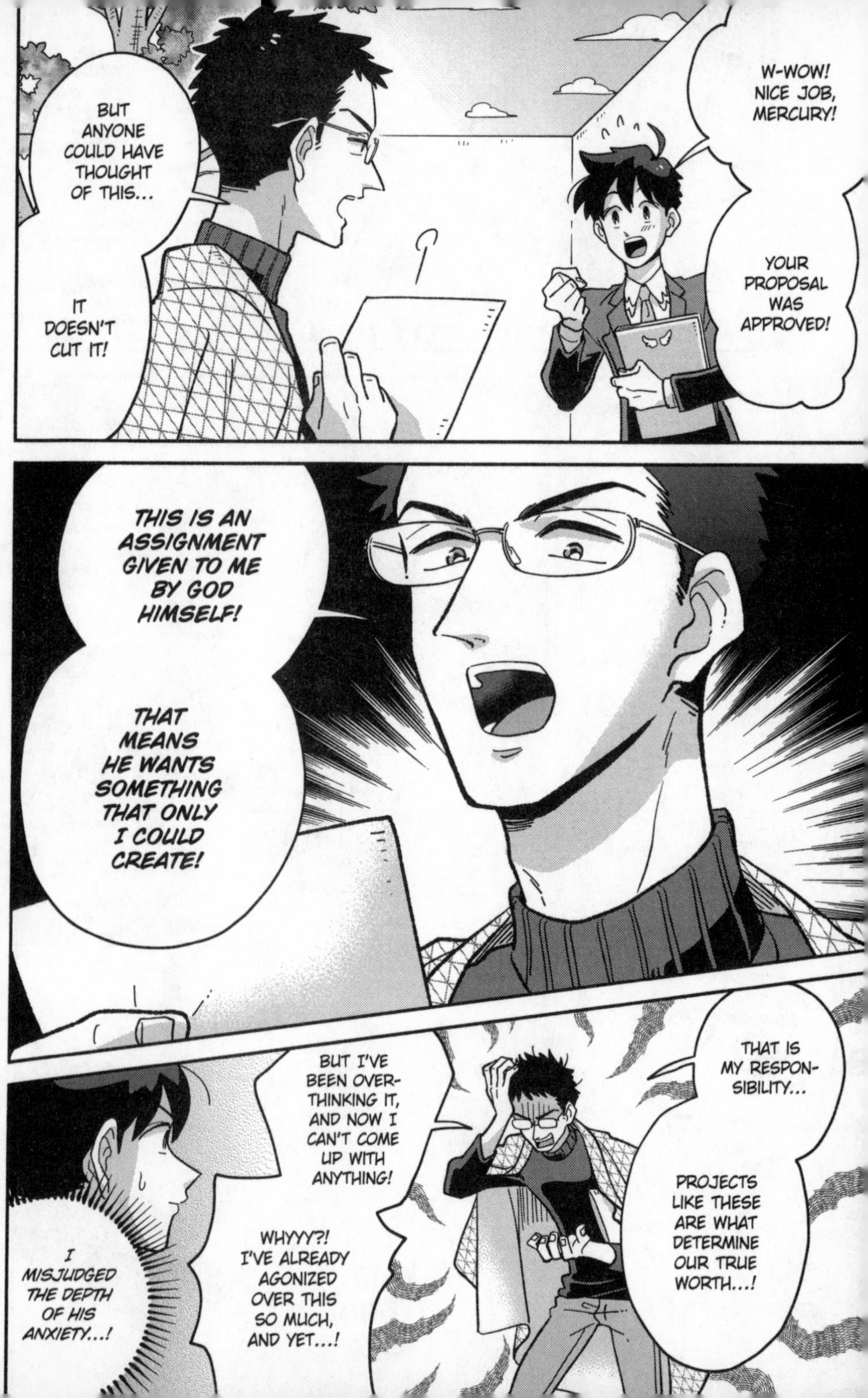
W-WOW! NICE JOB, MERCURY!
YOUR PROPOSAL WAS APPROVED!
BUT ANYONE COULD HAVE THOUGHT OF THIS...
IT DOESN'T CUT IT!
THIS IS AN ASSIGNMENT GIVEN TO ME BY GOD HIMSELF!
THAT MEANS HE WANTS SOMETHING THAT ONLY I COULD CREATE!
THAT IS MY RESPON-SIBILITY...
PROJECTS LIKE THESE ARE WHAT DETERMINE OUR TRUE WORTH...!
BUT I'VE BEEN OVER-THINKING IT, AND NOW I CAN'T COME UP WITH ANYTHING!
WHYYY?! I'VE ALREADY AGONIZED OVER THIS SO MUCH, AND YET...!
I MISJUDGED THE DEPTH OF HIS ANXIETY...!

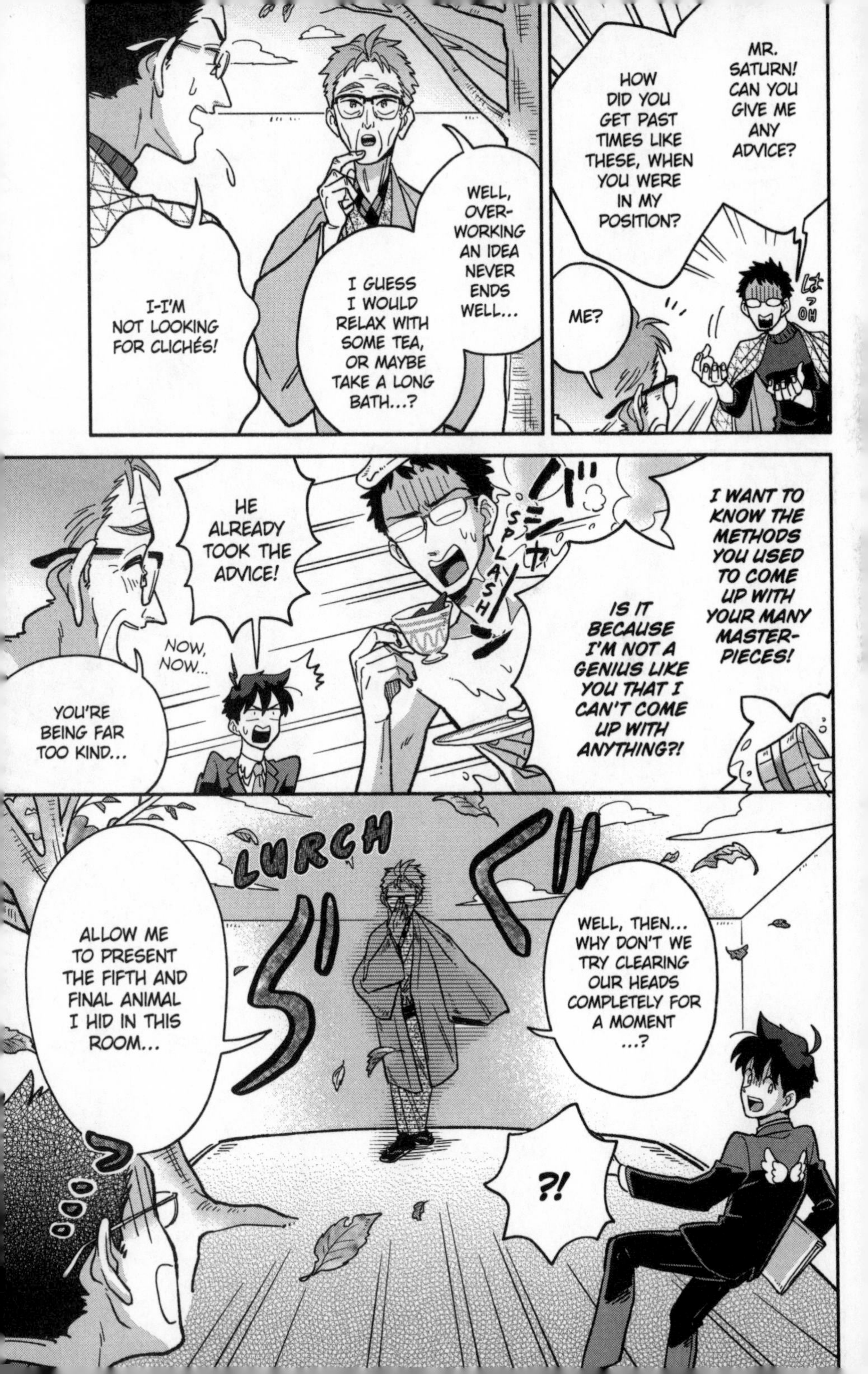
MR. SATURN! CAN YOU GIVE ME ANY ADVICE?
HOW DID YOU GET PAST TIMES LIKE THESE, WHEN YOU WERE IN MY POSITION?
はっ OH
ME?
WELL, OVER-WORKING AN IDEA NEVER ENDS WELL...
I GUESS I WOULD RELAX WITH SOME TEA, OR MAYBE TAKE A LONG BATH...?
I-I'M NOT LOOKING FOR CLICHÉS!
I WANT TO KNOW THE METHODS YOU USED TO COME UP WITH YOUR MANY MASTER-PIECES!
IS IT BECAUSE I'M NOT A GENIUS LIKE YOU THAT I CAN'T COME UP WITH ANYTHING?!
SPLASH
HE ALREADY TOOK THE ADVICE!
NOW, NOW...
YOU'RE BEING FAR TOO KIND...
WELL, THEN... WHY DON'T WE TRY CLEARING OUR HEADS COMPLETELY FOR A MOMENT ...?
?!
LURCH
ALLOW ME TO PRESENT THE FIFTH AND FINAL ANIMAL I HID IN THIS ROOM...

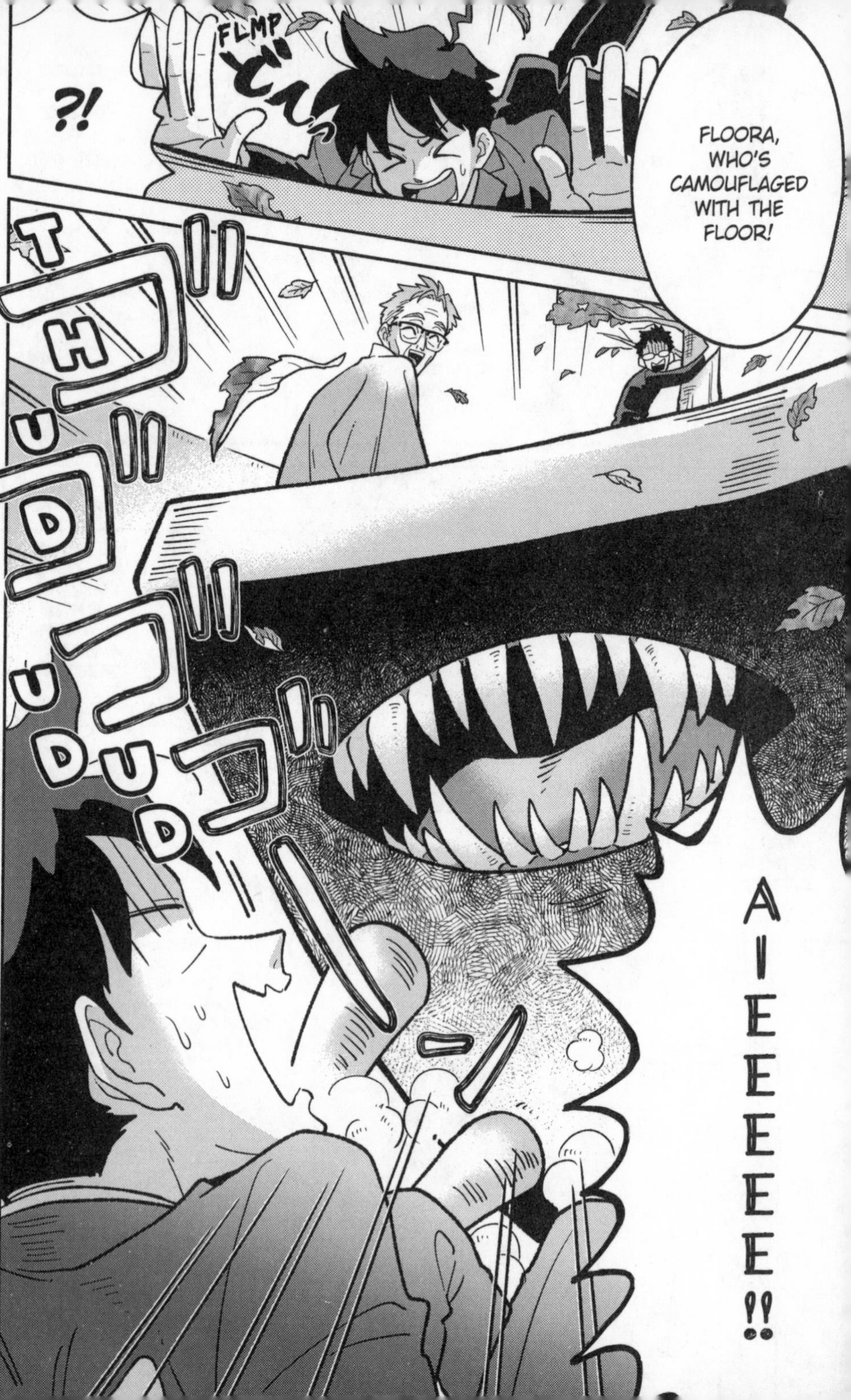
FLOORA, WHO'S CAMOUFLAGED WITH THE FLOOR!
FLMP
?!
AIEEEEEE!!
THUDUDUD

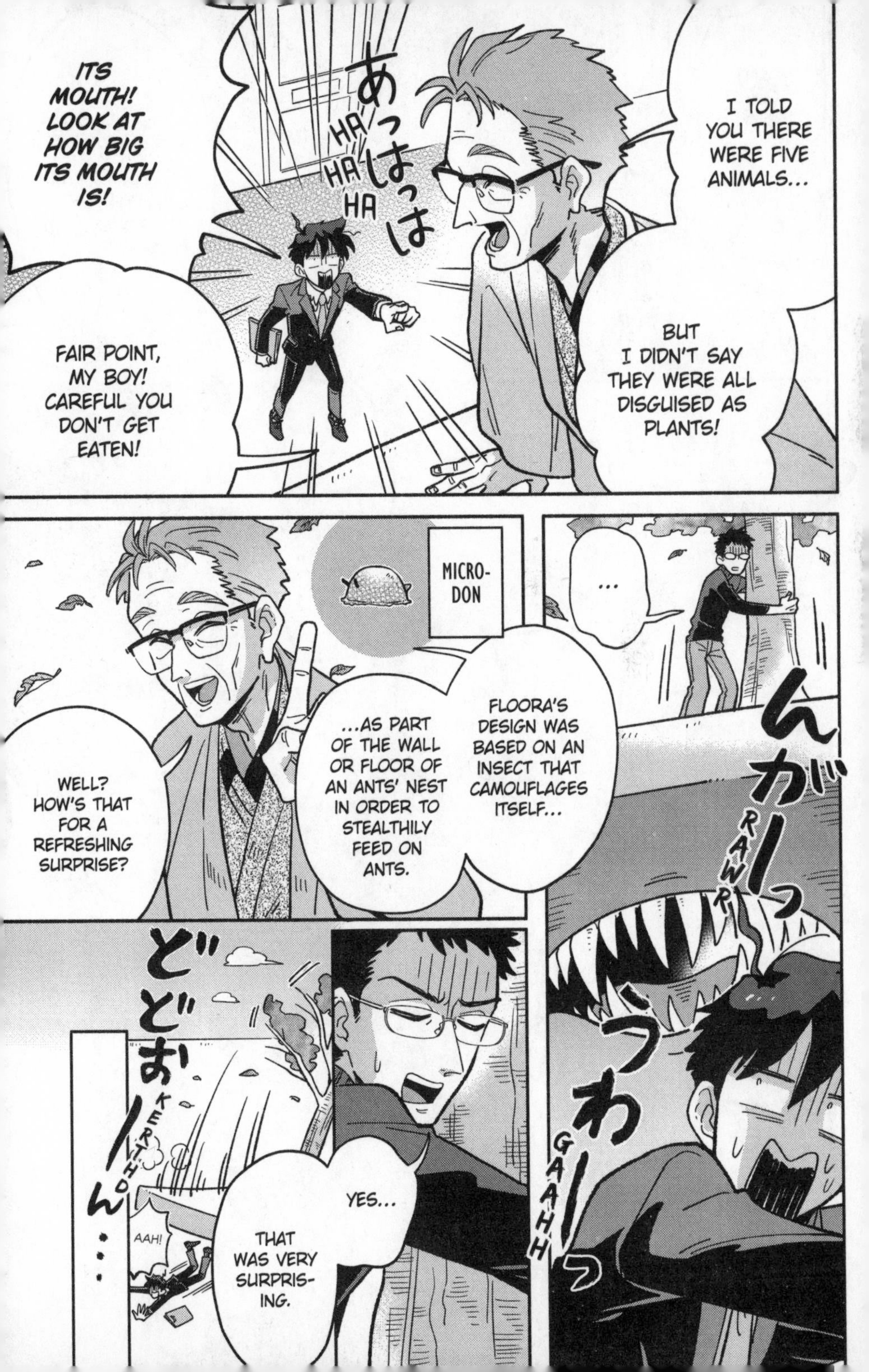
I TOLD YOU THERE WERE FIVE ANIMALS...
BUT I DIDN'T SAY THEY WERE ALL DISGUISED AS PLANTS!
あっはっは
HA HA HA
ITS MOUTH! LOOK AT HOW BIG ITS MOUTH IS!
FAIR POINT, MY BOY! CAREFUL YOU DON'T GET EATEN!
...
んがーっ
RAWR
うわーっ
GAAHH
MICRO-DON
FLOORA'S DESIGN WAS BASED ON AN INSECT THAT CAMOUFLAGES ITSELF...
...AS PART OF THE WALL OR FLOOR OF AN ANTS' NEST IN ORDER TO STEALTHILY FEED ON ANTS.
WELL? HOW'S THAT FOR A REFRESHING SURPRISE?
YES...
THAT WAS VERY SURPRIS-ING.
どどぉーん...
KERTHD
AAH!

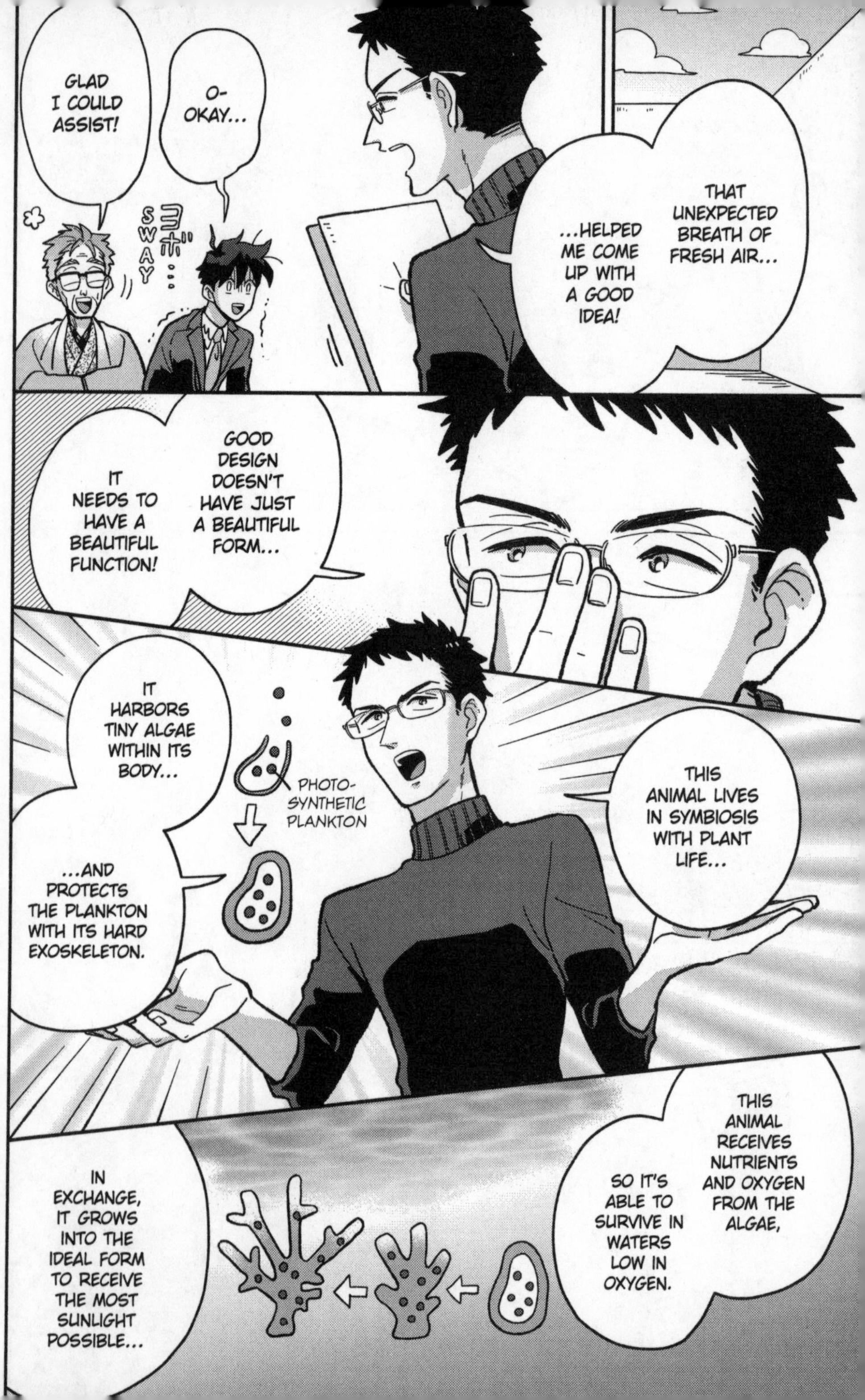
THAT UNEXPECTED BREATH OF FRESH AIR...
...HELPED ME COME UP WITH A GOOD IDEA!
O-OKAY...
SWAY
GLAD I COULD ASSIST!
GOOD DESIGN DOESN'T HAVE JUST A BEAUTIFUL FORM...
IT NEEDS TO HAVE A BEAUTIFUL FUNCTION!
THIS ANIMAL LIVES IN SYMBIOSIS WITH PLANT LIFE...
IT HARBORS TINY ALGAE WITHIN ITS BODY...
PHOTO-SYNTHETIC PLANKTON
...AND PROTECTS THE PLANKTON WITH ITS HARD EXOSKELETON.
THIS ANIMAL RECEIVES NUTRIENTS AND OXYGEN FROM THE ALGAE,
SO IT'S ABLE TO SURVIVE IN WATERS LOW IN OXYGEN.
IN EXCHANGE, IT GROWS INTO THE IDEAL FORM TO RECEIVE THE MOST SUNLIGHT POSSIBLE...

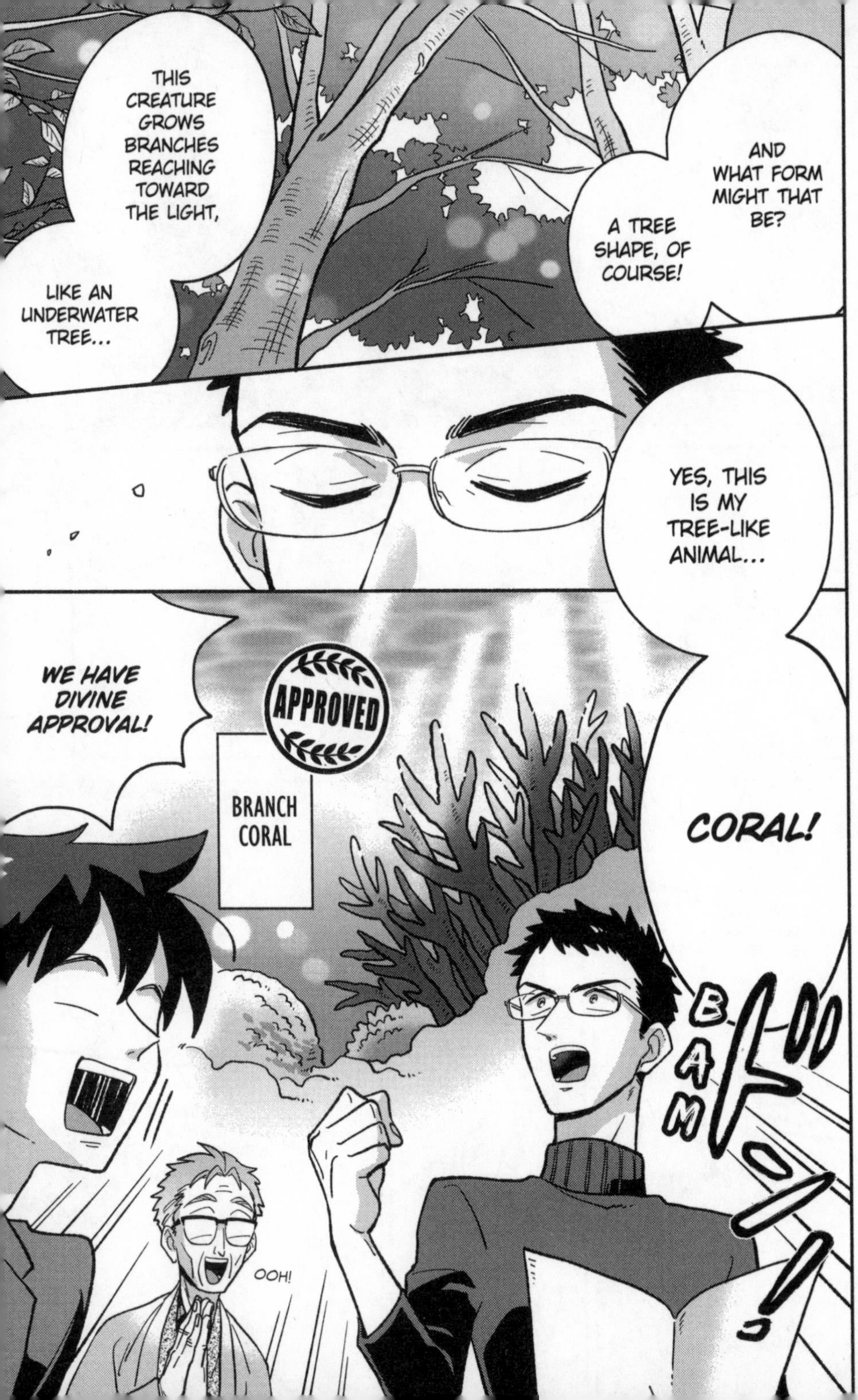
AND WHAT FORM MIGHT THAT BE?
A TREE SHAPE, OF COURSE!
THIS CREATURE GROWS BRANCHES REACHING TOWARD THE LIGHT,
LIKE AN UNDERWATER TREE...
YES, THIS IS MY TREE-LIKE ANIMAL...
CORAL!
BAM
APPROVED
BRANCH CORAL
WE HAVE DIVINE APPROVAL!
OOH!

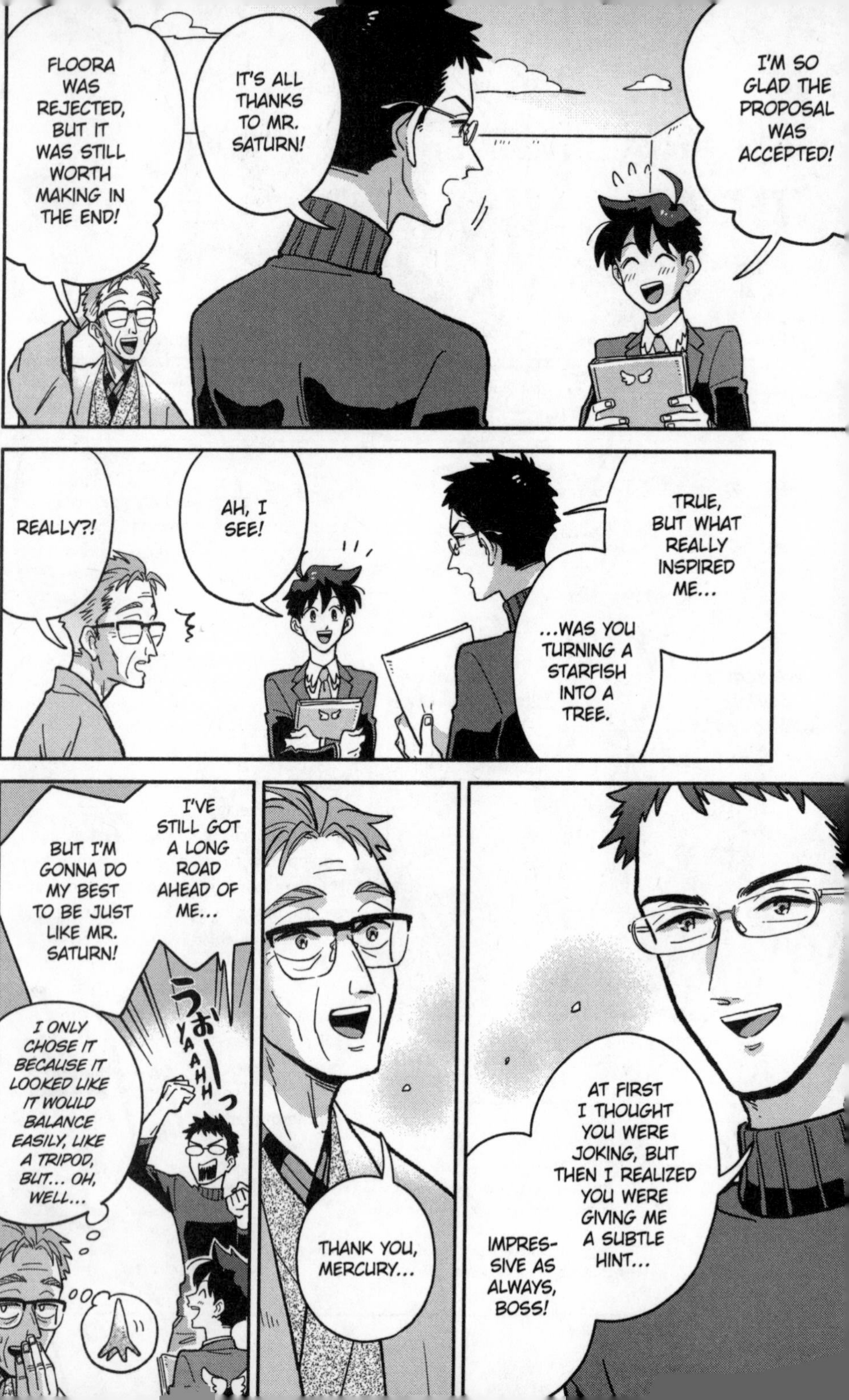
I'M SO GLAD THE PROPOSAL WAS ACCEPTED!
IT'S ALL THANKS TO MR. SATURN!
FLOORA WAS REJECTED, BUT IT WAS STILL WORTH MAKING IN THE END!
TRUE, BUT WHAT REALLY INSPIRED ME...
...WAS YOU TURNING A STARFISH INTO A TREE.
AH, I SEE!
REALLY?!
AT FIRST I THOUGHT YOU WERE JOKING, BUT THEN I REALIZED YOU WERE GIVING ME A SUBTLE HINT...
IMPRES-SIVE AS ALWAYS, BOSS!
THANK YOU, MERCURY...
I'VE STILL GOT A LONG ROAD AHEAD OF ME...
BUT I'M GONNA DO MY BEST TO BE JUST LIKE MR. SATURN!
うおーっ YAAHH
I ONLY CHOSE IT BECAUSE IT LOOKED LIKE IT WOULD BALANCE EASILY, LIKE A TRIPOD, BUT... OH, WELL...

THE ENCYCLOPEDIA OF REAL ANIMALS 31

ANIMAL 75 CORAL

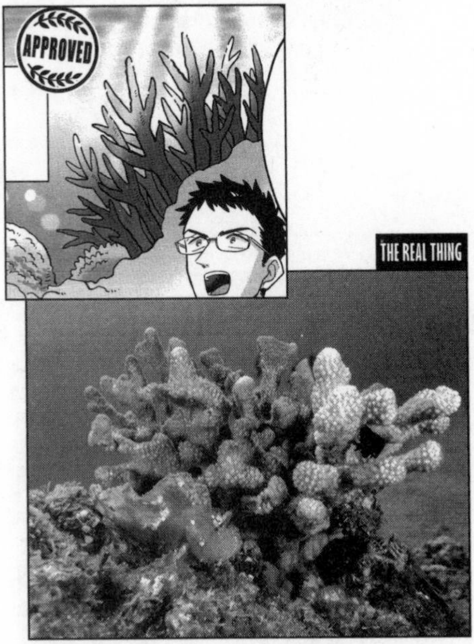
APPROVED
THE REAL THING

Lace coral has a distinct cauliflower shape.

Photo: Minden Pictures/Aflo

[Name] Coral
[Classification] Class: Anthozoa
[Habitat] Shallow, sunlit seas (hermatypic coral) / Deep seas (precious coral)
[Length] A few millimeters to tens of centimeters (per piece)

Coral is an animal belonging to the same phylum as anemones and jellyfish. In its larval stage, it is mobile and floats in the water until it matures and settles to form a new colony. It harbors a type of photosynthetic plankton known as zooxanthellae within its tissues, and relies on the oxygen and nutrients produced by the algae's photosynthesis to survive.

Zooxanthellae also benefit from this symbiotic relationship. Coral has a hard, fortress-like exoskeleton equipped with stinging cells which deter predators and protect the zooxanthellae living inside. Zooxanthellae can also feast on the carbon dioxide and waste material excreted by its host.

Because coral grows in shapes best suited for receiving maximum sunlight, it often looks like a plant. Some species do not enjoy a symbiotic relationship with plankton.

ANIMAL 76 STICK INSECT

STICK
INSECT

Photo: Minden Pictures/Aflo

THE REAL THING

A camouflaged *Entoria okinawaensis* hangs in the center of this photo, looking down.

Rather than flying away, most species of stick insect protect themselves by disguising themselves as sticks or leaves. In some species, the camouflage goes beyond appearance and the insects actually mimic the movement of twigs or leaves swaying in the breeze. The females of certain species are able to reproduce asexually, and the males are often difficult to find. Over 2,500 species exist, including some that reach over 50 cm (20 in) in length.

[Name]	Stick insect
[Classification]	Class: Insecta Order: Phasmatodea
[Habitat]	Forests and grasslands in temperate to tropical climates
[Length]	Approximately 5-60 cm (2-24 in)

ANIMAL 77 LONG-NOSED HORNED FROG

The long-nosed horned frog is a nocturnal species that looks exactly like a dead leaf—it even has markings that look like leaf veins and bite marks. Perhaps because its camouflage is so specialized, the long-nosed horned frog's legs are relatively thin compared to its body, and despite being a frog, it is a poor jumper. When it detects an enemy's presence, it folds its legs beneath its body and hunkers down. Its mouth is two-thirds the width of its body, and it ambushes insects and small reptiles before swallowing them whole.

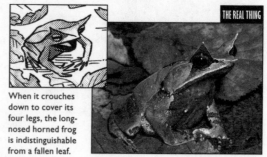

When it crouches down to cover its four legs, the long-nosed horned frog is indistinguishable from a fallen leaf.

THE REAL THING

Photo: Minden Pictures/Aflo

[Name]	*Megophrys nasuta*
[Classification]	Class: Amphibia Order: Anura Family: Megophryidae Genus: *Megophrys*
[Habitat]	Sumatra, Borneo, Peninsular Malaysia
[Length]	7-14 cm (2.7-5.5 in)

HEAVEN'S DESIGN TEAM

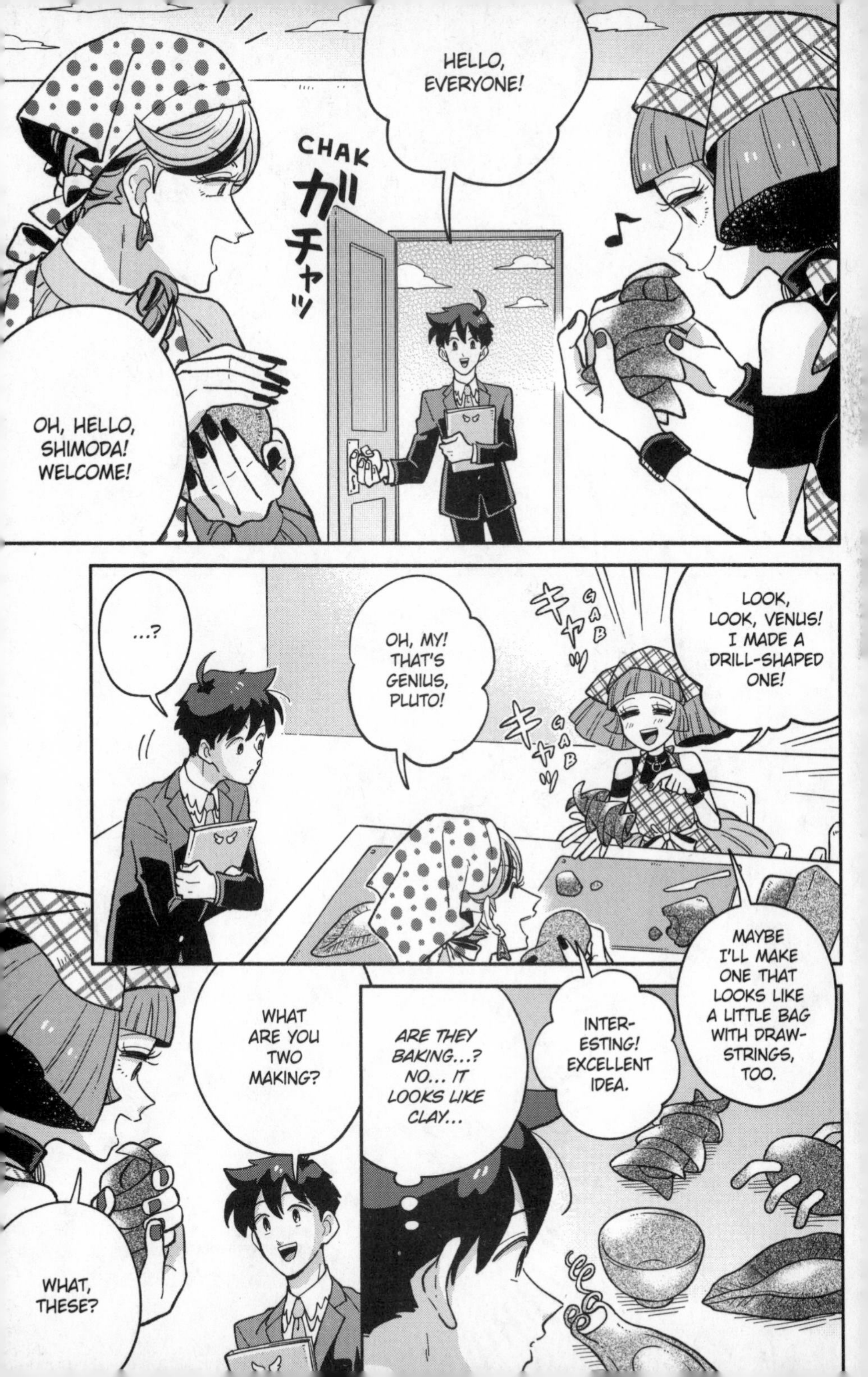
HELLO, EVERYONE!
CHAK
ガチャッ
OH, HELLO, SHIMODA! WELCOME!
LOOK, LOOK, VENUS! I MADE A DRILL-SHAPED ONE!
GAB
キャッ
GAB
キャッ
OH, MY! THAT'S GENIUS, PLUTO!
...?
MAYBE I'LL MAKE ONE THAT LOOKS LIKE A LITTLE BAG WITH DRAW-STRINGS, TOO.
INTER-ESTING! EXCELLENT IDEA.
ARE THEY BAKING...? NO... IT LOOKS LIKE CLAY...
WHAT ARE YOU TWO MAKING?
WHAT, THESE?

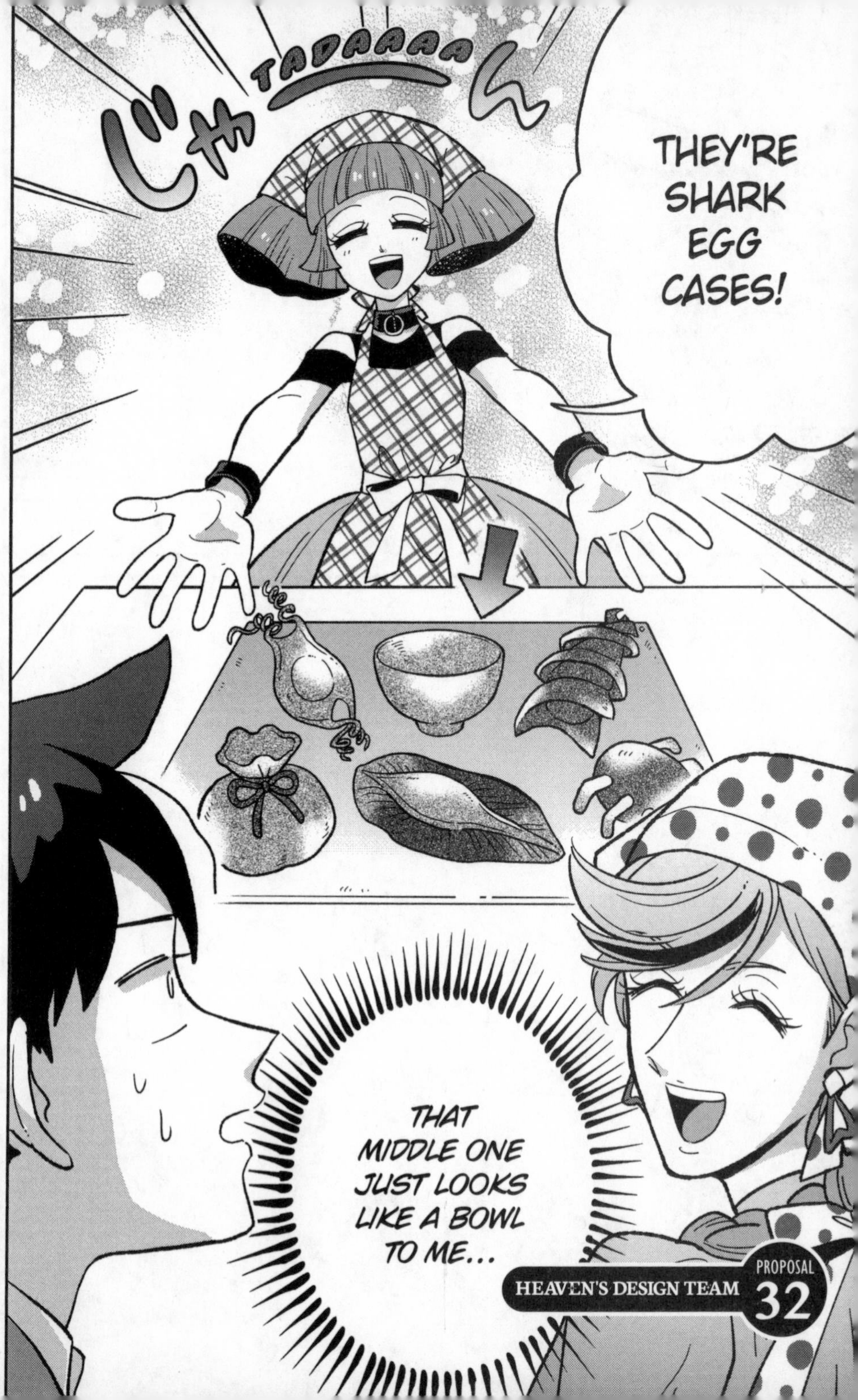
THEY'RE SHARK EGG CASES!
じゃ TADAAAA ん
THAT MIDDLE ONE JUST LOOKS LIKE A BOWL TO ME...
HEAVEN'S DESIGN TEAM
PROPOSAL 32

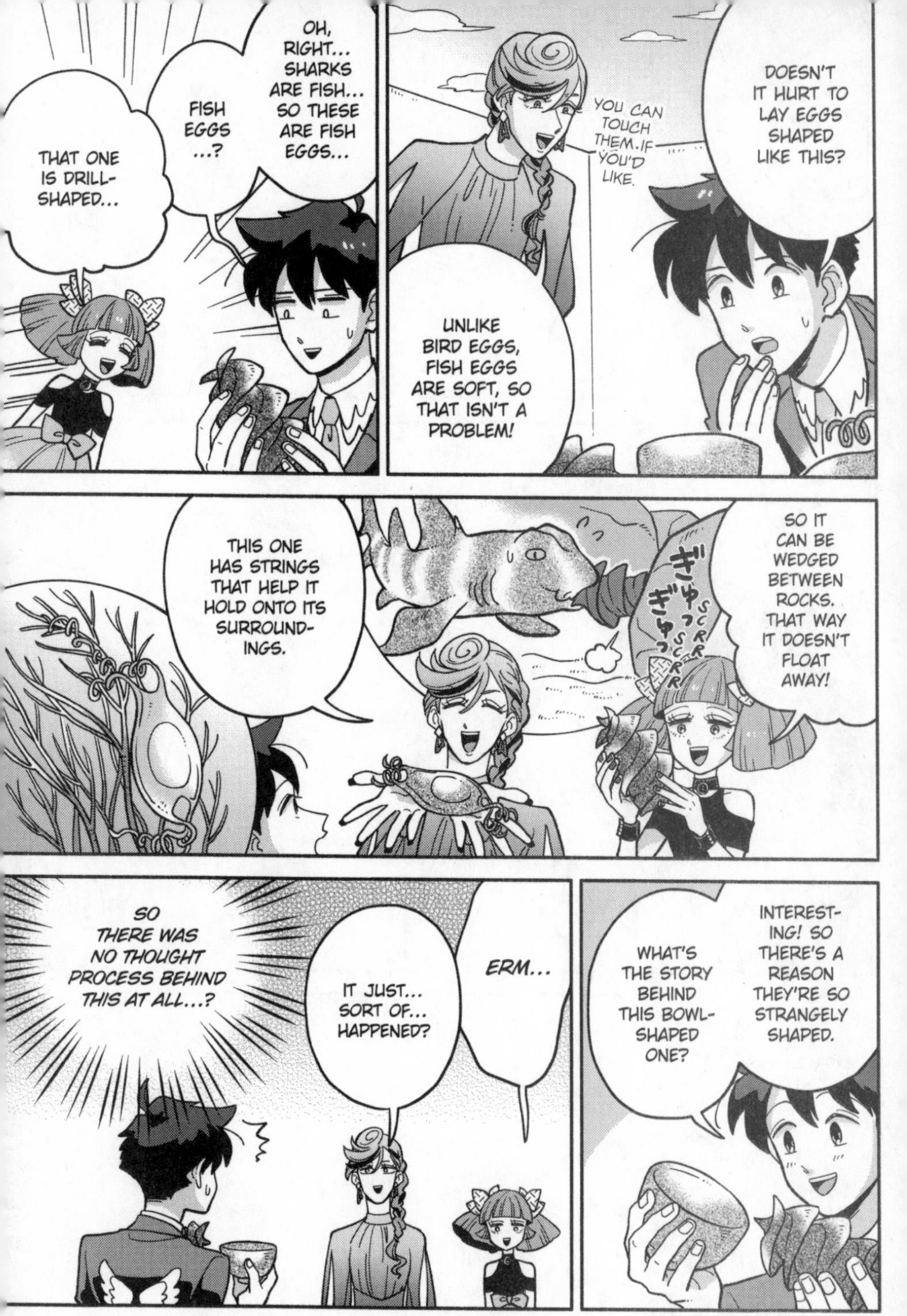
DOESN'T IT HURT TO LAY EGGS SHAPED LIKE THIS?
YOU CAN TOUCH THEM IF YOU'D LIKE.
UNLIKE BIRD EGGS, FISH EGGS ARE SOFT, SO THAT ISN'T A PROBLEM!
OH, RIGHT... SHARKS ARE FISH... SO THESE ARE FISH EGGS...
FISH EGGS ...?
THAT ONE IS DRILL-SHAPED...
SO IT CAN BE WEDGED BETWEEN ROCKS. THAT WAY IT DOESN'T FLOAT AWAY!
ぎゅっ ぎゅっ SCRR SCRR
THIS ONE HAS STRINGS THAT HELP IT HOLD ONTO ITS SURROUND-INGS.
INTEREST-ING! SO THERE'S A REASON THEY'RE SO STRANGELY SHAPED.
WHAT'S THE STORY BEHIND THIS BOWL-SHAPED ONE?
ERM...
IT JUST... SORT OF... HAPPENED?
SO THERE WAS NO THOUGHT PROCESS BEHIND THIS AT ALL...?

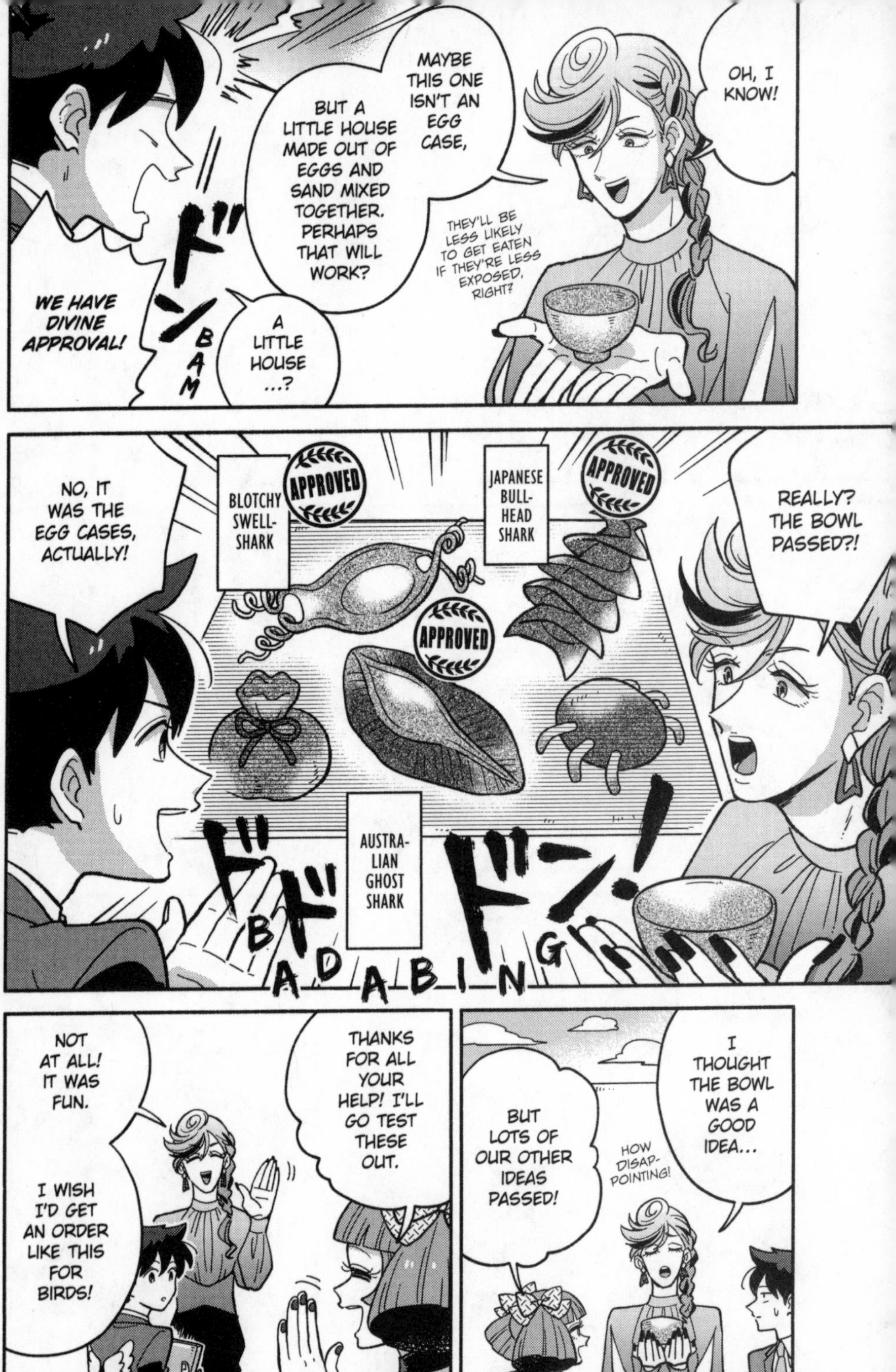
OH, I KNOW!
MAYBE THIS ONE ISN'T AN EGG CASE,
BUT A LITTLE HOUSE MADE OUT OF EGGS AND SAND MIXED TOGETHER. PERHAPS THAT WILL WORK?
THEY'LL BE LESS LIKELY TO GET EATEN IF THEY'RE LESS EXPOSED, RIGHT?
A LITTLE HOUSE ...?
BAM
WE HAVE DIVINE APPROVAL!
REALLY? THE BOWL PASSED?!
NO, IT WAS THE EGG CASES, ACTUALLY!
APPROVED
JAPANESE BULLHEAD SHARK
APPROVED
BLOTCHY SWELLSHARK
APPROVED
AUSTRALIAN GHOST SHARK
BADABING
I THOUGHT THE BOWL WAS A GOOD IDEA...
HOW DISAPPOINTING!
BUT LOTS OF OUR OTHER IDEAS PASSED!
THANKS FOR ALL YOUR HELP! I'LL GO TEST THESE OUT.
NOT AT ALL! IT WAS FUN.
I WISH I'D GET AN ORDER LIKE THIS FOR BIRDS!

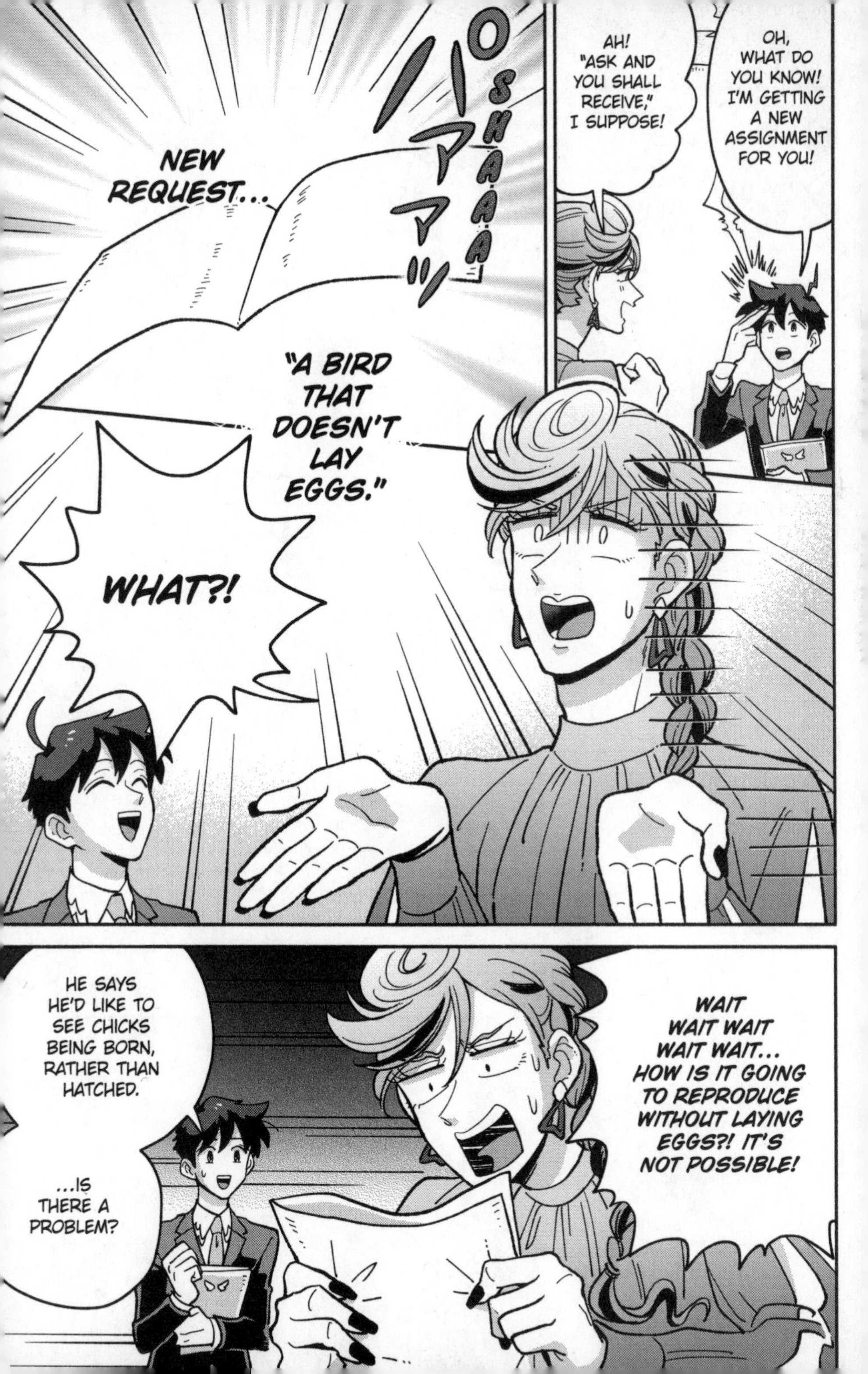
OH, WHAT DO YOU KNOW! I'M GETTING A NEW ASSIGNMENT FOR YOU!
AH! "ASK AND YOU SHALL RECEIVE," I SUPPOSE!
OSHAAAA
NEW REQUEST...
"A BIRD THAT DOESN'T LAY EGGS."
WHAT?!
WAIT WAIT WAIT WAIT WAIT... HOW IS IT GOING TO REPRODUCE WITHOUT LAYING EGGS?! IT'S NOT POSSIBLE!
HE SAYS HE'D LIKE TO SEE CHICKS BEING BORN, RATHER THAN HATCHED.
...IS THERE A PROBLEM?

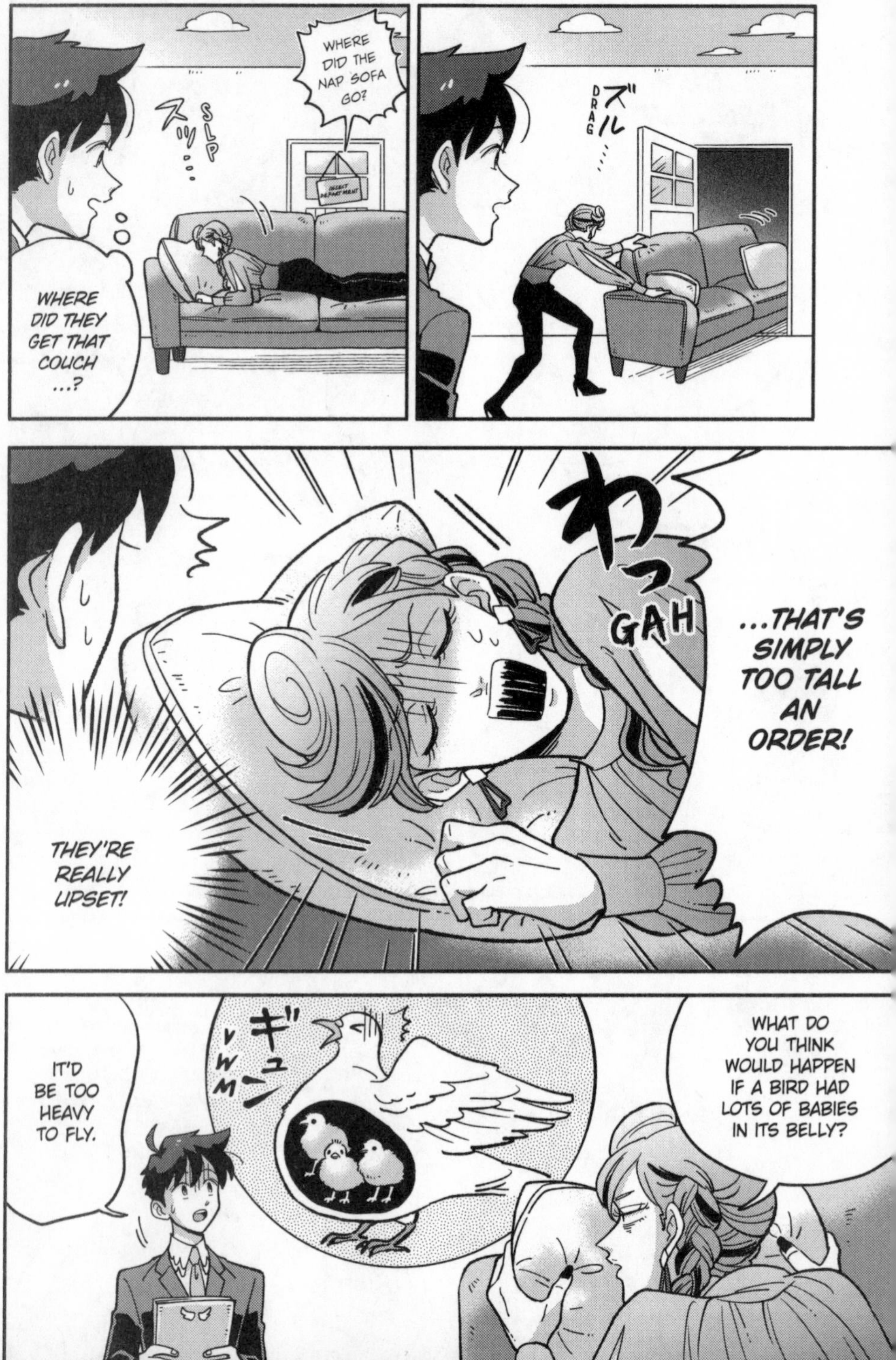
ズル
DRAG
WHERE DID THE NAP SOFA GO?
スッ…
SLP
WHERE DID THEY GET THAT COUCH …?
わっ
GAH
…THAT'S SIMPLY TOO TALL AN ORDER!
THEY'RE REALLY UPSET!
WHAT DO YOU THINK WOULD HAPPEN IF A BIRD HAD LOTS OF BABIES IN ITS BELLY?
ギュン
VWM
IT'D BE TOO HEAVY TO FLY.

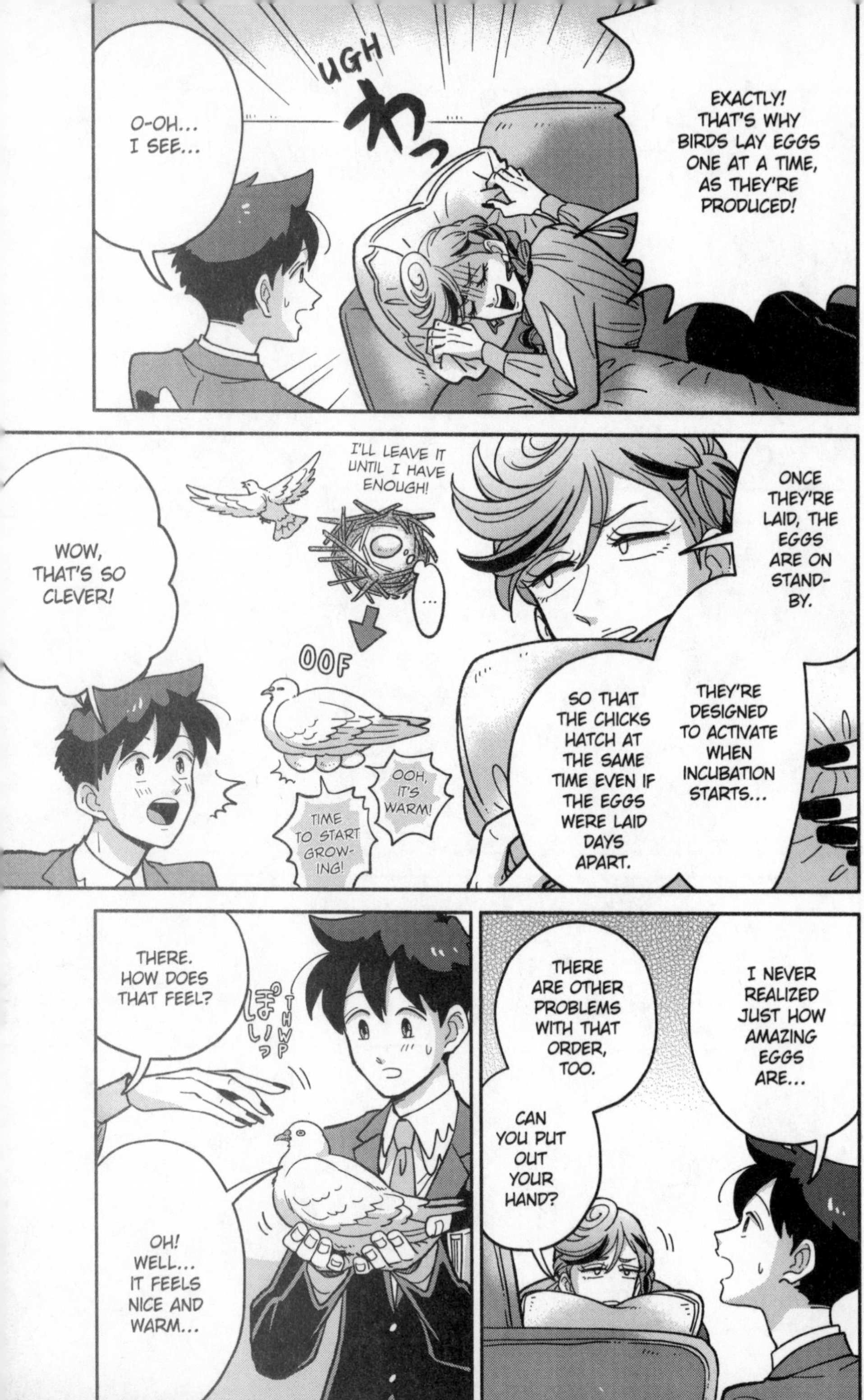
EXACTLY! THAT'S WHY BIRDS LAY EGGS ONE AT A TIME, AS THEY'RE PRODUCED!
UGH
わっ
O-OH... I SEE...
ONCE THEY'RE LAID, THE EGGS ARE ON STAND-BY.
I'LL LEAVE IT UNTIL I HAVE ENOUGH!
...
THEY'RE DESIGNED TO ACTIVATE WHEN INCUBATION STARTS...
SO THAT THE CHICKS HATCH AT THE SAME TIME EVEN IF THE EGGS WERE LAID DAYS APART.
OOF
OOH, IT'S WARM!
TIME TO START GROW-ING!
WOW, THAT'S SO CLEVER!
I NEVER REALIZED JUST HOW AMAZING EGGS ARE...
THERE ARE OTHER PROBLEMS WITH THAT ORDER, TOO.
CAN YOU PUT OUT YOUR HAND?
THERE. HOW DOES THAT FEEL?
THWP
ぽしっ
OH! WELL... IT FEELS NICE AND WARM...

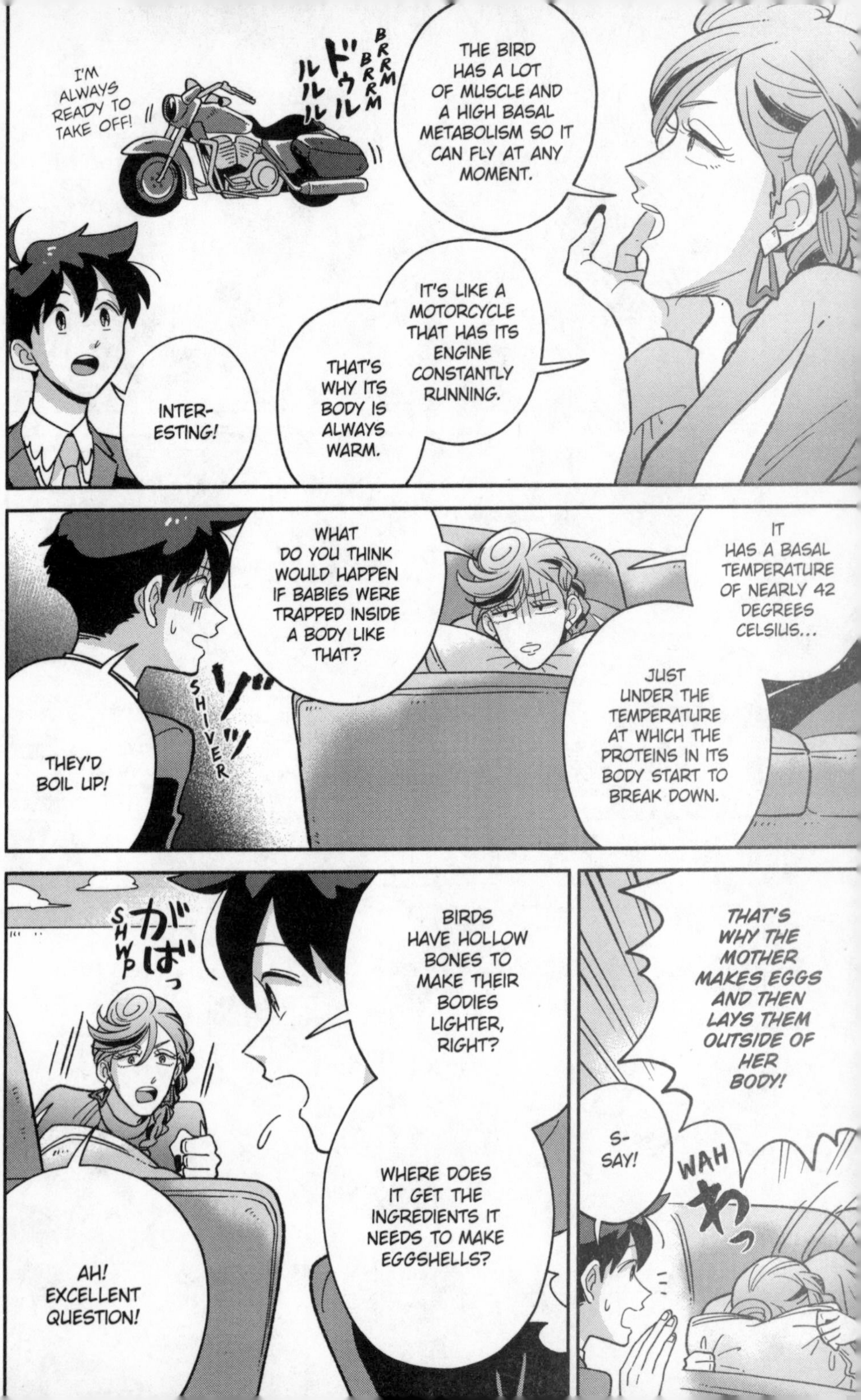
THE BIRD HAS A LOT OF MUSCLE AND A HIGH BASAL METABOLISM SO IT CAN FLY AT ANY MOMENT.
BRRM BRRM
ドゥルルル
I'M ALWAYS READY TO TAKE OFF!
IT'S LIKE A MOTORCYCLE THAT HAS ITS ENGINE CONSTANTLY RUNNING.
THAT'S WHY ITS BODY IS ALWAYS WARM.
INTER-ESTING!
IT HAS A BASAL TEMPERATURE OF NEARLY 42 DEGREES CELSIUS...
JUST UNDER THE TEMPERATURE AT WHICH THE PROTEINS IN ITS BODY START TO BREAK DOWN.
WHAT DO YOU THINK WOULD HAPPEN IF BABIES WERE TRAPPED INSIDE A BODY LIKE THAT?
SHIVER
ゾッ
THEY'D BOIL UP!
THAT'S WHY THE MOTHER MAKES EGGS AND THEN LAYS THEM OUTSIDE OF HER BODY!
WAH
わっ
S-SAY!
BIRDS HAVE HOLLOW BONES TO MAKE THEIR BODIES LIGHTER, RIGHT?
SHWP
がばっ
WHERE DOES IT GET THE INGREDIENTS IT NEEDS TO MAKE EGGSHELLS?
AH! EXCELLENT QUESTION!

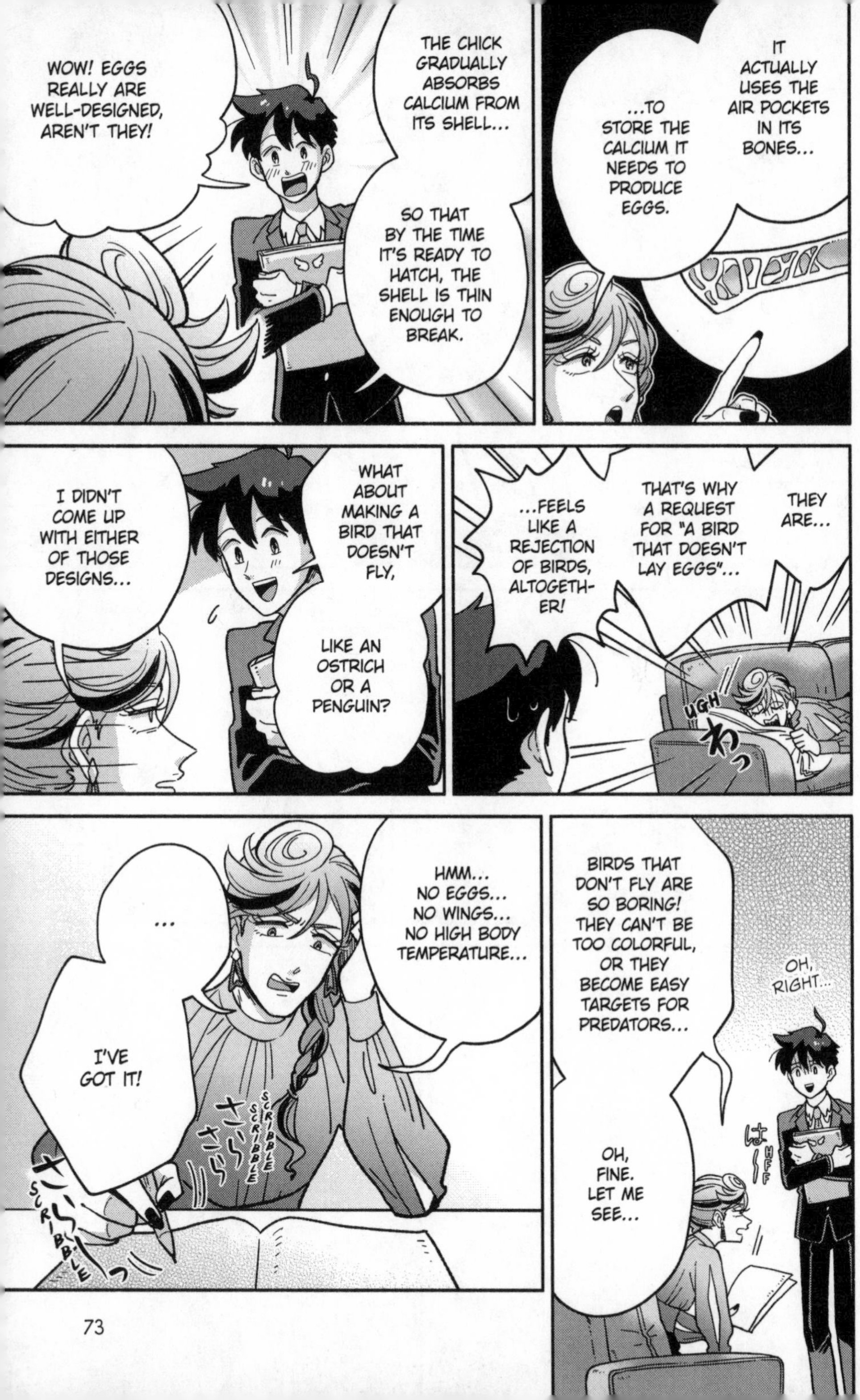
IT ACTUALLY USES THE AIR POCKETS IN ITS BONES...
...TO STORE THE CALCIUM IT NEEDS TO PRODUCE EGGS.
THE CHICK GRADUALLY ABSORBS CALCIUM FROM ITS SHELL...
SO THAT BY THE TIME IT'S READY TO HATCH, THE SHELL IS THIN ENOUGH TO BREAK.
WOW! EGGS REALLY ARE WELL-DESIGNED, AREN'T THEY!
THEY ARE...
THAT'S WHY A REQUEST FOR "A BIRD THAT DOESN'T LAY EGGS"...
...FEELS LIKE A REJECTION OF BIRDS, ALTOGETH-ER!
UGH
わっ
WHAT ABOUT MAKING A BIRD THAT DOESN'T FLY,
LIKE AN OSTRICH OR A PENGUIN?
I DIDN'T COME UP WITH EITHER OF THOSE DESIGNS...
BIRDS THAT DON'T FLY ARE SO BORING! THEY CAN'T BE TOO COLORFUL, OR THEY BECOME EASY TARGETS FOR PREDATORS...
OH, RIGHT...
はー
HFF
OH, FINE. LET ME SEE...
HMM... NO EGGS... NO WINGS... NO HIGH BODY TEMPERATURE...
...
I'VE GOT IT!
さらさら
SCRIBBLE SCRIBBLE
SCRIBBLE

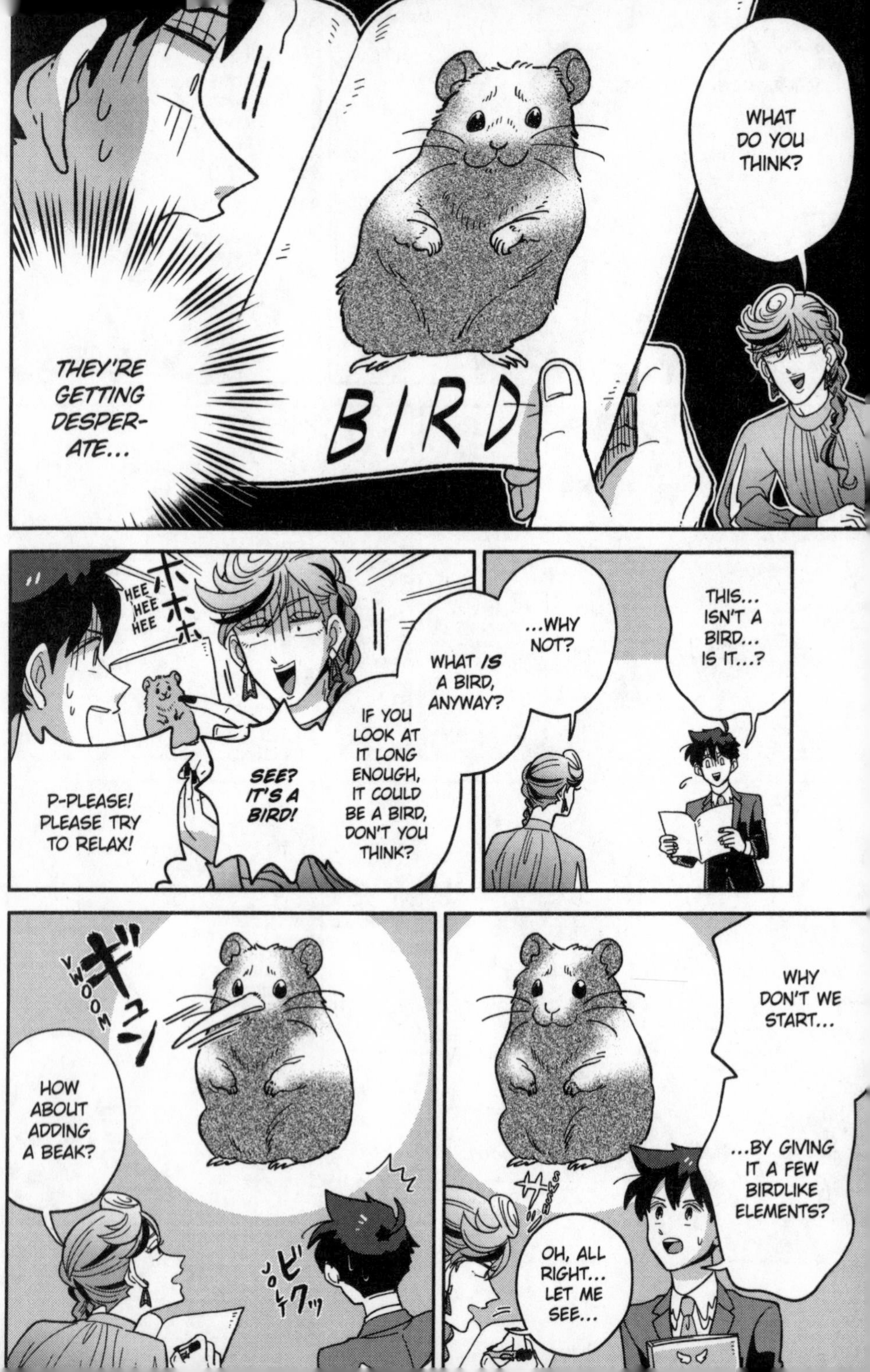
WHAT DO YOU THINK?
BIRD
THEY'RE GETTING DESPER-ATE...
THIS... ISN'T A BIRD... IS IT...?
...WHY NOT?
WHAT *IS* A BIRD, ANYWAY?
IF YOU LOOK AT IT LONG ENOUGH, IT COULD BE A BIRD, DON'T YOU THINK?
HEE HEE HEE
SEE? IT'S A BIRD!
P-PLEASE! PLEASE TRY TO RELAX!
WHY DON'T WE START...
...BY GIVING IT A FEW BIRDLIKE ELEMENTS?
OH, ALL RIGHT... LET ME SEE...
VWOOOM
HOW ABOUT ADDING A BEAK?
JOLT

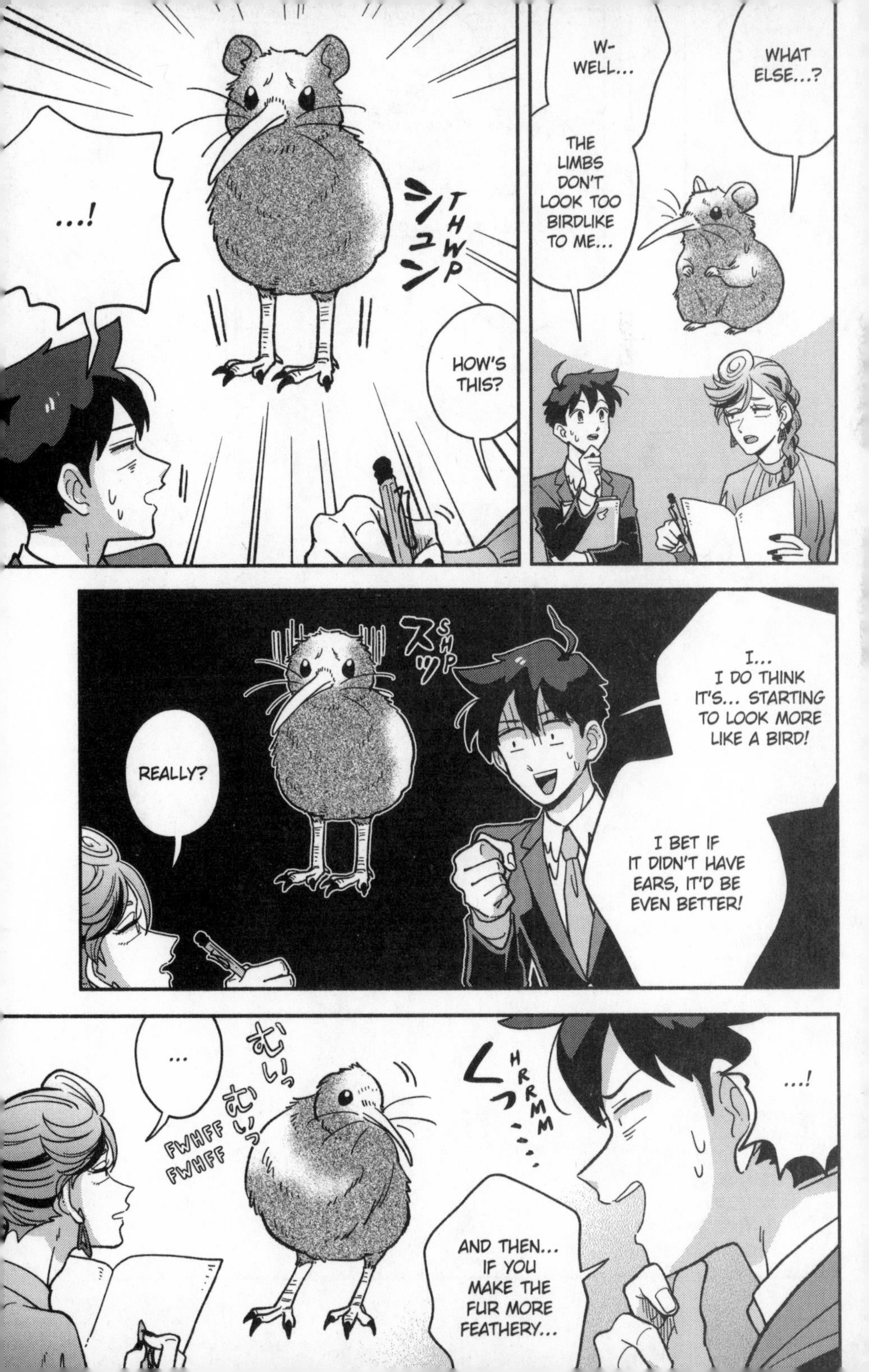
WHAT ELSE...?
W-WELL...
THE LIMBS DON'T LOOK TOO BIRDLIKE TO ME...
THWP
HOW'S THIS?
...!
I... I DO THINK IT'S... STARTING TO LOOK MORE LIKE A BIRD!
I BET IF IT DIDN'T HAVE EARS, IT'D BE EVEN BETTER!
SHP
REALLY?
...!
HRRMM
AND THEN... IF YOU MAKE THE FUR MORE FEATHERY...
FWHFF FWHFF
...

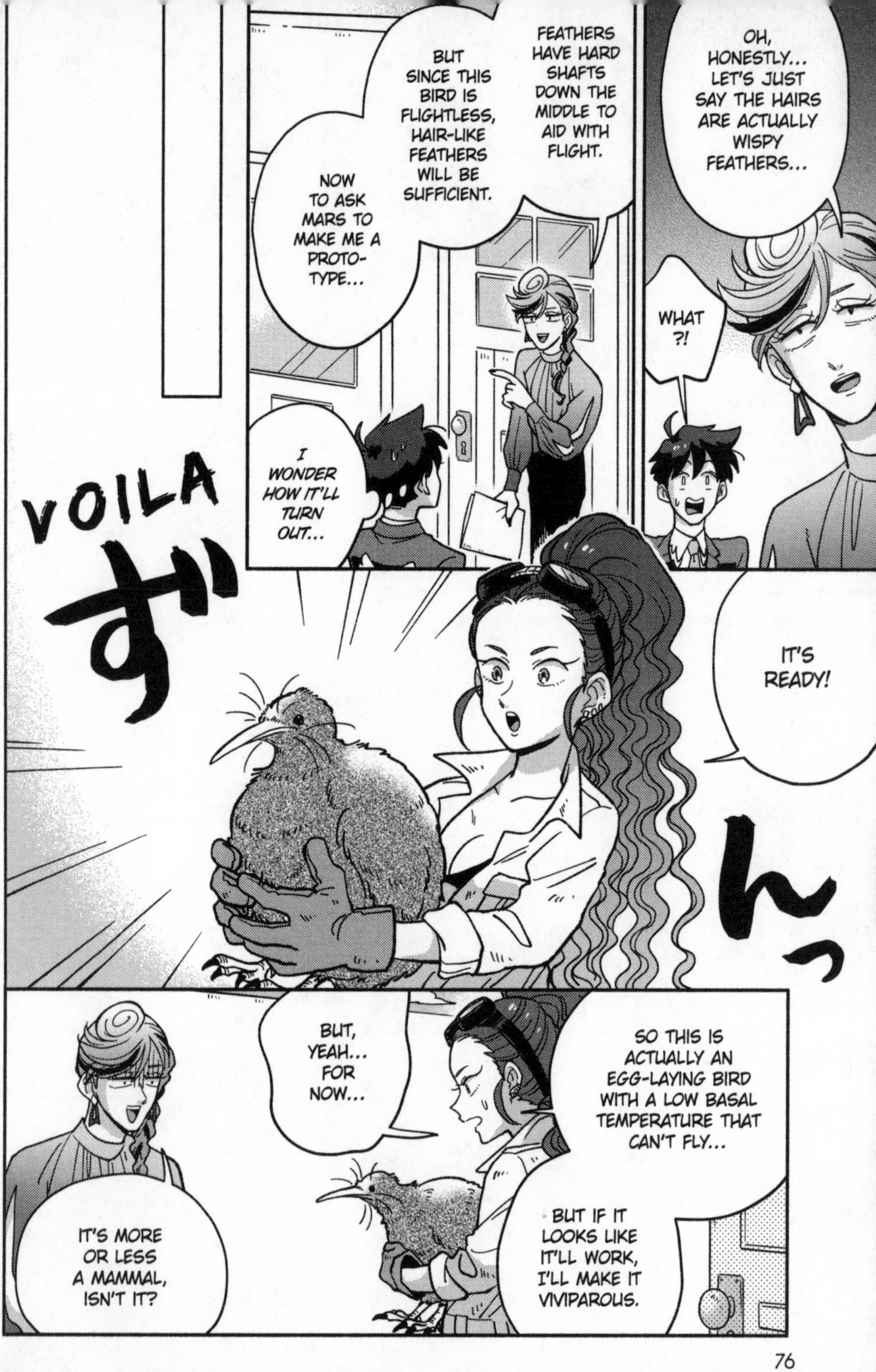
OH, HONESTLY... LET'S JUST SAY THE HAIRS ARE ACTUALLY WISPY FEATHERS...
WHAT ?!
FEATHERS HAVE HARD SHAFTS DOWN THE MIDDLE TO AID WITH FLIGHT.
BUT SINCE THIS BIRD IS FLIGHTLESS, HAIR-LIKE FEATHERS WILL BE SUFFICIENT.
NOW TO ASK MARS TO MAKE ME A PROTO-TYPE...
I WONDER HOW IT'LL TURN OUT...
IT'S READY!
んっ
VOILA
す
SO THIS IS ACTUALLY AN EGG-LAYING BIRD WITH A LOW BASAL TEMPERATURE THAT CAN'T FLY...
BUT IF IT LOOKS LIKE IT'LL WORK, I'LL MAKE IT VIVIPAROUS.
BUT, YEAH... FOR NOW...
IT'S MORE OR LESS A MAMMAL, ISN'T IT?

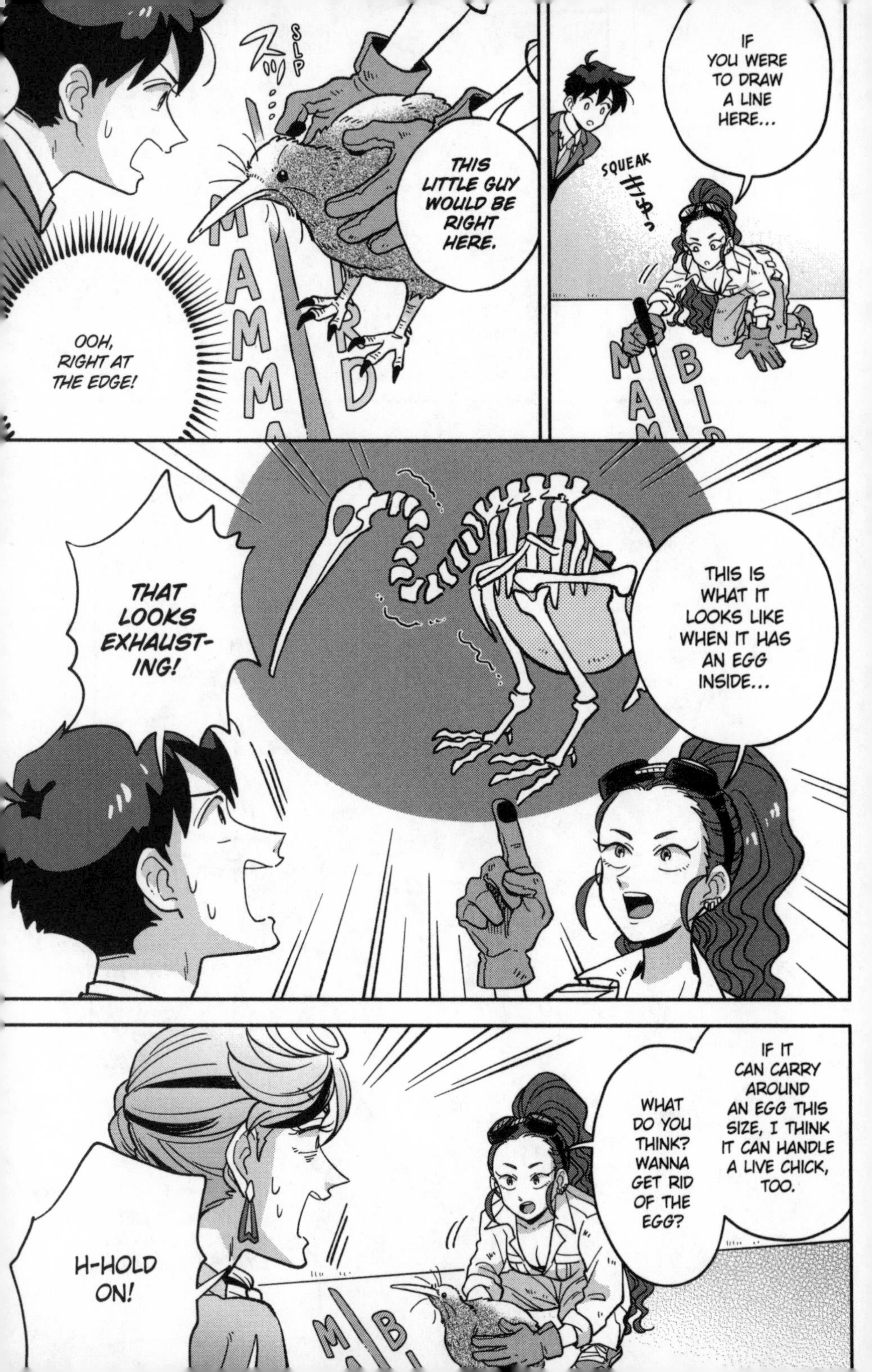

IF YOU WERE TO DRAW A LINE HERE...
SQUEAK
SLP
THIS LITTLE GUY WOULD BE RIGHT HERE.
OOH, RIGHT AT THE EDGE!
THIS IS WHAT IT LOOKS LIKE WHEN IT HAS AN EGG INSIDE...
THAT LOOKS EXHAUST-ING!
IF IT CAN CARRY AROUND AN EGG THIS SIZE, I THINK IT CAN HANDLE A LIVE CHICK, TOO.
WHAT DO YOU THINK? WANNA GET RID OF THE EGG?
H-HOLD ON!

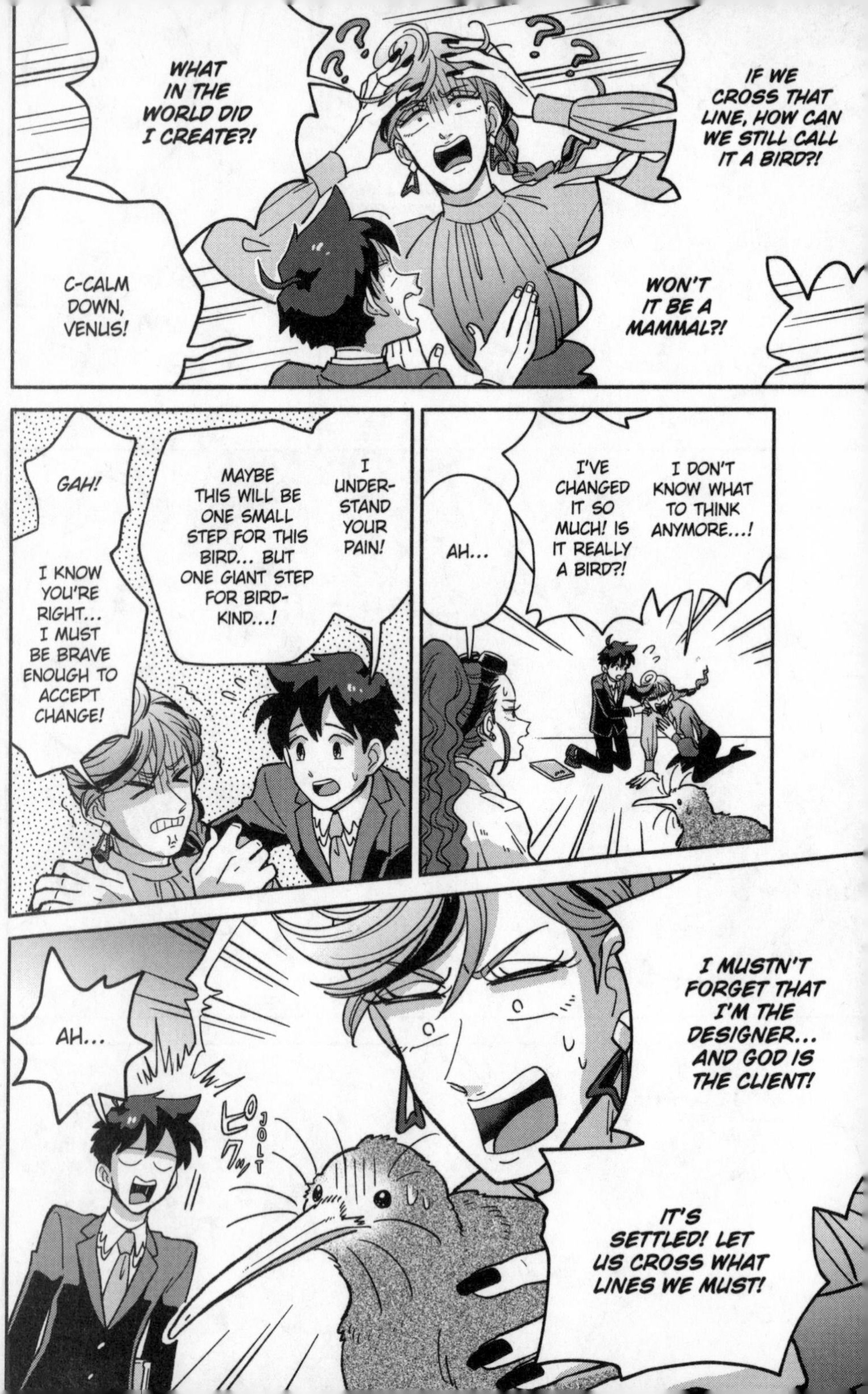
IF WE CROSS THAT LINE, HOW CAN WE STILL CALL IT A BIRD?!
WHAT IN THE WORLD DID I CREATE?!
WON'T IT BE A MAMMAL?!
C-CALM DOWN, VENUS!
I DON'T KNOW WHAT TO THINK ANYMORE...!
I'VE CHANGED IT SO MUCH! IS IT REALLY A BIRD?!
AH...
I UNDER-STAND YOUR PAIN!
MAYBE THIS WILL BE ONE SMALL STEP FOR THIS BIRD... BUT ONE GIANT STEP FOR BIRD-KIND...!
GAH!
I KNOW YOU'RE RIGHT... I MUST BE BRAVE ENOUGH TO ACCEPT CHANGE!
I MUSTN'T FORGET THAT I'M THE DESIGNER... AND GOD IS THE CLIENT!
IT'S SETTLED! LET US CROSS WHAT LINES WE MUST!
AH...
JOLT

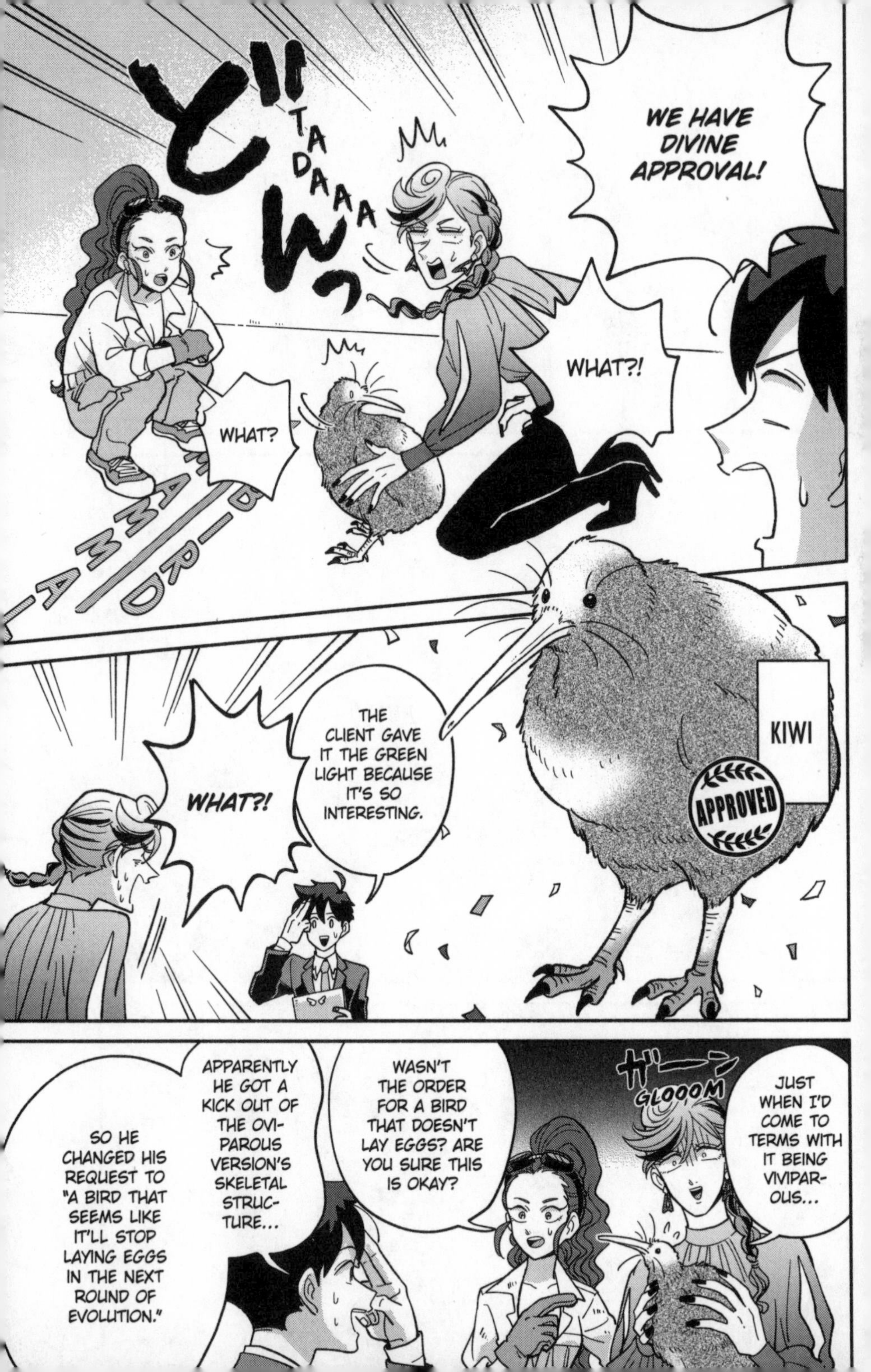
WE HAVE DIVINE APPROVAL!
WHAT?!
どんっ
TADAAAA
WHAT?
KIWI
APPROVED
THE CLIENT GAVE IT THE GREEN LIGHT BECAUSE IT'S SO INTERESTING.
WHAT?!
JUST WHEN I'D COME TO TERMS WITH IT BEING VIVIPAROUS...
ガーン
GLOOOM
WASN'T THE ORDER FOR A BIRD THAT DOESN'T LAY EGGS? ARE YOU SURE THIS IS OKAY?
APPARENTLY HE GOT A KICK OUT OF THE OVIPAROUS VERSION'S SKELETAL STRUCTURE...
SO HE CHANGED HIS REQUEST TO "A BIRD THAT SEEMS LIKE IT'LL STOP LAYING EGGS IN THE NEXT ROUND OF EVOLUTION."

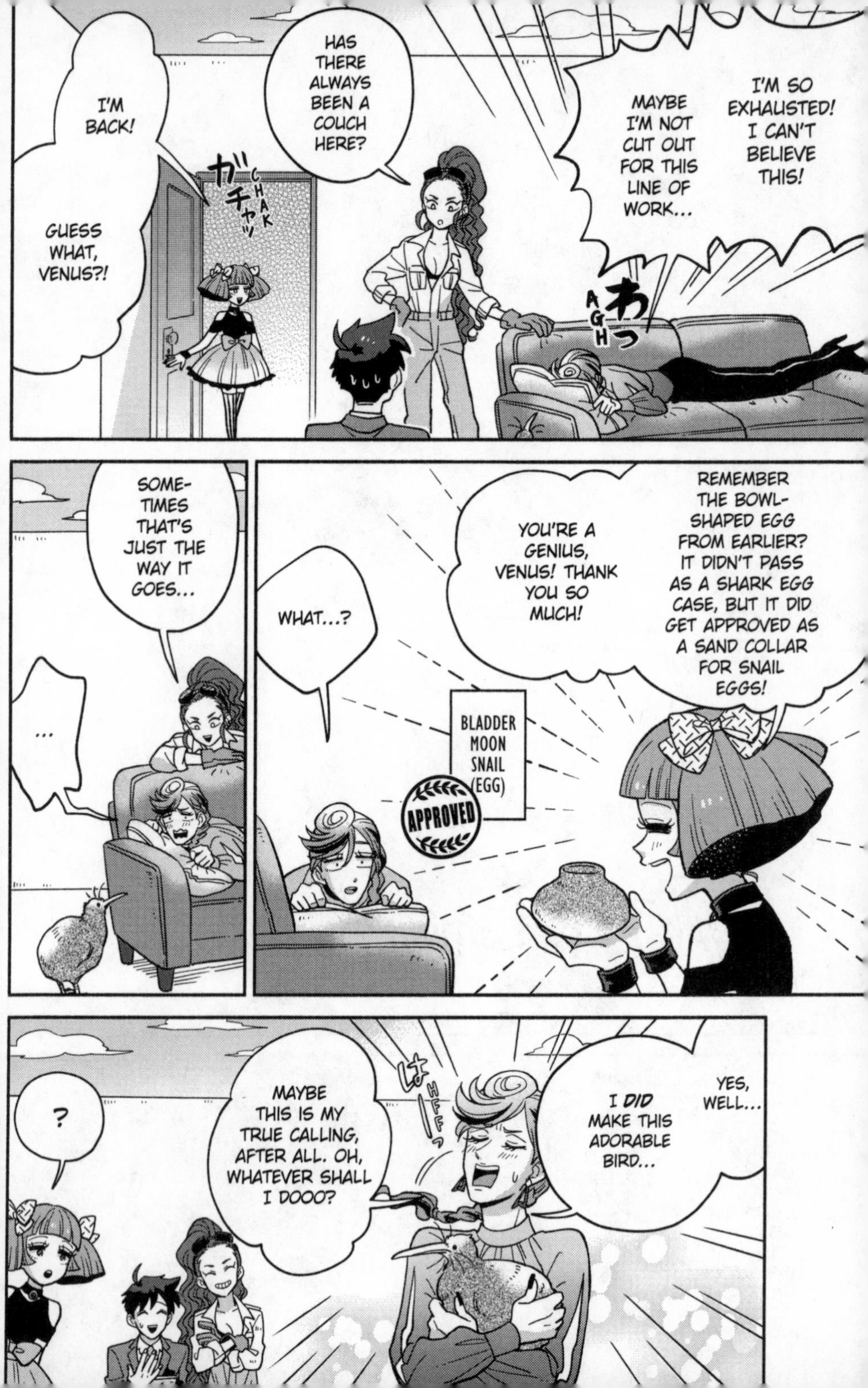
I'M SO EXHAUSTED! I CAN'T BELIEVE THIS!
MAYBE I'M NOT CUT OUT FOR THIS LINE OF WORK...
わっ AGH
HAS THERE ALWAYS BEEN A COUCH HERE?
I'M BACK!
ガチャッ CHAK
GUESS WHAT, VENUS?!
REMEMBER THE BOWL-SHAPED EGG FROM EARLIER? IT DIDN'T PASS AS A SHARK EGG CASE, BUT IT DID GET APPROVED AS A SAND COLLAR FOR SNAIL EGGS!
YOU'RE A GENIUS, VENUS! THANK YOU SO MUCH!
WHAT...?
BLADDER MOON SNAIL (EGG)
APPROVED
SOME-TIMES THAT'S JUST THE WAY IT GOES...
...
YES, WELL...
I *DID* MAKE THIS ADORABLE BIRD...
はーっ HFF
MAYBE THIS IS MY TRUE CALLING, AFTER ALL. OH, WHATEVER SHALL I DOOO?
?

THE ENCYCLOPEDIA OF REAL ANIMALS 32

ANIMAL 78 | KIWI

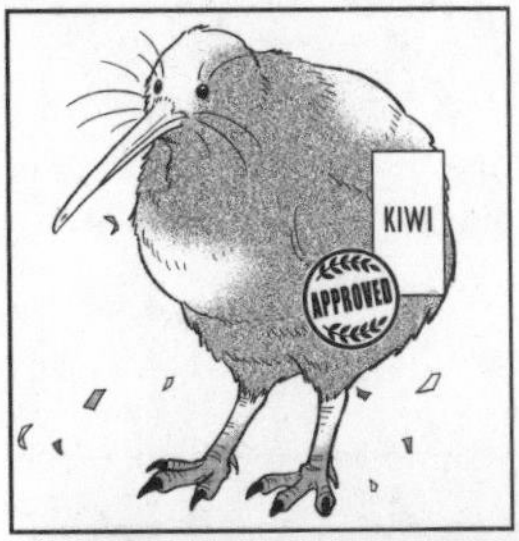
KIWI
APPROVED

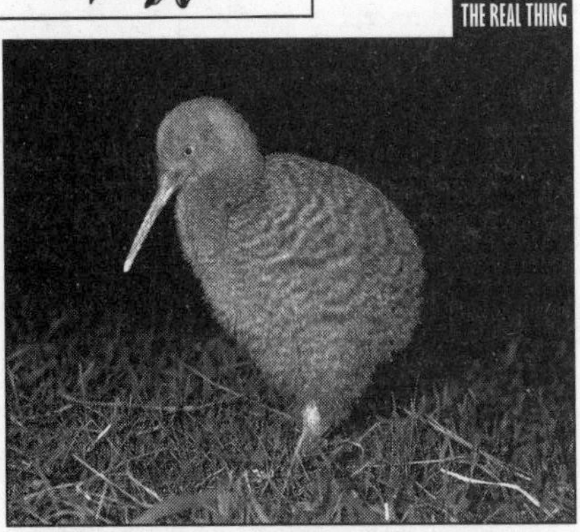
THE REAL THING

The nocturnal kiwi hunts for food using its long beak.

Photo: Minden Pictures/Aflo

[Name] Kiwi
[Classification] Class: Aves
Order: Apterygiformes
Family: Apterygidae
Class: Apteryx
[Habitat] New Zealand
[Length] 40-50 cm (1.3-1.6 ft)

The kiwi is a flightless bird endemic to New Zealand. Its wings are only a few centimeters long and invisible at first glance. The feathers that cover its body are soft like mammal fur, and it has a strong skeletal structure. It has a significantly lower basal body temperature than other birds, hovering around 38 degrees Celsius (approximately 100 degrees Fahrenheit). Because of these characteristics, some researchers call the kiwi a "mammal-like bird."

The kiwi lays eggs that are extremely large in proportion to its body size—up to four to five times the size of those of similarly sized birds. Sixty-one percent of the eggs' contents is made up of the yolk, which allows the robust chick to survive for several days without food after it is hatched. In most species, the male incubates the eggs. Though the kiwi's eyes are small and its vision is weak, it has an excellent sense of smell. It uses the nostrils located at the end of its beak to sniff out worms and other prey from the ground.

SPECIAL FEATURE — SHARK EGG CASES

APPROVED
THE REAL THING

The long tendrils of the small-spotted catshark's egg case wrap around seaweed to anchor it in place.

Photo: Minden Pictures/Aflo

Sharks reproduce in a wide variety of ways. Some are viviparous, while others are oviparous, and the eggs of the latter come in all shapes and sizes. The Japanese bullhead shark, for example, lays drill-shaped egg cases that can be pushed between rocks for safekeeping.

The wide range of unusual shapes is possible because the egg cases are soft when they're first deposited and only later become harder. Catsharks lay egg cases with long tendrils that wrap around seaweed and keep them in place.

On another note, the fish eggs best known as expensive "caviar" are those of sturgeons, which may resemble sharks, but are actually more closely related to mackerels.

ANIMAL 79 — BLADDER MOON SNAIL

The bladder moon snail is a type of conch that creates sand collars for its eggs that look like upside-down bowls lying on the beach. These structures are made from a mixture of eggs, sand, and mucus.

The bladder moon snail is carnivorous and drills small holes in the shells of its prey to eat their insides. When the snail is inactive, it looks like a normal conch, but when it starts moving, its large foot extends beyond its shell, making it look like a pancake with a shell on top.

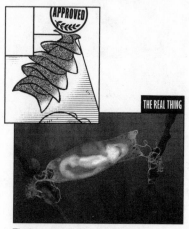

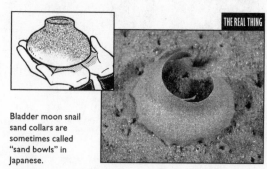

THE REAL THING

Bladder moon snail sand collars are sometimes called "sand bowls" in Japanese.

Photo: Minden Pictures/Aflo

[Name]	*Glossaulax didyma*
[Classification]	Class: Gastropoda Family: Naticidae Genus: *Neverita*
[Habitat]	Oceans of Japan (south of Hokkaido), India, and the western Pacific
[Length]	Approximately 7 cm (3 in)

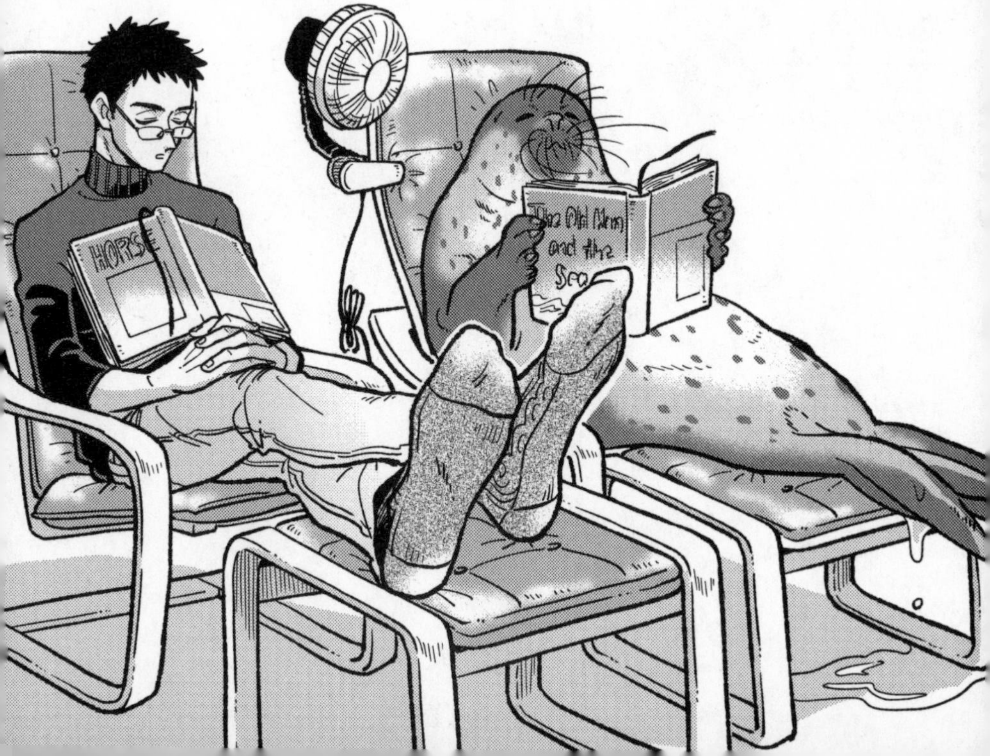
HORSE
The Old Man and the Sea

**HEAVEN'S
DESIGN TEAM**

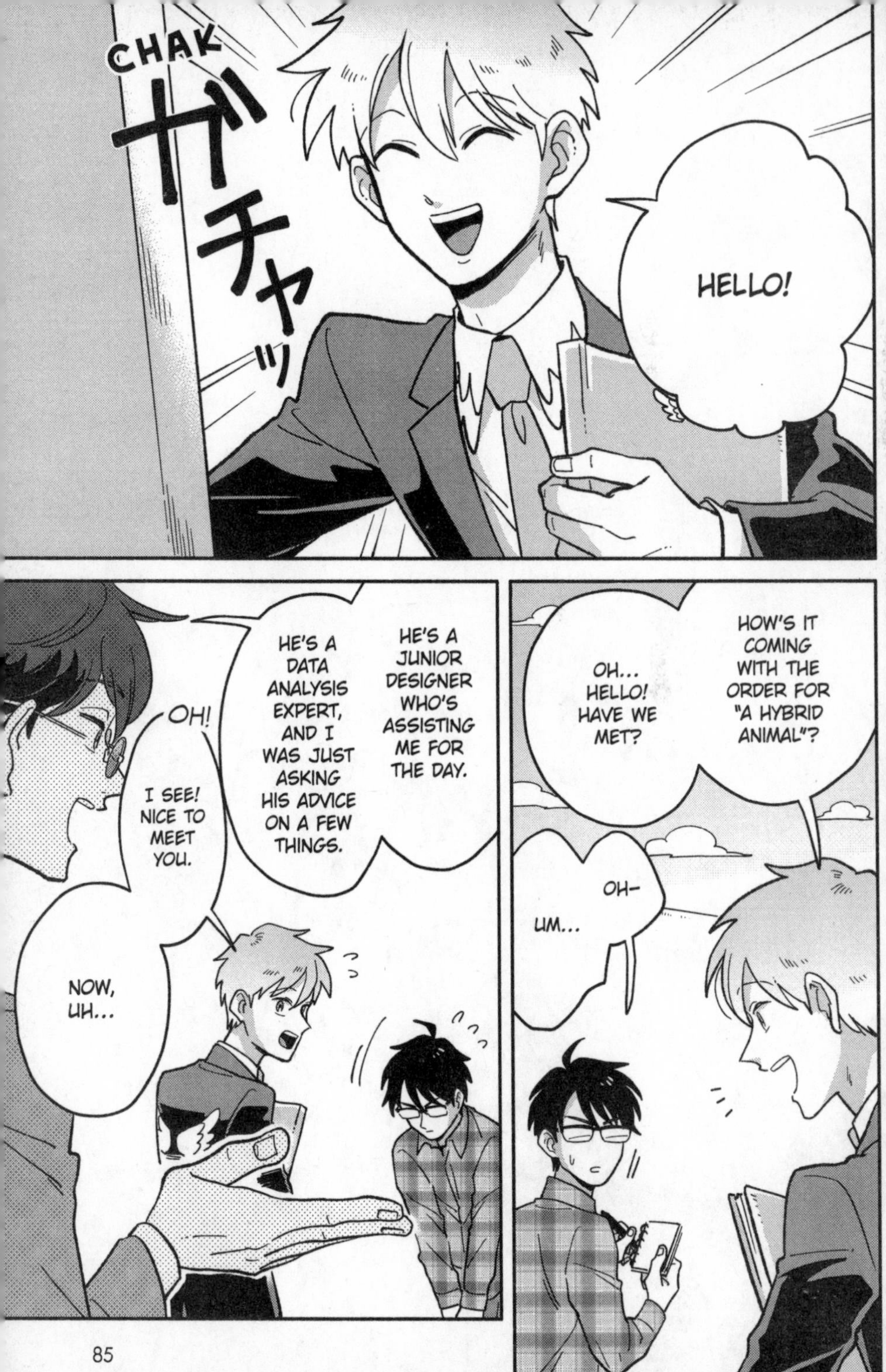
CHAK
ガチャッ
HELLO!
HOW'S IT COMING WITH THE ORDER FOR "A HYBRID ANIMAL"?
OH... HELLO! HAVE WE MET?
OH—
UM...
HE'S A JUNIOR DESIGNER WHO'S ASSISTING ME FOR THE DAY.
HE'S A DATA ANALYSIS EXPERT, AND I WAS JUST ASKING HIS ADVICE ON A FEW THINGS.
OH!
I SEE! NICE TO MEET YOU.
NOW, UH...

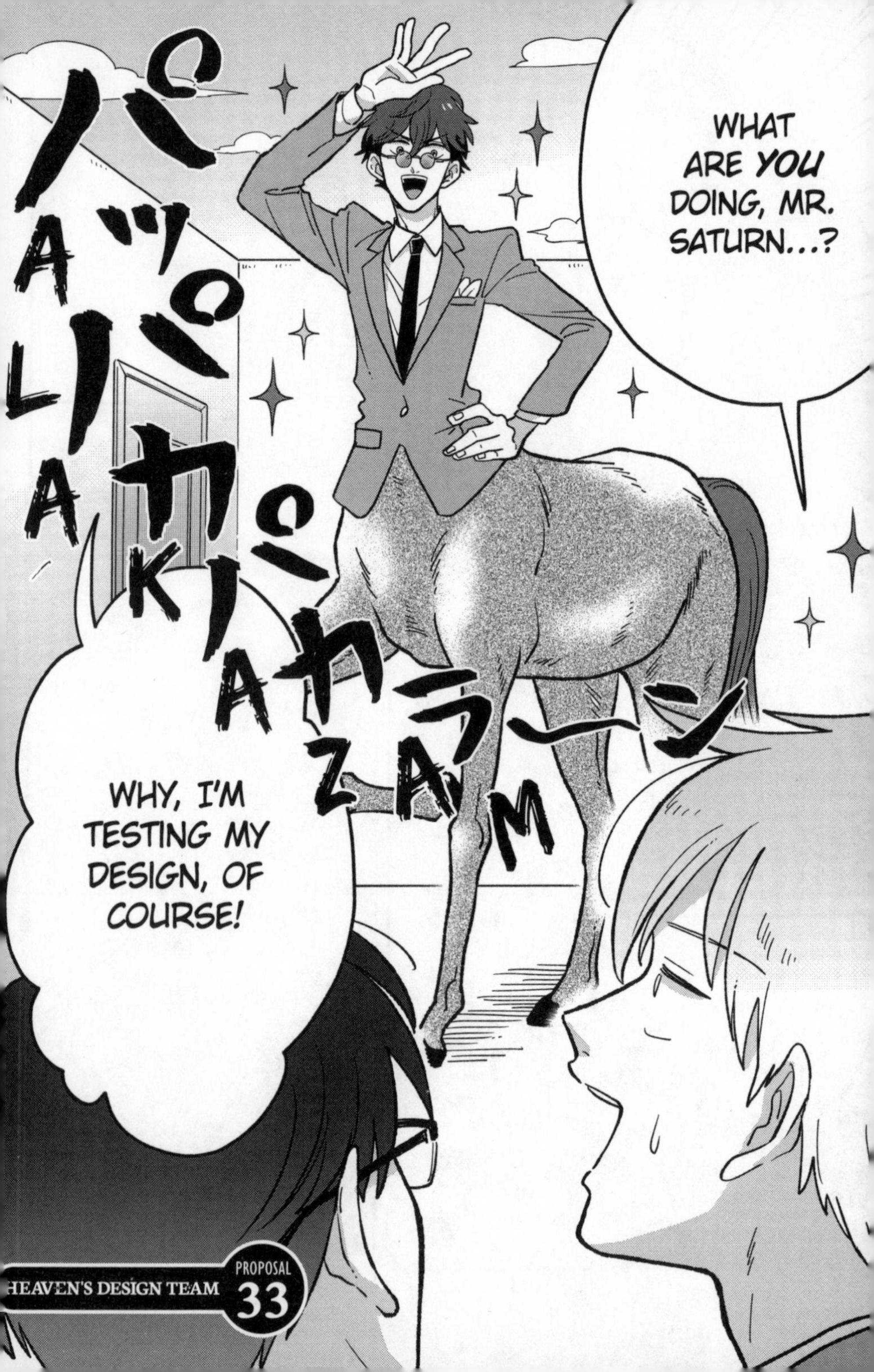
WHAT ARE YOU DOING, MR. SATURN...?
WHY, I'M TESTING MY DESIGN, OF COURSE!

HEAVEN'S DESIGN TEAM PROPOSAL 33

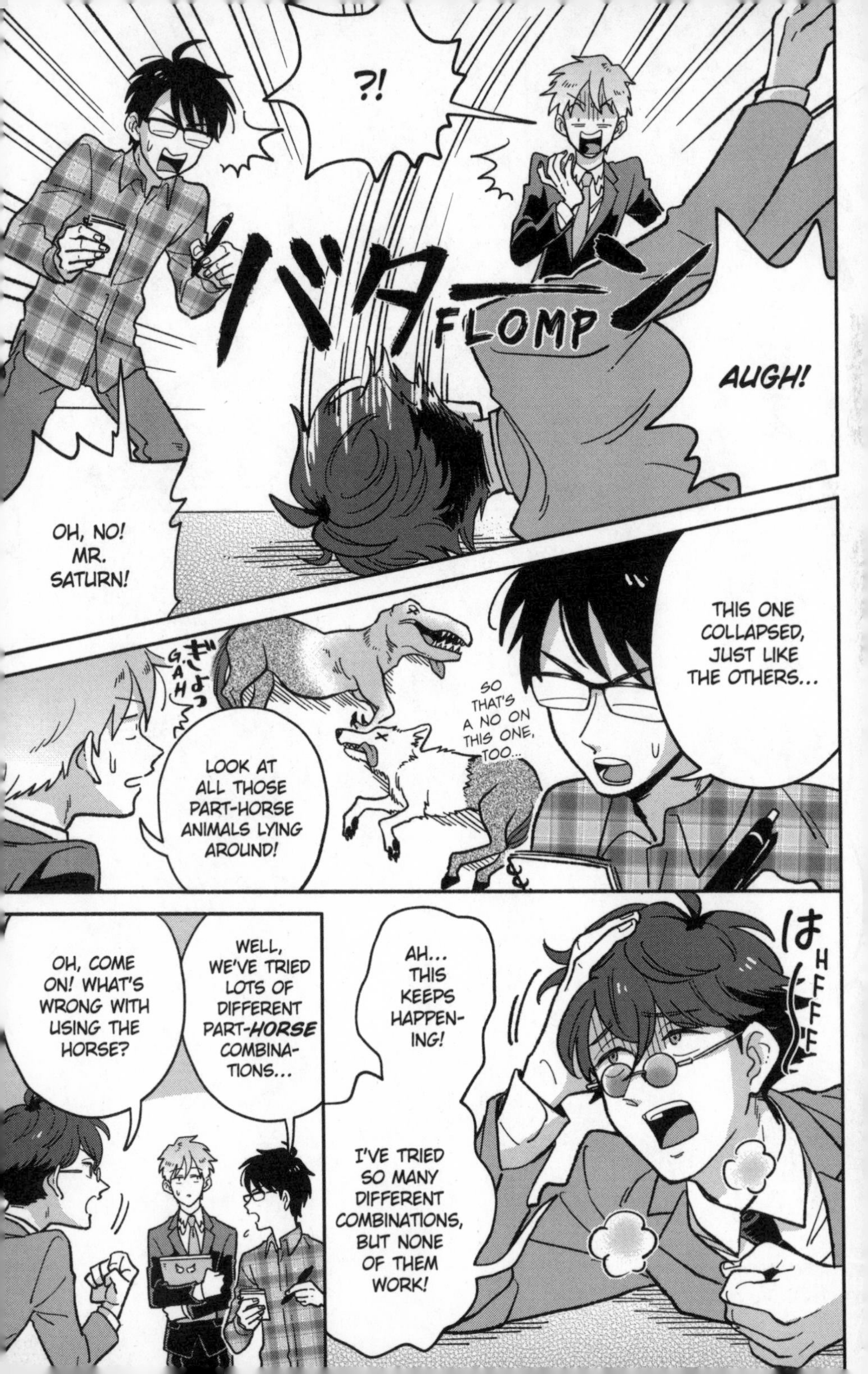
?!
バター
FLOMP
AUGH!
OH, NO! MR. SATURN!
THIS ONE COLLAPSED, JUST LIKE THE OTHERS...
SO THAT'S A NO ON THIS ONE, TOO...
ぎょっ
GAH
LOOK AT ALL THOSE PART-HORSE ANIMALS LYING AROUND!
は
HFFF
AH... THIS KEEPS HAPPEN-ING!
I'VE TRIED SO MANY DIFFERENT COMBINATIONS, BUT NONE OF THEM WORK!
WELL, WE'VE TRIED LOTS OF DIFFERENT PART-*HORSE* COMBINA-TIONS...
OH, COME ON! WHAT'S WRONG WITH USING THE HORSE?

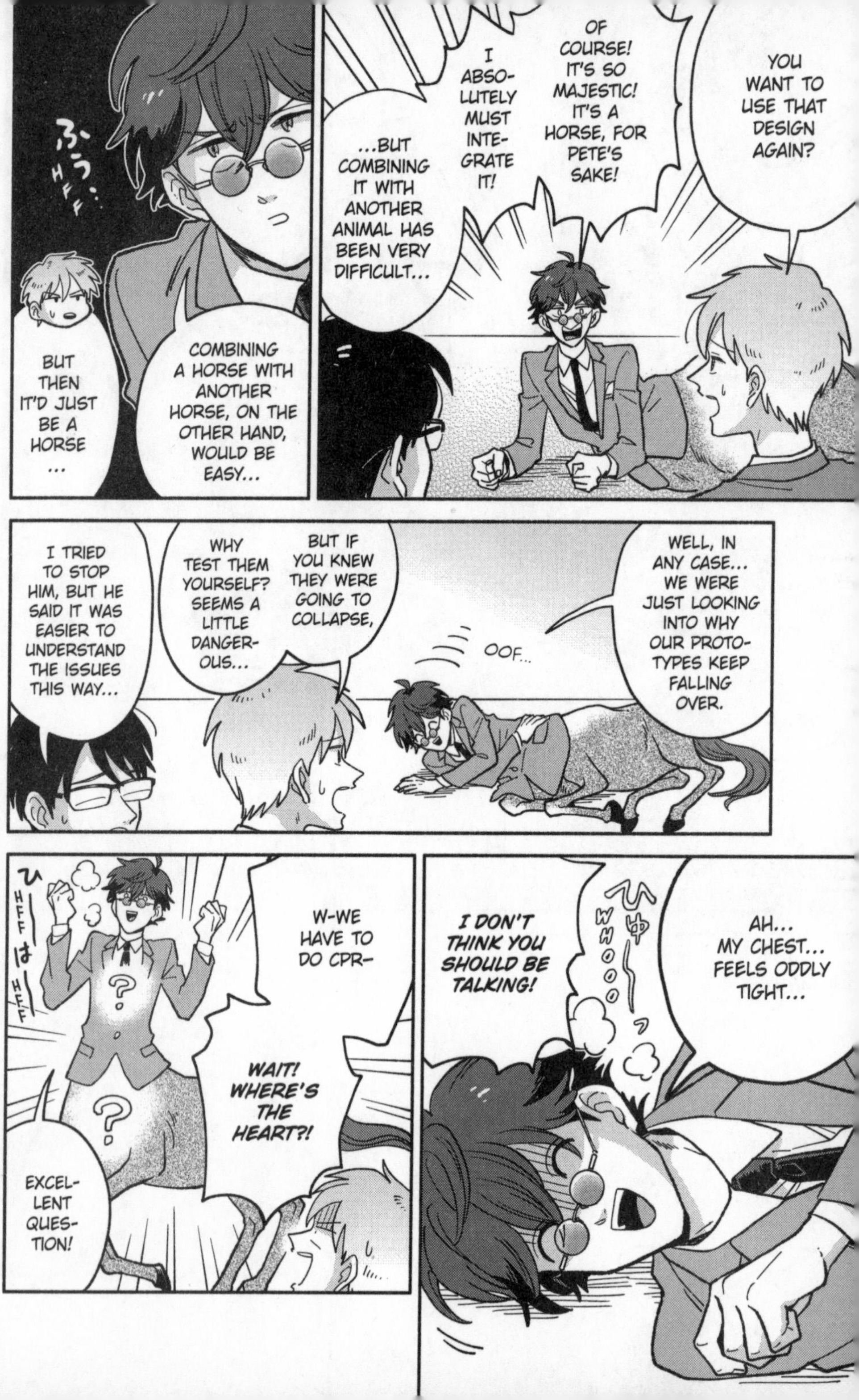
YOU WANT TO USE THAT DESIGN AGAIN?
OF COURSE! IT'S SO MAJESTIC! IT'S A HORSE, FOR PETE'S SAKE!
I ABSOLUTELY MUST INTEGRATE IT!
...BUT COMBINING IT WITH ANOTHER ANIMAL HAS BEEN VERY DIFFICULT...
ふう… HFF
COMBINING A HORSE WITH ANOTHER HORSE, ON THE OTHER HAND, WOULD BE EASY...
BUT THEN IT'D JUST BE A HORSE...
WELL, IN ANY CASE... WE WERE JUST LOOKING INTO WHY OUR PROTOTYPES KEEP FALLING OVER.
OOF...
BUT IF YOU KNEW THEY WERE GOING TO COLLAPSE,
WHY TEST THEM YOURSELF? SEEMS A LITTLE DANGEROUS...
I TRIED TO STOP HIM, BUT HE SAID IT WAS EASIER TO UNDERSTAND THE ISSUES THIS WAY...
AH... MY CHEST... FEELS ODDLY TIGHT...
ひゅー WHOOO
I DON'T THINK YOU SHOULD BE TALKING!
W-WE HAVE TO DO CPR-
WAIT! WHERE'S THE HEART?!
ひ HFF は HFF
EXCELLENT QUESTION!

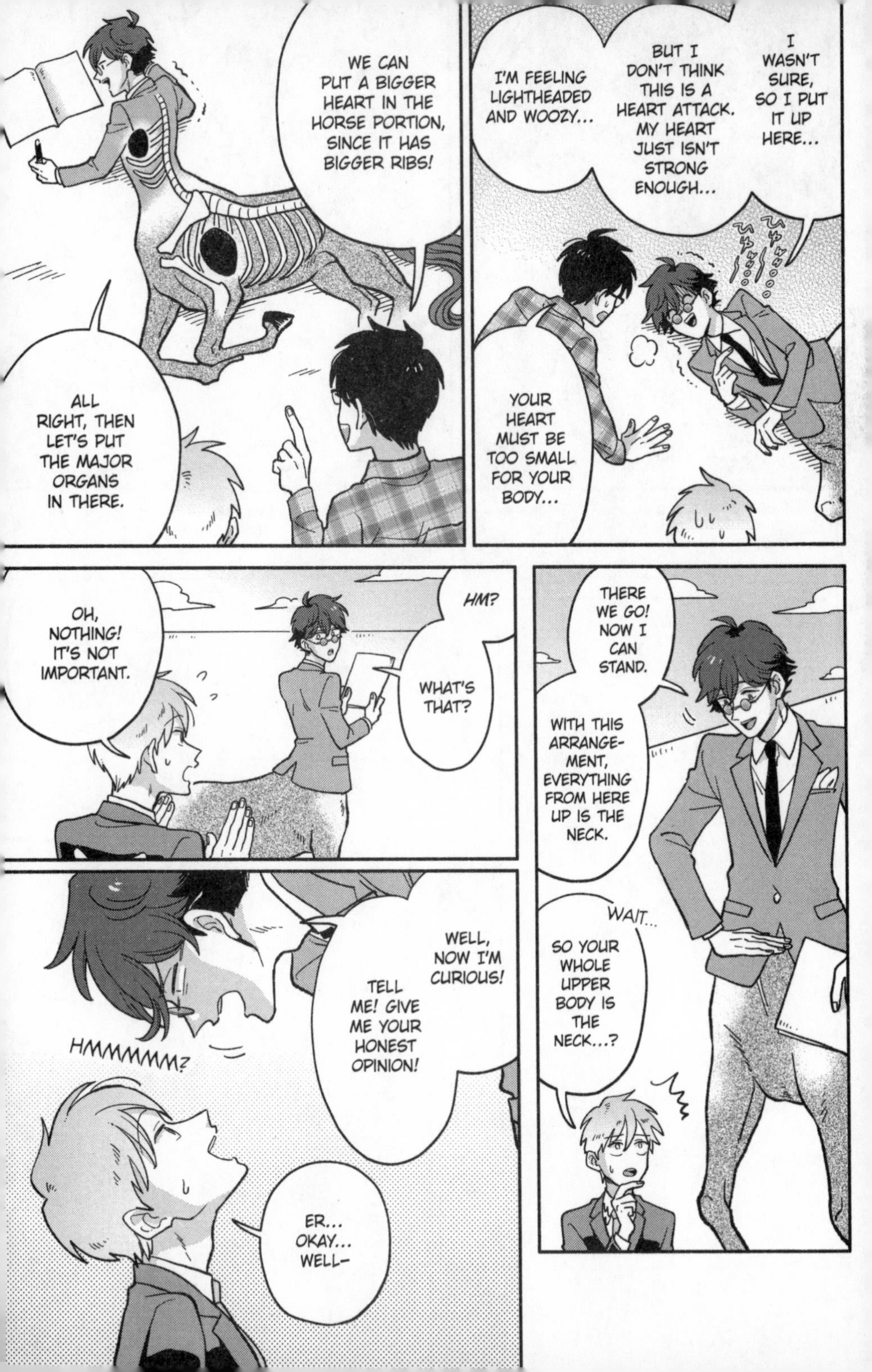
I WASN'T SURE, SO I PUT IT UP HERE...
BUT I DON'T THINK THIS IS A HEART ATTACK. MY HEART JUST ISN'T STRONG ENOUGH...
I'M FEELING LIGHTHEADED AND WOOZY...
YOUR HEART MUST BE TOO SMALL FOR YOUR BODY...
WE CAN PUT A BIGGER HEART IN THE HORSE PORTION, SINCE IT HAS BIGGER RIBS!
ALL RIGHT, THEN LET'S PUT THE MAJOR ORGANS IN THERE.
THERE WE GO! NOW I CAN STAND.
WITH THIS ARRANGE-MENT, EVERYTHING FROM HERE UP IS THE NECK.
WAIT...
SO YOUR WHOLE UPPER BODY IS THE NECK...?
HM?
WHAT'S THAT?
OH, NOTHING! IT'S NOT IMPORTANT.
WELL, NOW I'M CURIOUS!
TELL ME! GIVE ME YOUR HONEST OPINION!
HMMMMMM?
ER... OKAY... WELL-

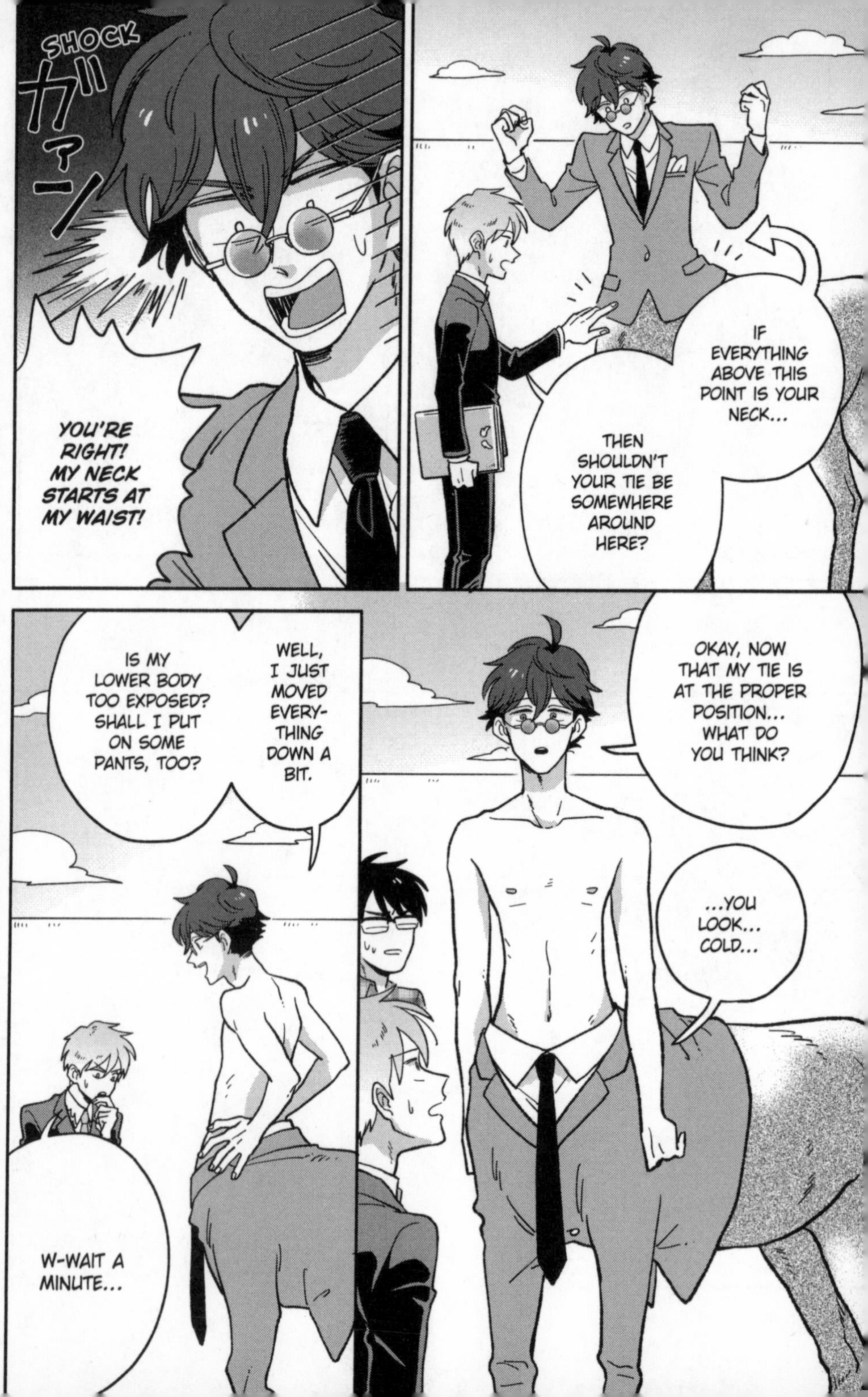
IF EVERYTHING ABOVE THIS POINT IS YOUR NECK...
THEN SHOULDN'T YOUR TIE BE SOMEWHERE AROUND HERE?
SHOCK
カァーン
YOU'RE RIGHT! MY NECK STARTS AT MY WAIST!
OKAY, NOW THAT MY TIE IS AT THE PROPER POSITION... WHAT DO YOU THINK?
...YOU LOOK... COLD...
WELL, I JUST MOVED EVERYTHING DOWN A BIT.
IS MY LOWER BODY TOO EXPOSED? SHALL I PUT ON SOME PANTS, TOO?
W-WAIT A MINUTE...

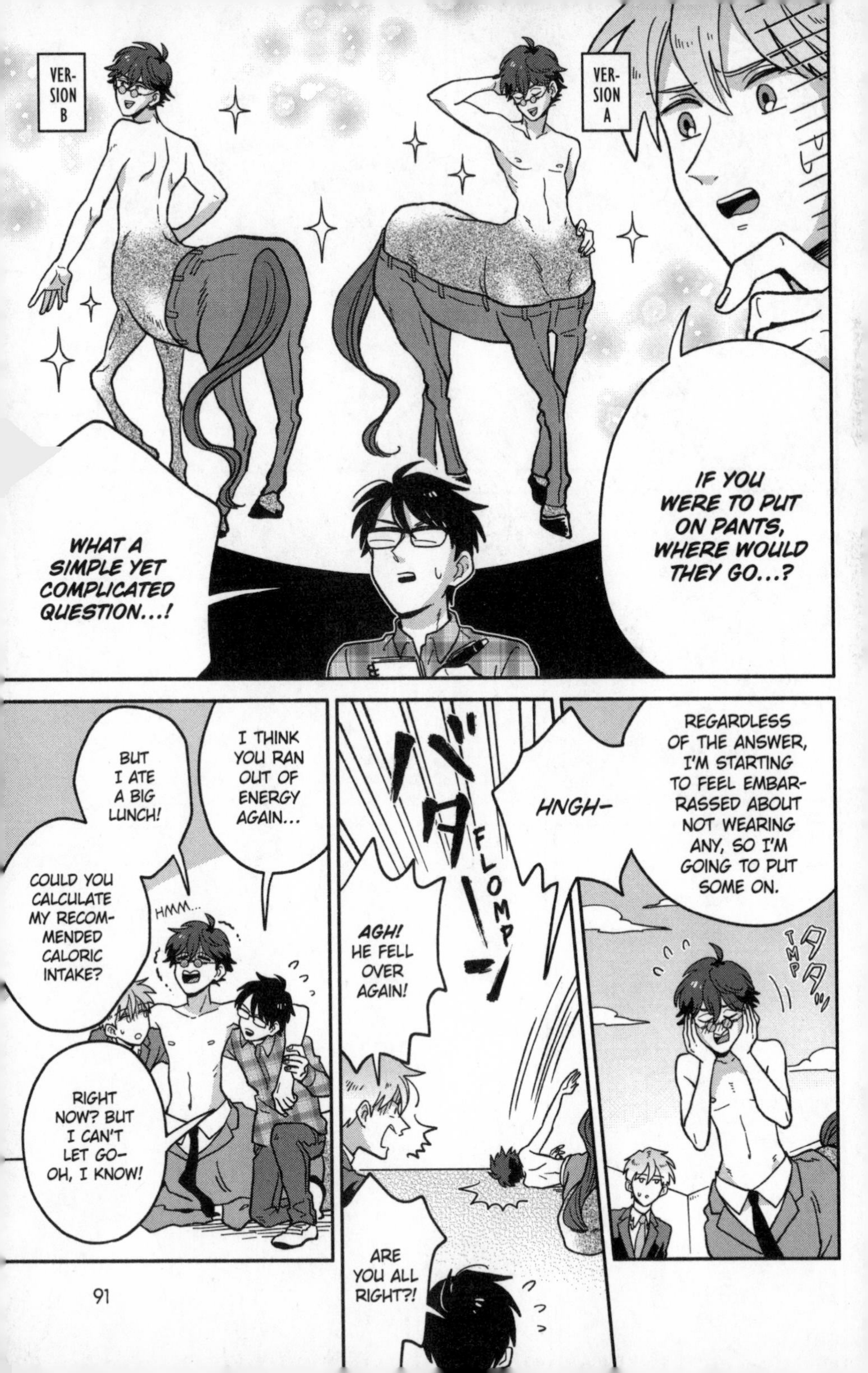
IF YOU WERE TO PUT ON PANTS, WHERE WOULD THEY GO...?
VER-SION A
VER-SION B
WHAT A SIMPLE YET COMPLICATED QUESTION...!
REGARDLESS OF THE ANSWER, I'M STARTING TO FEEL EMBAR-RASSED ABOUT NOT WEARING ANY, SO I'M GOING TO PUT SOME ON.
タタ
TMP
HNGH-
バタ
FLOMP
AGH! HE FELL OVER AGAIN!
ARE YOU ALL RIGHT?!
I THINK YOU RAN OUT OF ENERGY AGAIN...
BUT I ATE A BIG LUNCH!
HMM...
COULD YOU CALCULATE MY RECOM-MENDED CALORIC INTAKE?
RIGHT NOW? BUT I CAN'T LET GO—OH, I KNOW!

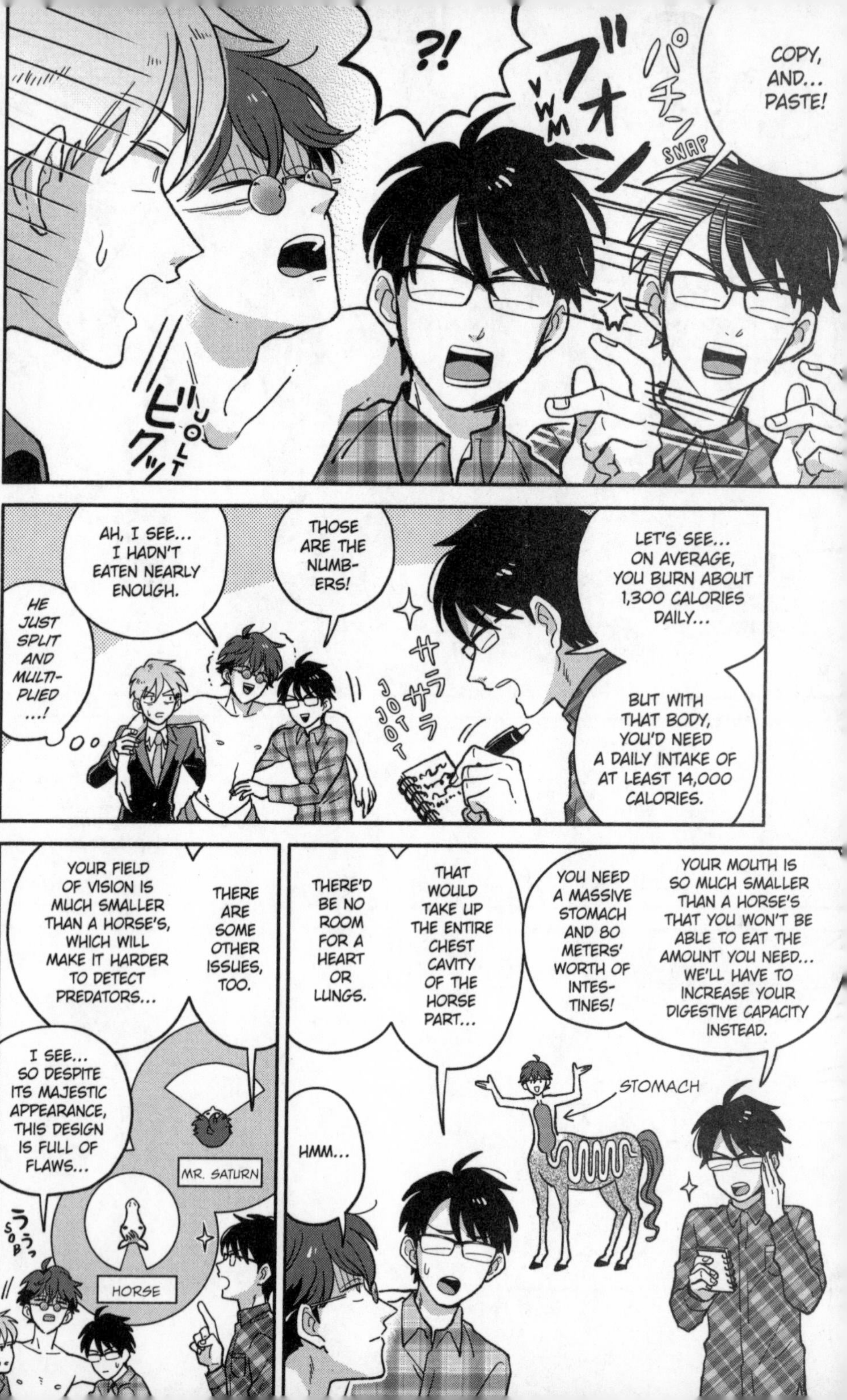
COPY, AND... PASTE!
パチーン
SNAP
ブォーン
VWM
?!
ビクッ
JOLT
LET'S SEE... ON AVERAGE, YOU BURN ABOUT 1,300 CALORIES DAILY...
BUT WITH THAT BODY, YOU'D NEED A DAILY INTAKE OF AT LEAST 14,000 CALORIES.
サラサラ
JOT JOT
THOSE ARE THE NUMB-ERS!
AH, I SEE... I HADN'T EATEN NEARLY ENOUGH.
HE JUST SPLIT AND MULTI-PLIED ...!
YOUR MOUTH IS SO MUCH SMALLER THAN A HORSE'S THAT YOU WON'T BE ABLE TO EAT THE AMOUNT YOU NEED... WE'LL HAVE TO INCREASE YOUR DIGESTIVE CAPACITY INSTEAD.
YOU NEED A MASSIVE STOMACH AND 80 METERS' WORTH OF INTES-TINES!
THAT WOULD TAKE UP THE ENTIRE CHEST CAVITY OF THE HORSE PART...
THERE'D BE NO ROOM FOR A HEART OR LUNGS.
STOMACH
HMM...
THERE ARE SOME OTHER ISSUES, TOO.
YOUR FIELD OF VISION IS MUCH SMALLER THAN A HORSE'S, WHICH WILL MAKE IT HARDER TO DETECT PREDATORS...
MR. SATURN
I SEE... SO DESPITE ITS MAJESTIC APPEARANCE, THIS DESIGN IS FULL OF FLAWS...
HORSE
うぅ
SOB

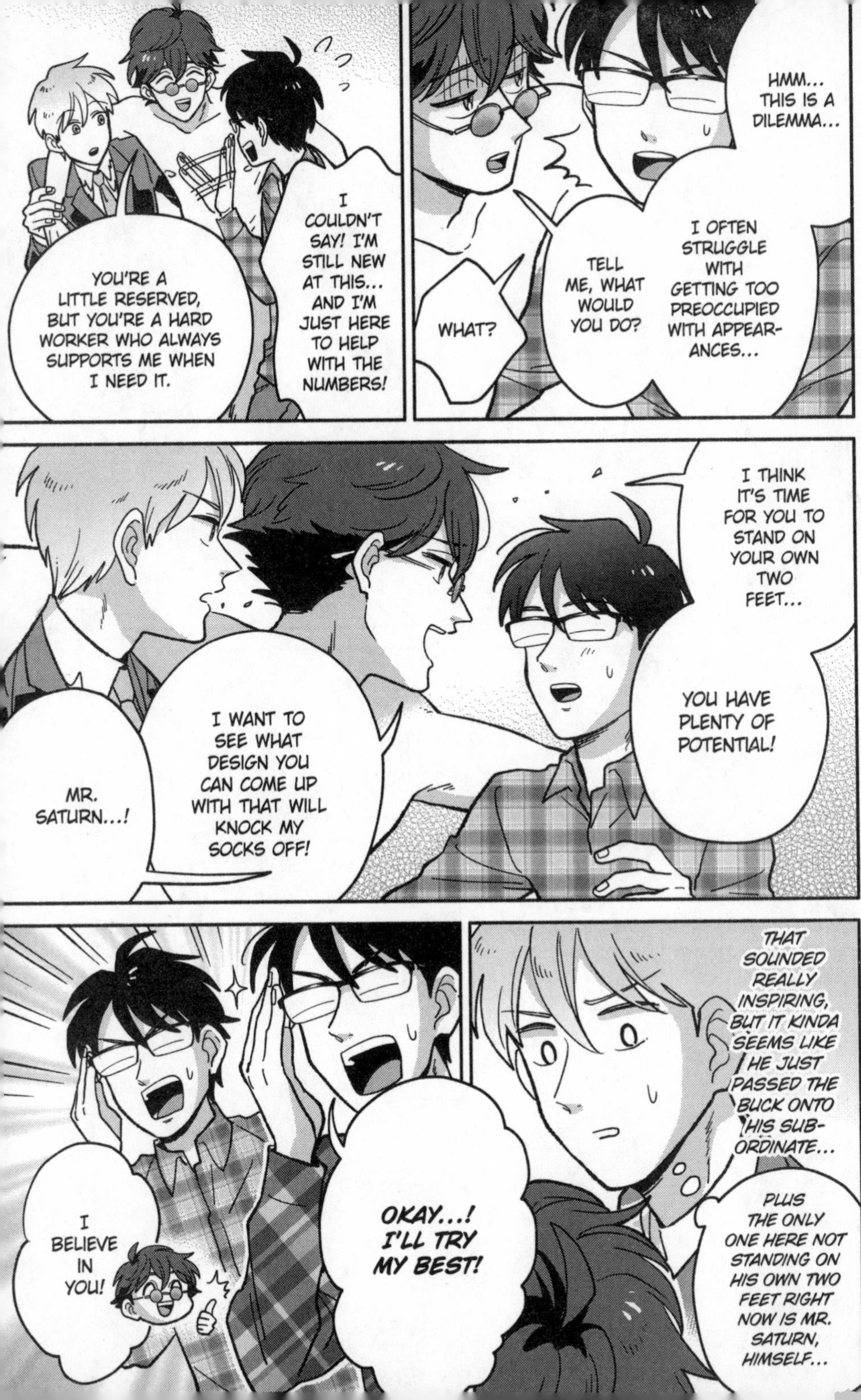
HMM... THIS IS A DILEMMA...
I OFTEN STRUGGLE WITH GETTING TOO PREOCCUPIED WITH APPEAR-ANCES...
TELL ME, WHAT WOULD YOU DO?
WHAT?
I COULDN'T SAY! I'M STILL NEW AT THIS... AND I'M JUST HERE TO HELP WITH THE NUMBERS!
YOU'RE A LITTLE RESERVED, BUT YOU'RE A HARD WORKER WHO ALWAYS SUPPORTS ME WHEN I NEED IT.
I THINK IT'S TIME FOR YOU TO STAND ON YOUR OWN TWO FEET...
YOU HAVE PLENTY OF POTENTIAL!
I WANT TO SEE WHAT DESIGN YOU CAN COME UP WITH THAT WILL KNOCK MY SOCKS OFF!
MR. SATURN...!
THAT SOUNDED REALLY INSPIRING, BUT IT KINDA SEEMS LIKE HE JUST PASSED THE BUCK ONTO HIS SUB-ORDINATE...
PLUS THE ONLY ONE HERE NOT STANDING ON HIS OWN TWO FEET RIGHT NOW IS MR. SATURN, HIMSELF...
OKAY...! I'LL TRY MY BEST!
I BELIEVE IN YOU!

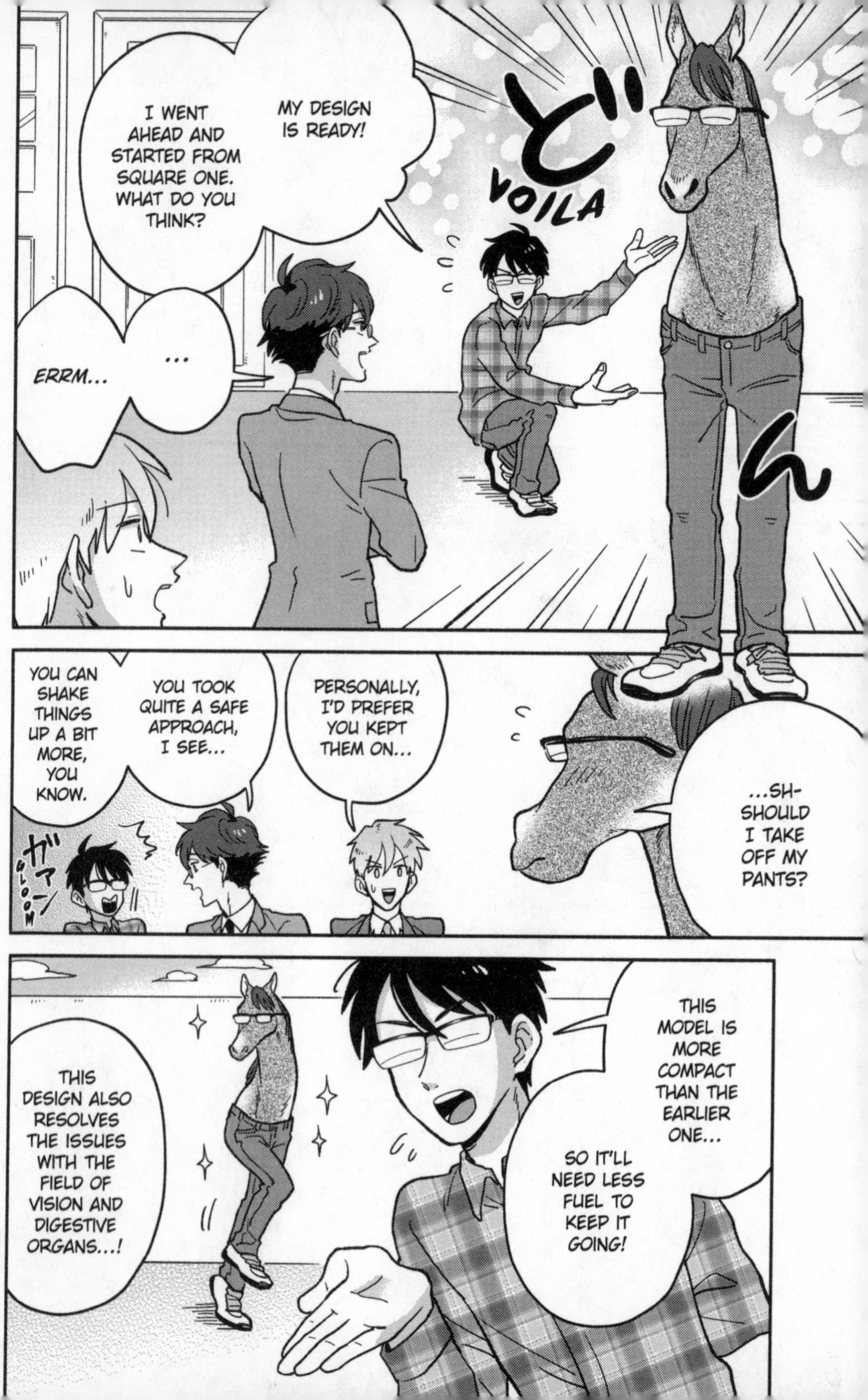

MY DESIGN IS READY!
I WENT AHEAD AND STARTED FROM SQUARE ONE. WHAT DO YOU THINK?
どん
VOILA
...
ERRM...
...SH-SHOULD I TAKE OFF MY PANTS?
PERSONALLY, I'D PREFER YOU KEPT THEM ON...
YOU TOOK QUITE A SAFE APPROACH, I SEE...
YOU CAN SHAKE THINGS UP A BIT MORE, YOU KNOW.
ガァーン
GLOOM
THIS MODEL IS MORE COMPACT THAN THE EARLIER ONE...
SO IT'LL NEED LESS FUEL TO KEEP IT GOING!
THIS DESIGN ALSO RESOLVES THE ISSUES WITH THE FIELD OF VISION AND DIGESTIVE ORGANS...!

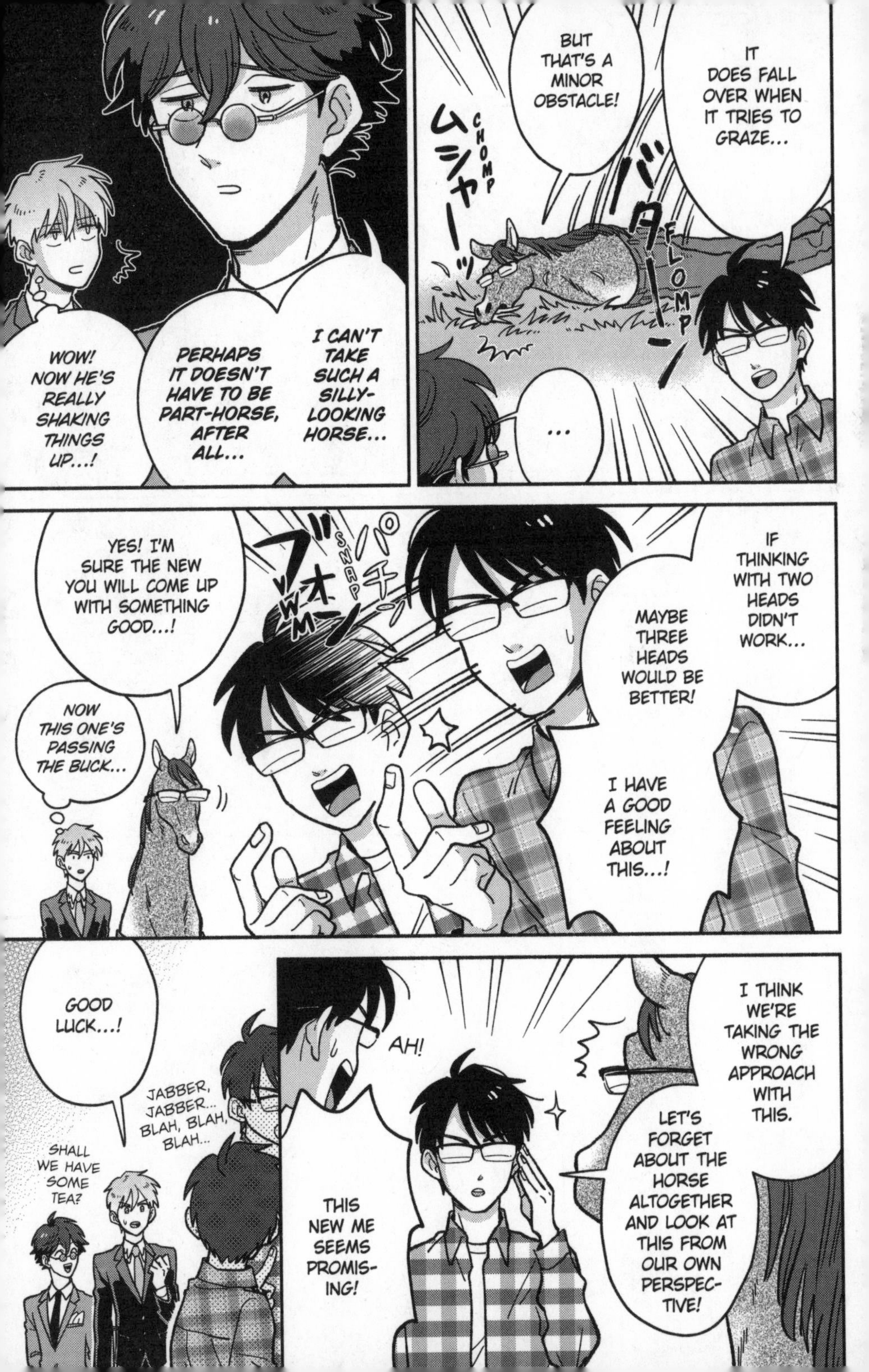
IT DOES FALL OVER WHEN IT TRIES TO GRAZE...
BUT THAT'S A MINOR OBSTACLE!
ムシャーッ
CHOMP
FLOMP
...
I CAN'T TAKE SUCH A SILLY-LOOKING HORSE...
PERHAPS IT DOESN'T HAVE TO BE PART-HORSE, AFTER ALL...
WOW! NOW HE'S REALLY SHAKING THINGS UP...!
IF THINKING WITH TWO HEADS DIDN'T WORK...
MAYBE THREE HEADS WOULD BE BETTER!
I HAVE A GOOD FEELING ABOUT THIS...!
SNAP
VWM
YES! I'M SURE THE NEW YOU WILL COME UP WITH SOMETHING GOOD...!
NOW THIS ONE'S PASSING THE BUCK...
I THINK WE'RE TAKING THE WRONG APPROACH WITH THIS.
LET'S FORGET ABOUT THE HORSE ALTOGETHER AND LOOK AT THIS FROM OUR OWN PERSPECTIVE!
AH!
THIS NEW ME SEEMS PROMISING!
GOOD LUCK...!
JABBER, JABBER... BLAH, BLAH, BLAH...
SHALL WE HAVE SOME TEA?

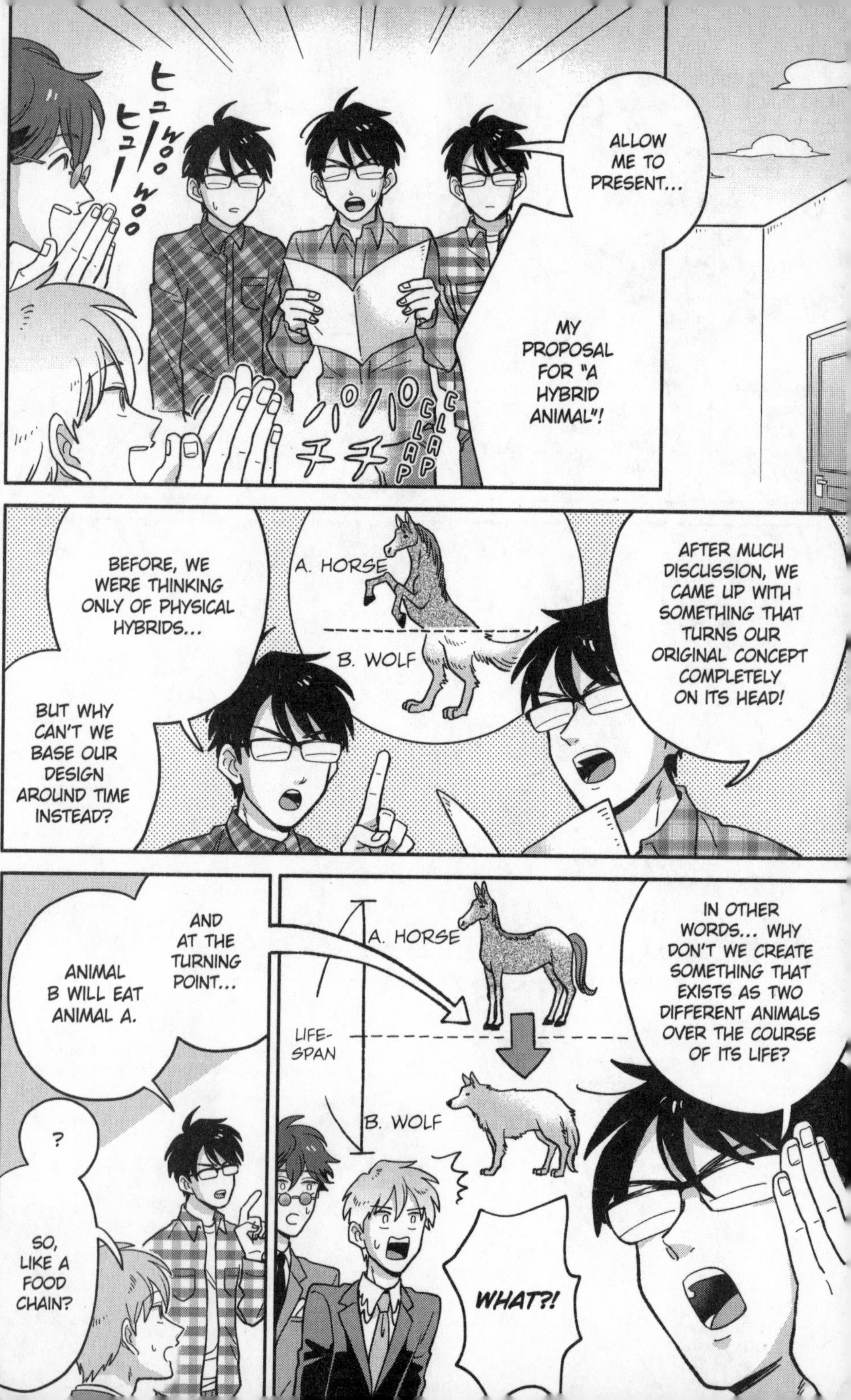
ALLOW ME TO PRESENT...
MY PROPOSAL FOR "A HYBRID ANIMAL"!
パチパチ CLAP CLAP
ヒューヒュー WOO WOO
AFTER MUCH DISCUSSION, WE CAME UP WITH SOMETHING THAT TURNS OUR ORIGINAL CONCEPT COMPLETELY ON ITS HEAD!
A. HORSE
B. WOLF
BEFORE, WE WERE THINKING ONLY OF PHYSICAL HYBRIDS...
BUT WHY CAN'T WE BASE OUR DESIGN AROUND TIME INSTEAD?
IN OTHER WORDS... WHY DON'T WE CREATE SOMETHING THAT EXISTS AS TWO DIFFERENT ANIMALS OVER THE COURSE OF ITS LIFE?
A. HORSE
LIFE-SPAN
B. WOLF
WHAT?!
AND AT THE TURNING POINT...
ANIMAL B WILL EAT ANIMAL A.
?
SO, LIKE A FOOD CHAIN?

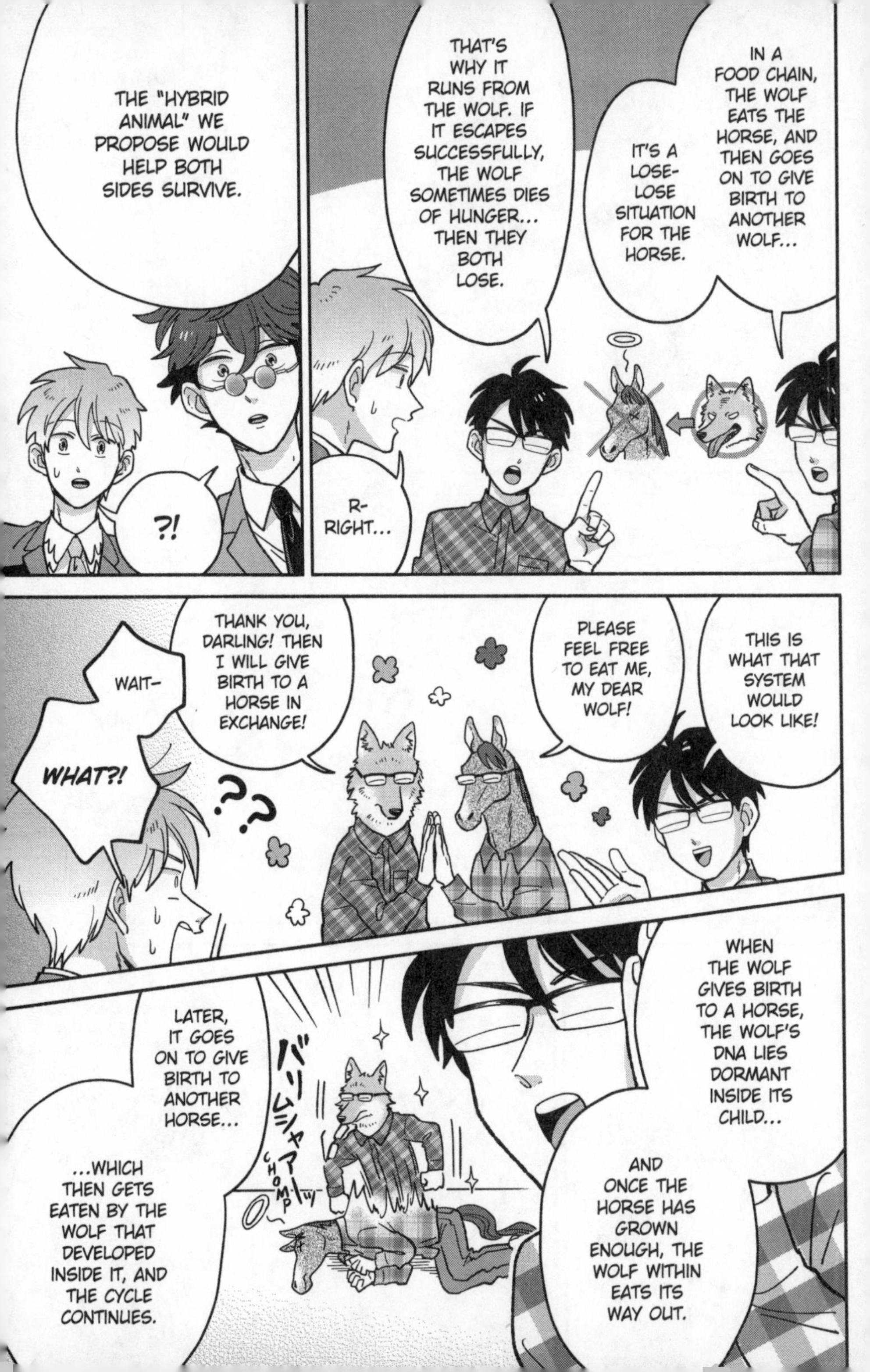
IN A FOOD CHAIN, THE WOLF EATS THE HORSE, AND THEN GOES ON TO GIVE BIRTH TO ANOTHER WOLF...
IT'S A LOSE-LOSE SITUATION FOR THE HORSE.
THAT'S WHY IT RUNS FROM THE WOLF. IF IT ESCAPES SUCCESSFULLY, THE WOLF SOMETIMES DIES OF HUNGER... THEN THEY BOTH LOSE.
R-RIGHT...
THE "HYBRID ANIMAL" WE PROPOSE WOULD HELP BOTH SIDES SURVIVE.
?!
THIS IS WHAT THAT SYSTEM WOULD LOOK LIKE!
PLEASE FEEL FREE TO EAT ME, MY DEAR WOLF!
THANK YOU, DARLING! THEN I WILL GIVE BIRTH TO A HORSE IN EXCHANGE!
??
WAIT-
WHAT?!
WHEN THE WOLF GIVES BIRTH TO A HORSE, THE WOLF'S DNA LIES DORMANT INSIDE ITS CHILD...
AND ONCE THE HORSE HAS GROWN ENOUGH, THE WOLF WITHIN EATS ITS WAY OUT.
バリムシャアーッ
CHOMP
LATER, IT GOES ON TO GIVE BIRTH TO ANOTHER HORSE...
...WHICH THEN GETS EATEN BY THE WOLF THAT DEVELOPED INSIDE IT, AND THE CYCLE CONTINUES.

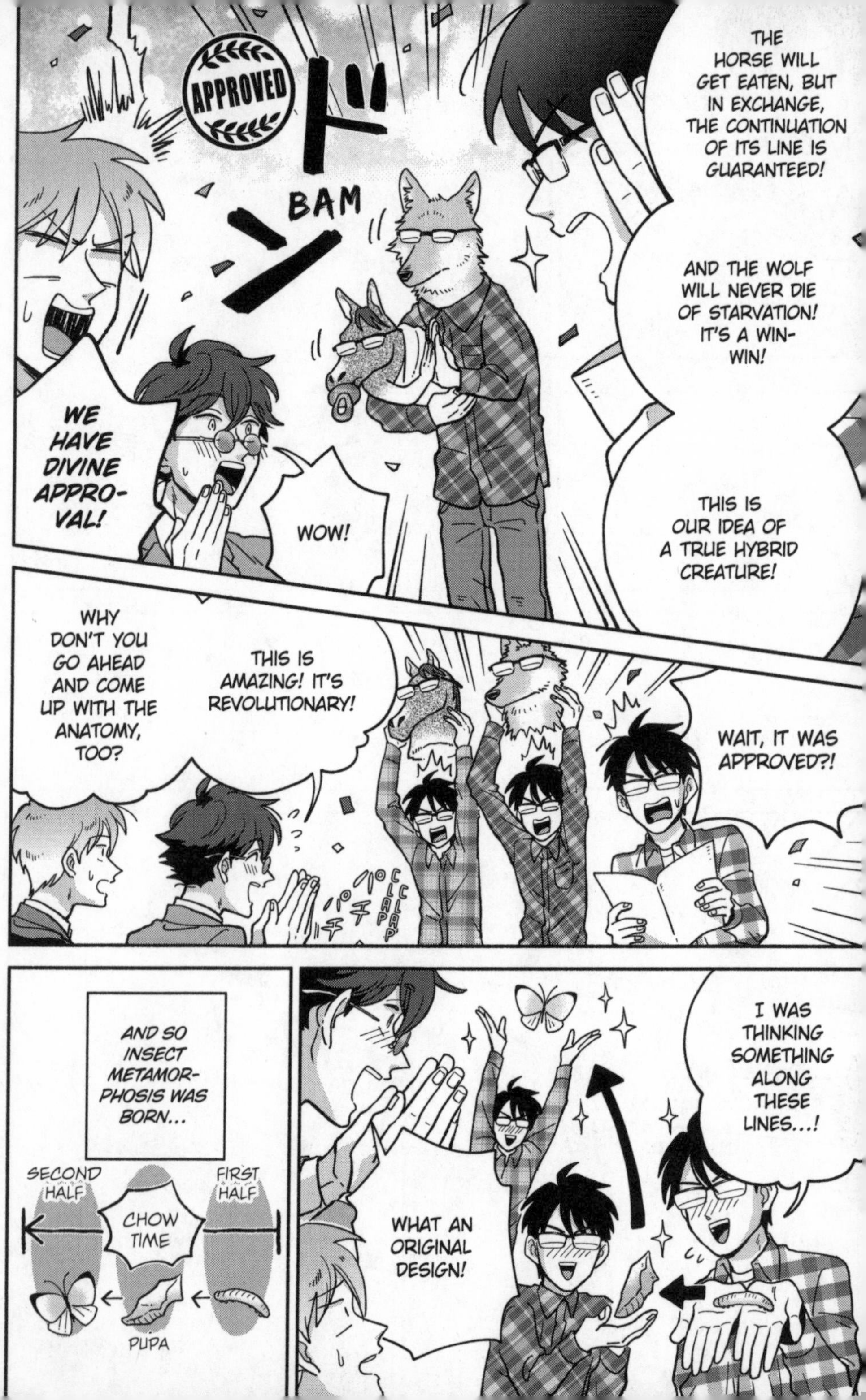
THE HORSE WILL GET EATEN, BUT IN EXCHANGE, THE CONTINUATION OF ITS LINE IS GUARANTEED!
AND THE WOLF WILL NEVER DIE OF STARVATION! IT'S A WIN-WIN!
THIS IS OUR IDEA OF A TRUE HYBRID CREATURE!
APPROVED
ドン
BAM
WOW!
WE HAVE DIVINE APPROVAL!
WAIT, IT WAS APPROVED?!
THIS IS AMAZING! IT'S REVOLUTIONARY!
WHY DON'T YOU GO AHEAD AND COME UP WITH THE ANATOMY, TOO?
パチパチ
CLAP CLAP
I WAS THINKING SOMETHING ALONG THESE LINES...!
WHAT AN ORIGINAL DESIGN!
AND SO INSECT METAMORPHOSIS WAS BORN...
FIRST HALF
SECOND HALF
CHOW TIME
PUPA

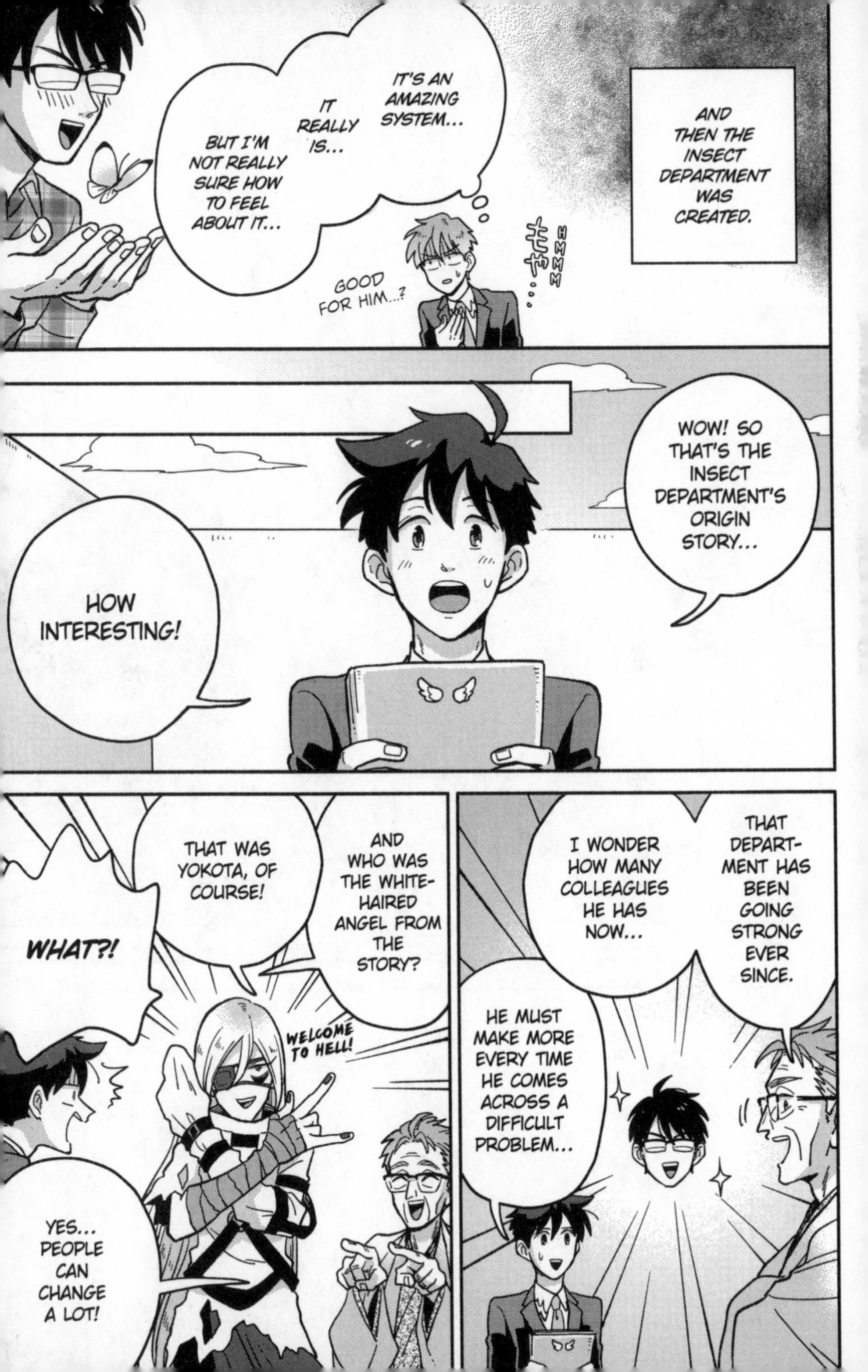
AND THEN THE INSECT DEPARTMENT WAS CREATED.
HMMMM
GOOD FOR HIM...?
IT'S AN AMAZING SYSTEM...
IT REALLY IS...
BUT I'M NOT REALLY SURE HOW TO FEEL ABOUT IT...
WOW! SO THAT'S THE INSECT DEPARTMENT'S ORIGIN STORY...
HOW INTERESTING!
THAT DEPARTMENT HAS BEEN GOING STRONG EVER SINCE.
I WONDER HOW MANY COLLEAGUES HE HAS NOW...
HE MUST MAKE MORE EVERY TIME HE COMES ACROSS A DIFFICULT PROBLEM...
AND WHO WAS THE WHITE-HAIRED ANGEL FROM THE STORY?
THAT WAS YOKOTA, OF COURSE!
WELCOME TO HELL!
WHAT?!
YES... PEOPLE CAN CHANGE A LOT!

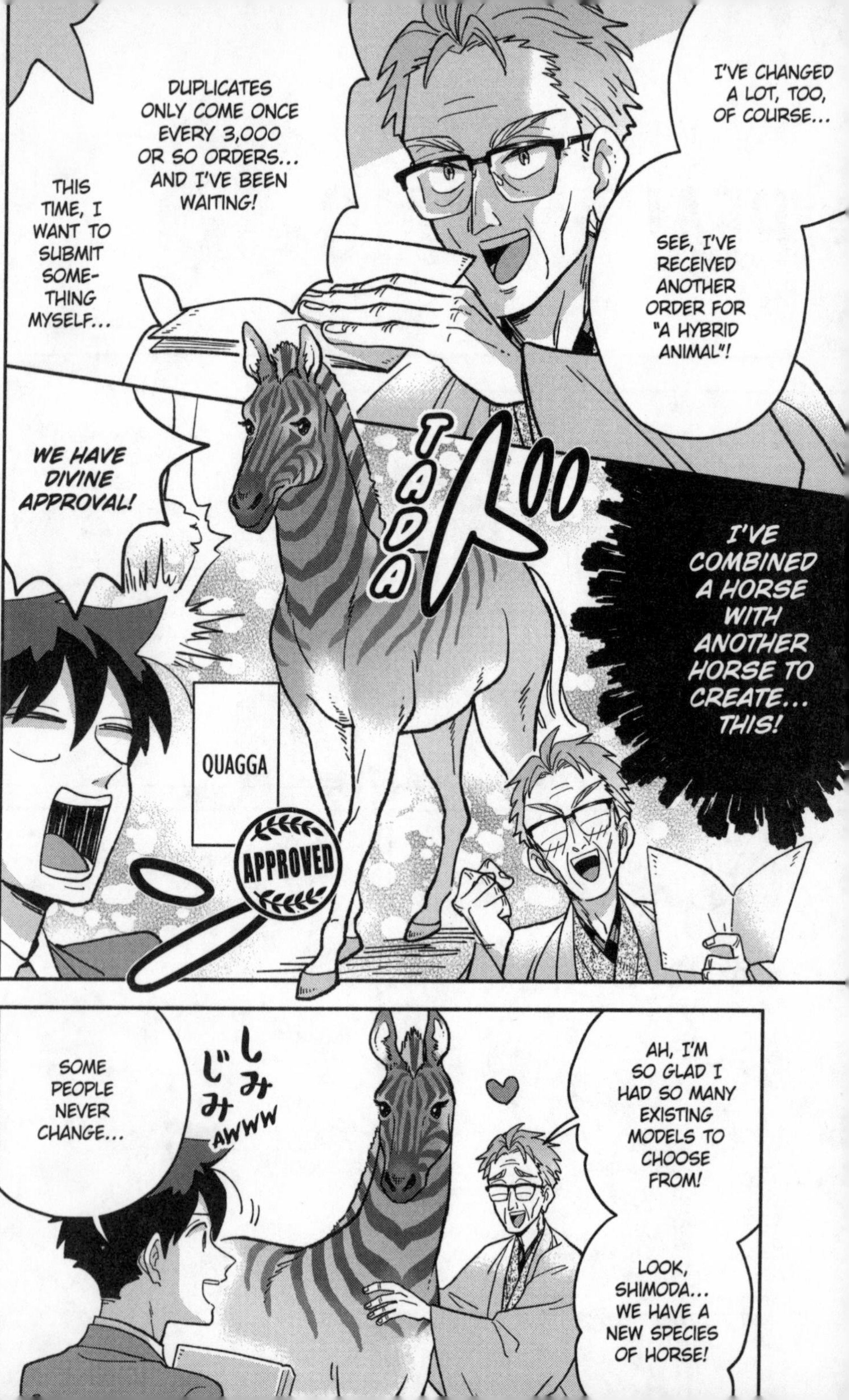
I'VE CHANGED A LOT, TOO, OF COURSE...
SEE, I'VE RECEIVED ANOTHER ORDER FOR "A HYBRID ANIMAL"!
DUPLICATES ONLY COME ONCE EVERY 3,000 OR SO ORDERS... AND I'VE BEEN WAITING!
THIS TIME, I WANT TO SUBMIT SOME-THING MYSELF...
I'VE COMBINED A HORSE WITH ANOTHER HORSE TO CREATE... THIS!
TADA
QUAGGA
APPROVED
WE HAVE DIVINE APPROVAL!
AH, I'M SO GLAD I HAD SO MANY EXISTING MODELS TO CHOOSE FROM!
LOOK, SHIMODA... WE HAVE A NEW SPECIES OF HORSE!
しみじみ AWWW
SOME PEOPLE NEVER CHANGE...

THE ENCYCLOPEDIA OF
REAL ANIMALS 33

ANIMAL 80	QUAGGA

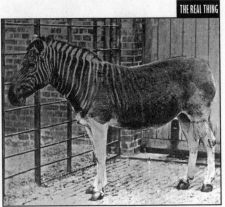

THE REAL THING

Though the quagga was a subspecies of the zebra, it had stripes only on its front half.

Photo: Alamy/Aflo

Striped from its head to its shoulders and solid from its midsection to the ends of its legs, the quagga looked like a combination of a zebra and a horse. This brown and white ungulate was once found in great numbers in the savannahs of South Africa, but was hunted extensively by humans until its extinction in the wild in 1878. In 1883, the last captive quagga died in Amsterdam.

One hundred years later, scientists recovered samples from a mounted specimen and conducted DNA analysis, which showed that the quagga was a member of the plains zebra species. The quagga is the first extinct animal in history whose DNA was recovered and analyzed.

[Name]	*Equus quagga quagga*
[Classification]	Class: Mammalia
	Order: Perissodactyla
	Family: Equidae
	Genus: *Equus*
[Habitat]	Pre-19th century southern Africa (now extinct)
[Length]	Approximately 260 cm (8.5 ft)

SPECIAL FEATURE | INSECT METAMORPHOSIS

Insects develop in roughly three different ways: those that undergo a series of molts without much change to their appearance, those that grow gradually and change in appearance, and those that transform entirely during the pupal stage of what's known as complete metamorphosis. In complete metamorphosis, the larva breaks down into a gooey substance within the pupal case and becomes the base material that forms the adult insect. Adults and larvae look different both outwardly and inwardly, and because they have different diets do not need to compete with each other for food.

One theory claims the pupal stage developed as a survival mechanism during the Ice Age. This manga purposely proposed the radical idea that insect metamorphosis originated as an extreme form of symbiosis between two different animals. The origins of the process remain unclear, and there is still no established explanation.

FIRST HALF
CHOW TIME
SECOND HALF
PUPA

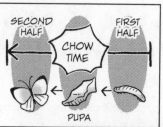

THE REAL THING

Photo: Masao Akiyama/Aflo

HEAVEN'S DESIGN TEAM

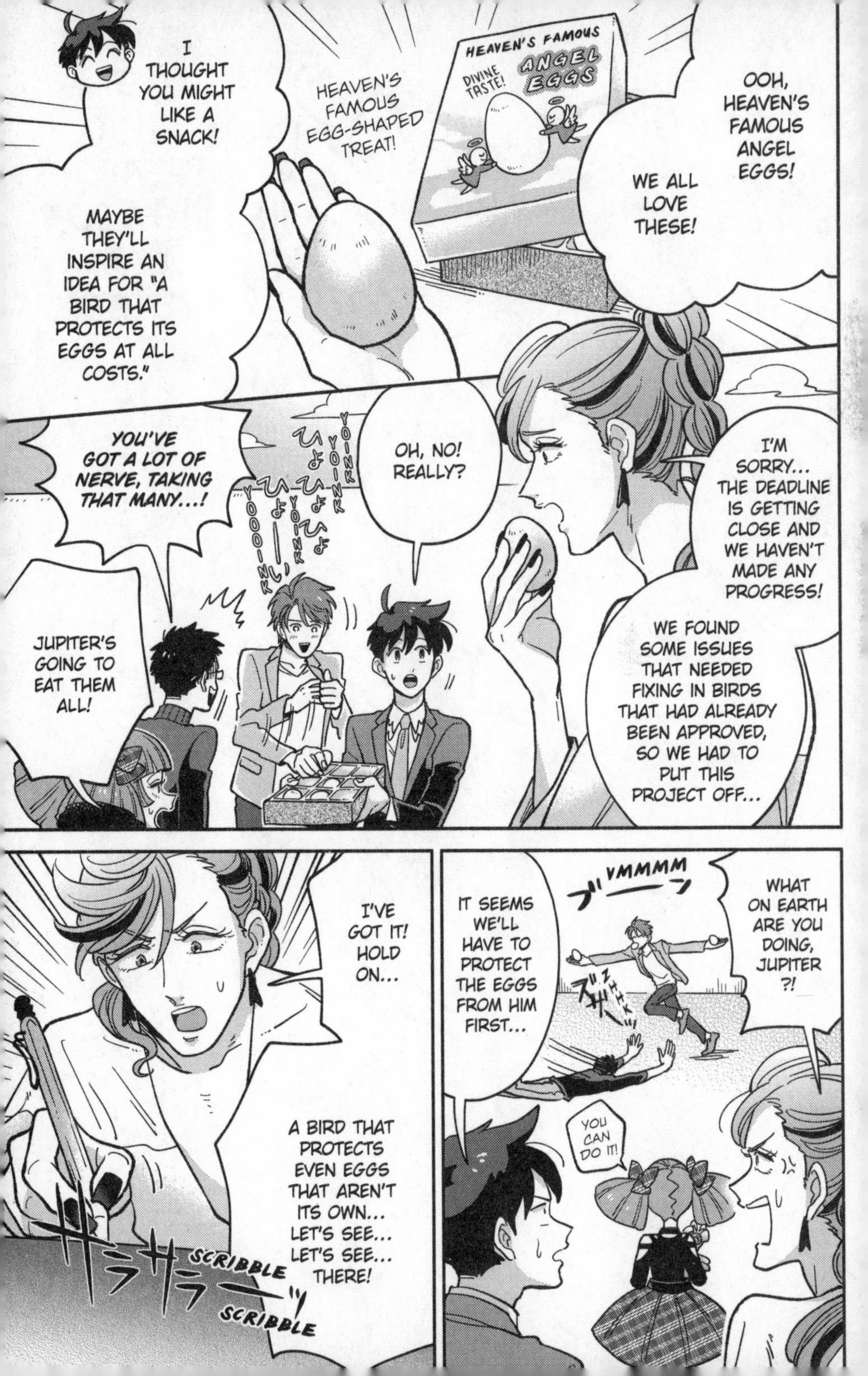
HEAVEN'S FAMOUS
ANGEL EGGS
DIVINE TASTE!
OOH, HEAVEN'S FAMOUS ANGEL EGGS!
WE ALL LOVE THESE!
I THOUGHT YOU MIGHT LIKE A SNACK!
HEAVEN'S FAMOUS EGG-SHAPED TREAT!
MAYBE THEY'LL INSPIRE AN IDEA FOR "A BIRD THAT PROTECTS ITS EGGS AT ALL COSTS."
I'M SORRY... THE DEADLINE IS GETTING CLOSE AND WE HAVEN'T MADE ANY PROGRESS!
WE FOUND SOME ISSUES THAT NEEDED FIXING IN BIRDS THAT HAD ALREADY BEEN APPROVED, SO WE HAD TO PUT THIS PROJECT OFF...
OH, NO! REALLY?
YOINK
YOINK
YOINK
YOOOINK
YOU'VE GOT A LOT OF NERVE, TAKING THAT MANY...!
JUPITER'S GOING TO EAT THEM ALL!
WHAT ON EARTH ARE YOU DOING, JUPITER?!
VMMMM
IT SEEMS WE'LL HAVE TO PROTECT THE EGGS FROM HIM FIRST...
YOU CAN DO IT!
I'VE GOT IT! HOLD ON...
A BIRD THAT PROTECTS EVEN EGGS THAT AREN'T ITS OWN... LET'S SEE... LET'S SEE... THERE!
SCRIBBLE
SCRIBBLE

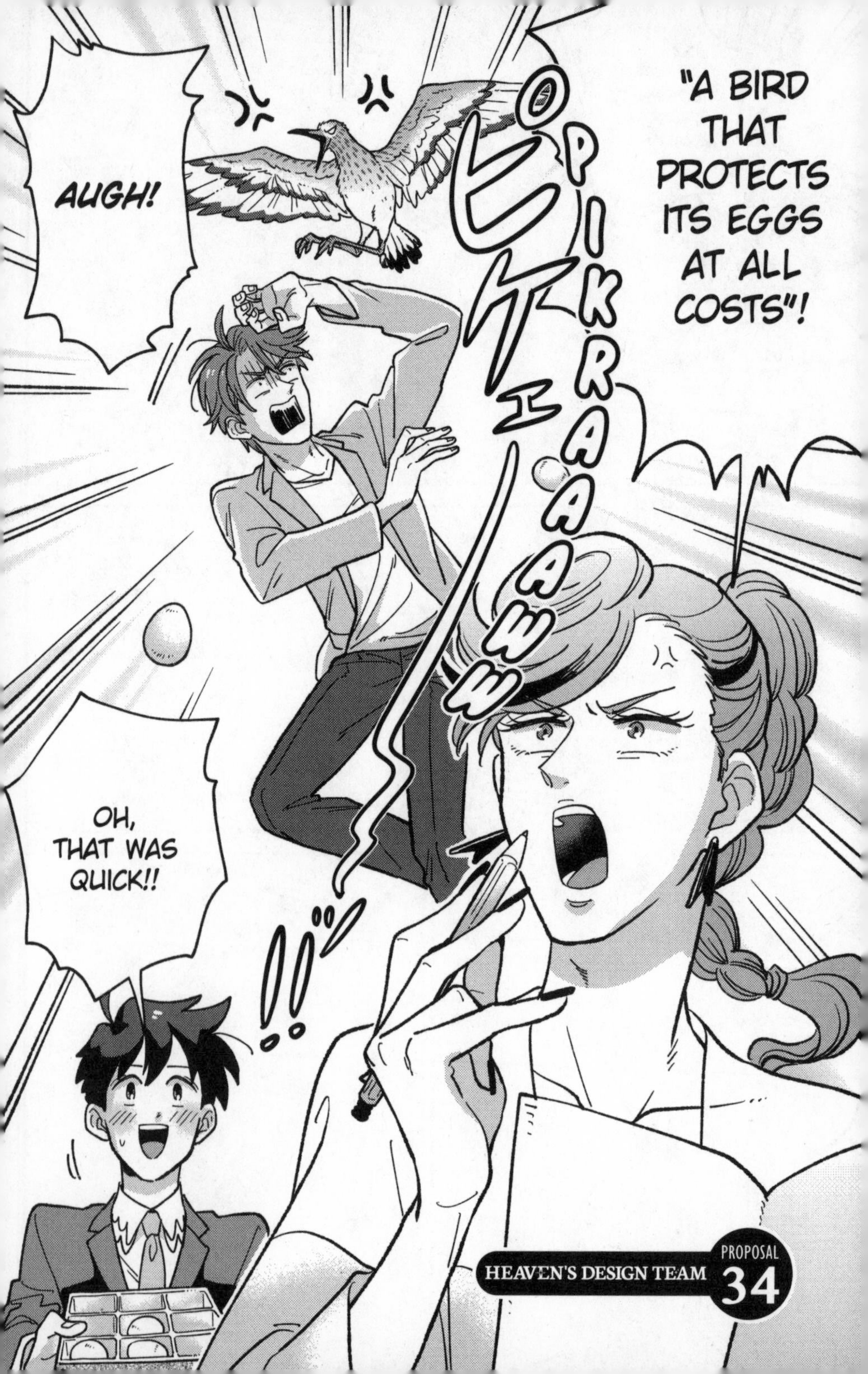
"A BIRD THAT PROTECTS ITS EGGS AT ALL COSTS"!
PIKRAAAAWWW
AUGH!
OH, THAT WAS QUICK!!
HEAVEN'S DESIGN TEAM
PROPOSAL 34

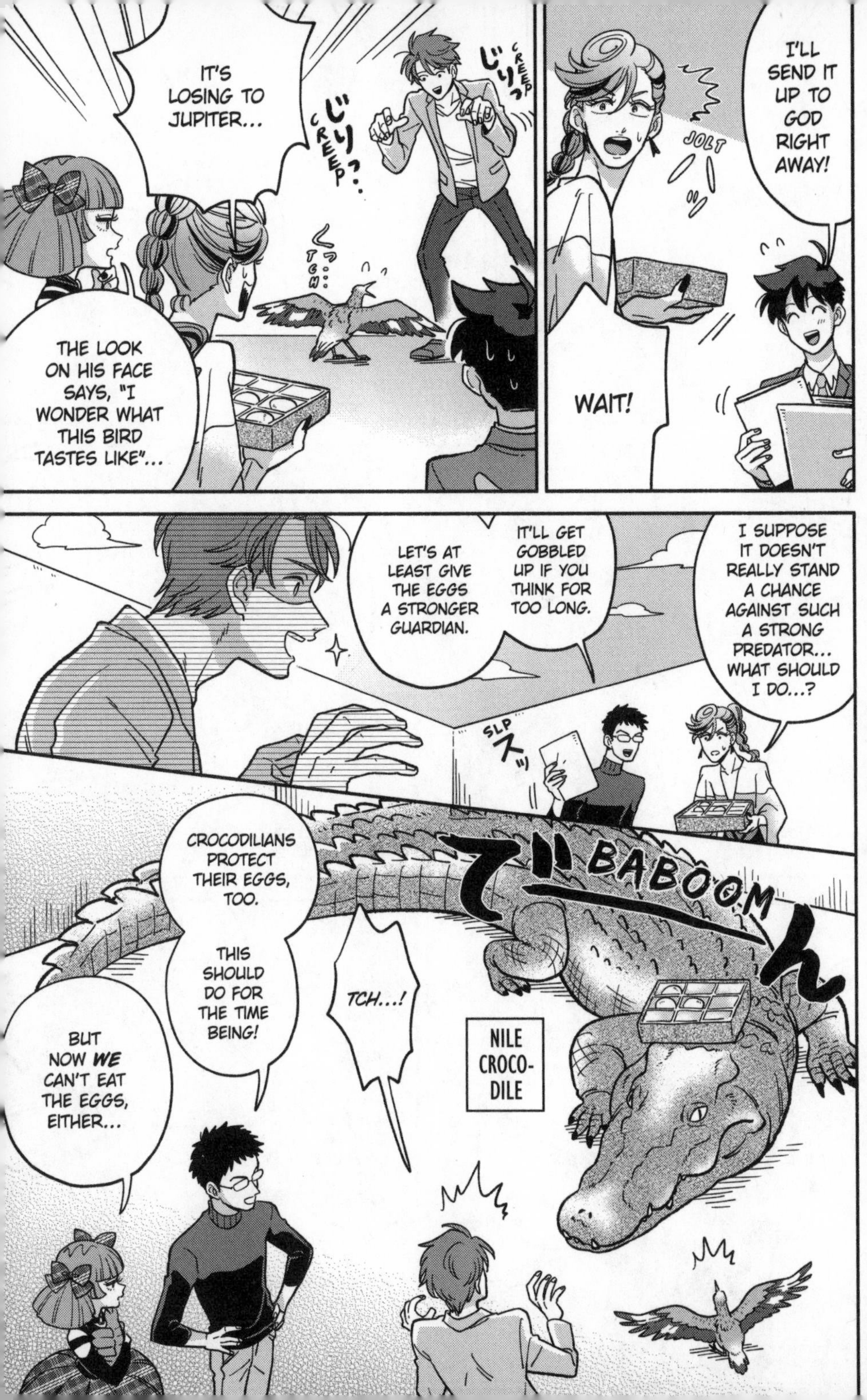

I'LL SEND IT UP TO GOD RIGHT AWAY!
JOLT
WAIT!
IT'S LOSING TO JUPITER...
じりっ
CREEP
じりっ…
CREEP
くっ…
TCH
THE LOOK ON HIS FACE SAYS, "I WONDER WHAT THIS BIRD TASTES LIKE"...
I SUPPOSE IT DOESN'T REALLY STAND A CHANCE AGAINST SUCH A STRONG PREDATOR... WHAT SHOULD I DO...?
IT'LL GET GOBBLED UP IF YOU THINK FOR TOO LONG.
LET'S AT LEAST GIVE THE EGGS A STRONGER GUARDIAN.
スッ
SLP
BABOOM
CROCODILIANS PROTECT THEIR EGGS, TOO.
THIS SHOULD DO FOR THE TIME BEING!
TCH...!
NILE CROCO-DILE
BUT NOW *WE* CAN'T EAT THE EGGS, EITHER...

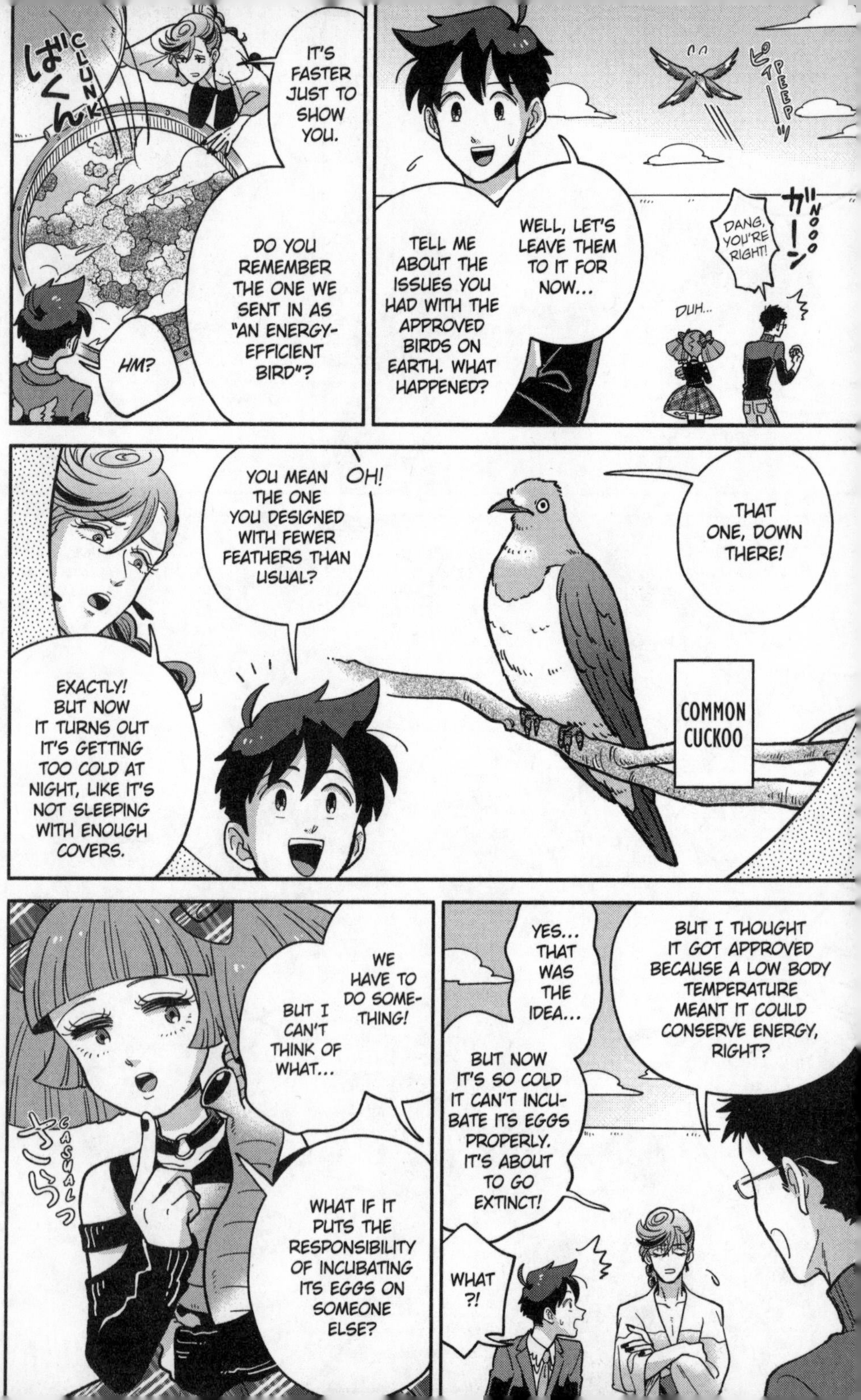
ピィー
PEEP
ガーン
NOOO
DANG, YOU'RE RIGHT!
DUH...
WELL, LET'S LEAVE THEM TO IT FOR NOW...
TELL ME ABOUT THE ISSUES YOU HAD WITH THE APPROVED BIRDS ON EARTH. WHAT HAPPENED?
ばくん
CLUNK
IT'S FASTER JUST TO SHOW YOU.
DO YOU REMEMBER THE ONE WE SENT IN AS "AN ENERGY-EFFICIENT BIRD"?
HM?
THAT ONE, DOWN THERE!
COMMON CUCKOO
OH!
YOU MEAN THE ONE YOU DESIGNED WITH FEWER FEATHERS THAN USUAL?
EXACTLY! BUT NOW IT TURNS OUT IT'S GETTING TOO COLD AT NIGHT, LIKE IT'S NOT SLEEPING WITH ENOUGH COVERS.
BUT I THOUGHT IT GOT APPROVED BECAUSE A LOW BODY TEMPERATURE MEANT IT COULD CONSERVE ENERGY, RIGHT?
YES... THAT WAS THE IDEA...
BUT NOW IT'S SO COLD IT CAN'T INCU-BATE ITS EGGS PROPERLY. IT'S ABOUT TO GO EXTINCT!
WHAT ?!
WE HAVE TO DO SOME-THING!
BUT I CAN'T THINK OF WHAT...
さらっ
CASUAL
WHAT IF IT PUTS THE RESPONSIBILITY OF INCUBATING ITS EGGS ON SOMEONE ELSE?

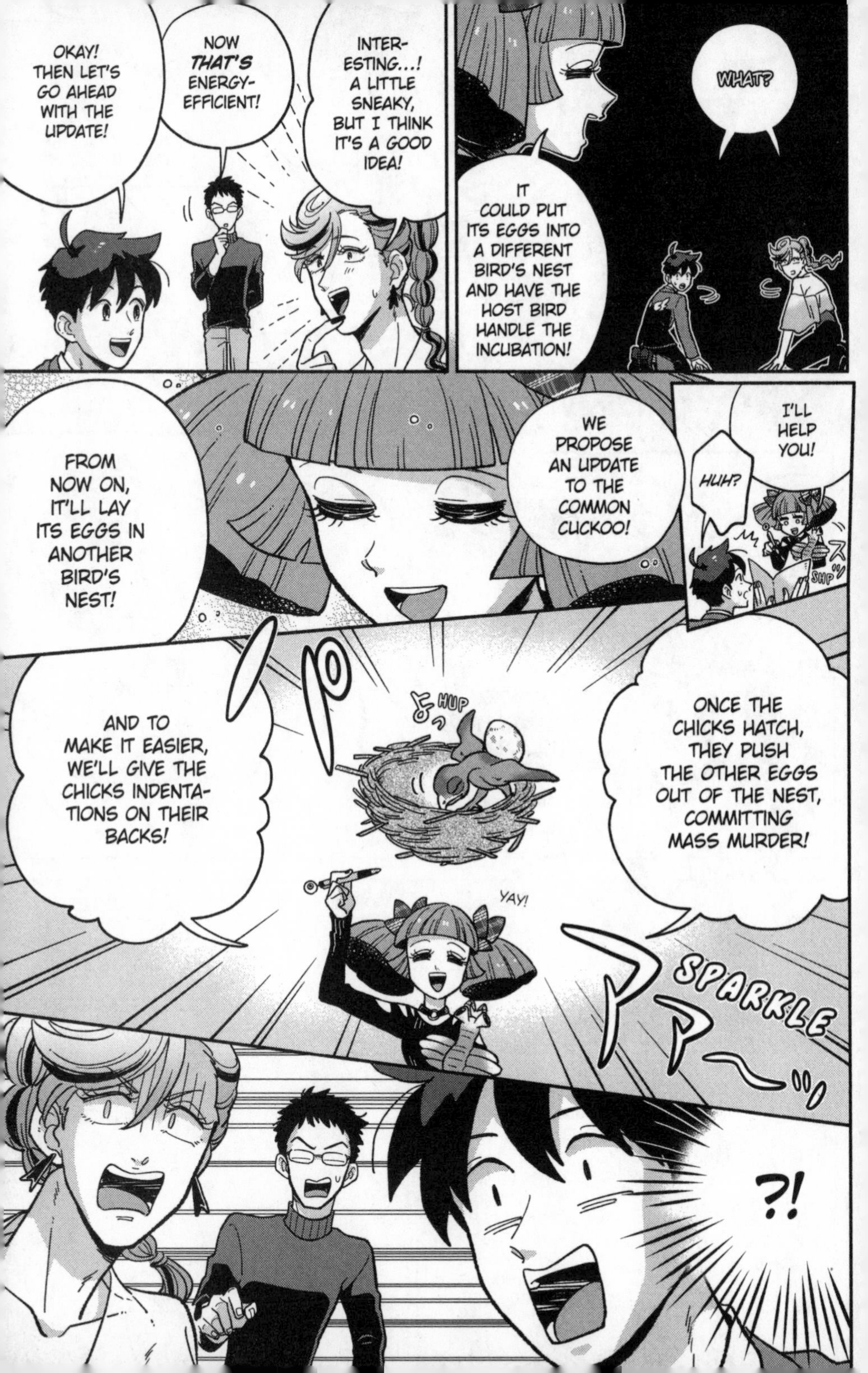
WHAT?
IT COULD PUT ITS EGGS INTO A DIFFERENT BIRD'S NEST AND HAVE THE HOST BIRD HANDLE THE INCUBATION!
INTER-ESTING...! A LITTLE SNEAKY, BUT I THINK IT'S A GOOD IDEA!
NOW *THAT'S* ENERGY-EFFICIENT!
OKAY! THEN LET'S GO AHEAD WITH THE UPDATE!
I'LL HELP YOU!
HUH?
SHP
WE PROPOSE AN UPDATE TO THE COMMON CUCKOO!
FROM NOW ON, IT'LL LAY ITS EGGS IN ANOTHER BIRD'S NEST!
ONCE THE CHICKS HATCH, THEY PUSH THE OTHER EGGS OUT OF THE NEST, COMMITTING MASS MURDER!
HUP
AND TO MAKE IT EASIER, WE'LL GIVE THE CHICKS INDENTATIONS ON THEIR BACKS!
YAY!
SPARKLE
?!

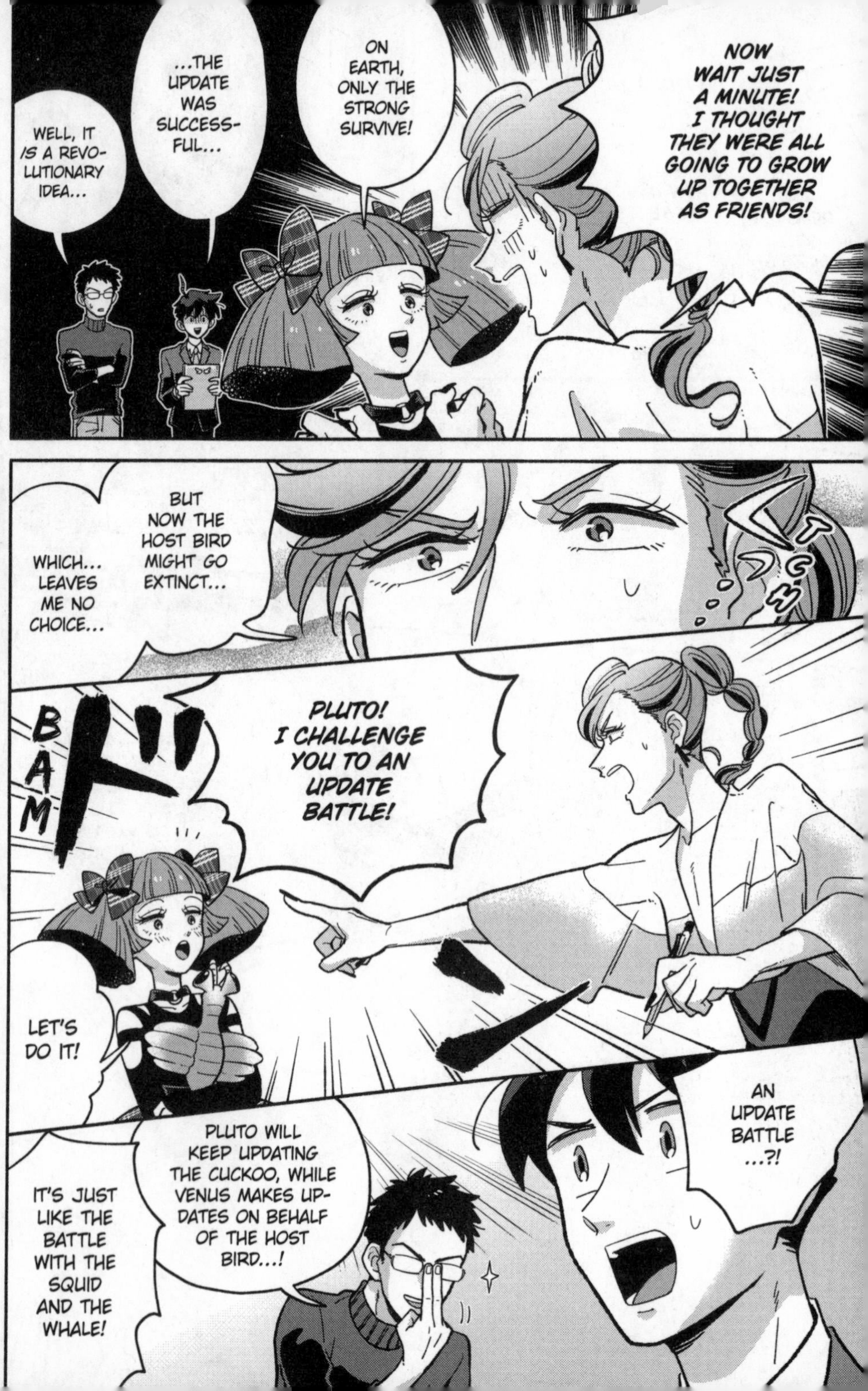
NOW WAIT JUST A MINUTE! I THOUGHT THEY WERE ALL GOING TO GROW UP TOGETHER AS FRIENDS!
ON EARTH, ONLY THE STRONG SURVIVE!
...THE UPDATE WAS SUCCESSFUL...
WELL, IT IS A REVOLUTIONARY IDEA...
TCH
BUT NOW THE HOST BIRD MIGHT GO EXTINCT...
WHICH... LEAVES ME NO CHOICE...
PLUTO! I CHALLENGE YOU TO AN UPDATE BATTLE!
BAM
LET'S DO IT!
AN UPDATE BATTLE...?!
PLUTO WILL KEEP UPDATING THE CUCKOO, WHILE VENUS MAKES UPDATES ON BEHALF OF THE HOST BIRD...!
IT'S JUST LIKE THE BATTLE WITH THE SQUID AND THE WHALE!

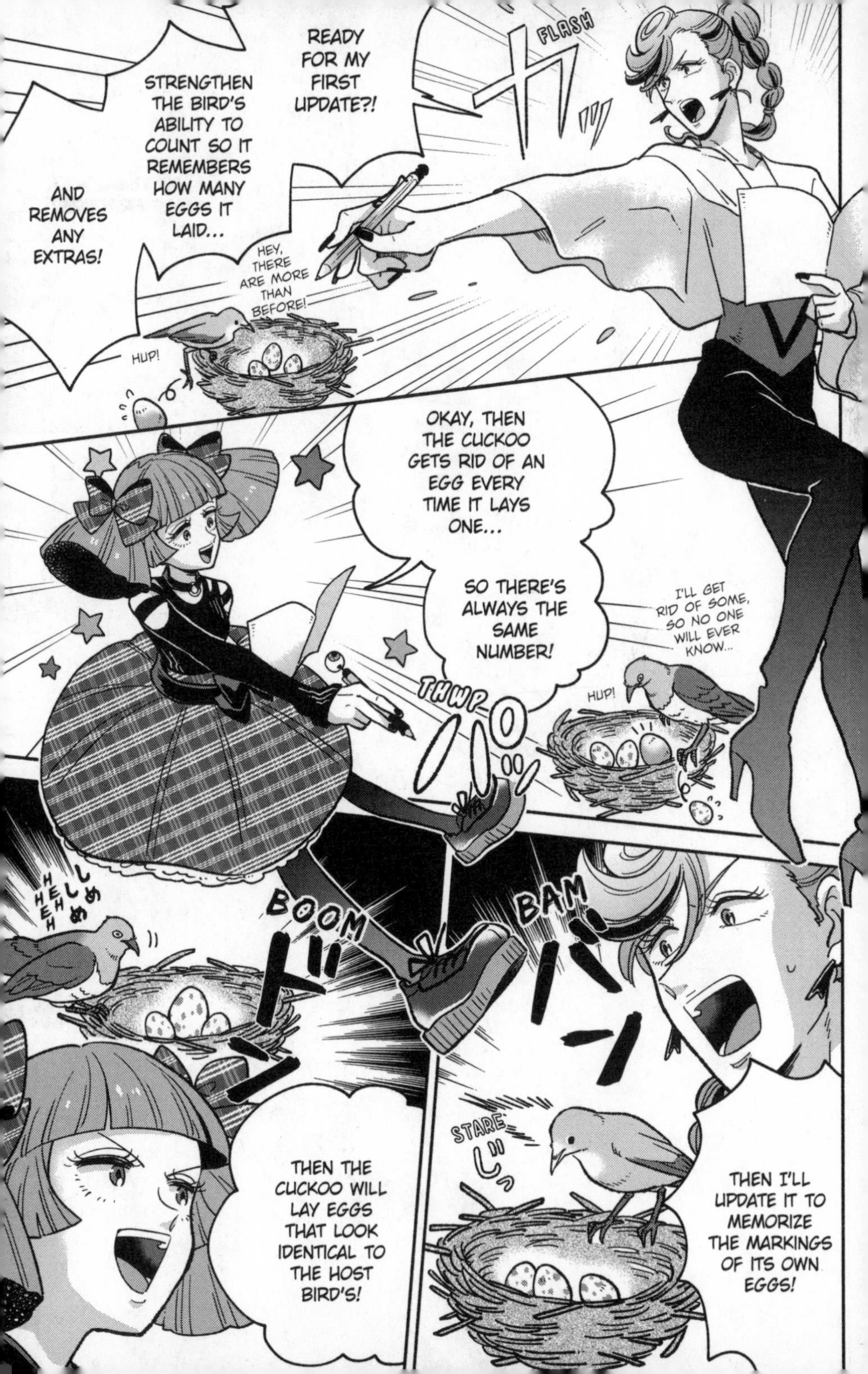
FLASH
READY FOR MY FIRST UPDATE?!
STRENGTHEN THE BIRD'S ABILITY TO COUNT SO IT REMEMBERS HOW MANY EGGS IT LAID...
AND REMOVES ANY EXTRAS!
HEY, THERE ARE MORE THAN BEFORE!
HUP!
OKAY, THEN THE CUCKOO GETS RID OF AN EGG EVERY TIME IT LAYS ONE...
SO THERE'S ALWAYS THE SAME NUMBER!
I'LL GET RID OF SOME, SO NO ONE WILL EVER KNOW...
HUP!
THWP
BAM
STARE
THEN I'LL UPDATE IT TO MEMORIZE THE MARKINGS OF ITS OWN EGGS!
BOOM
HEH HEH HEH
THEN THE CUCKOO WILL LAY EGGS THAT LOOK IDENTICAL TO THE HOST BIRD'S!

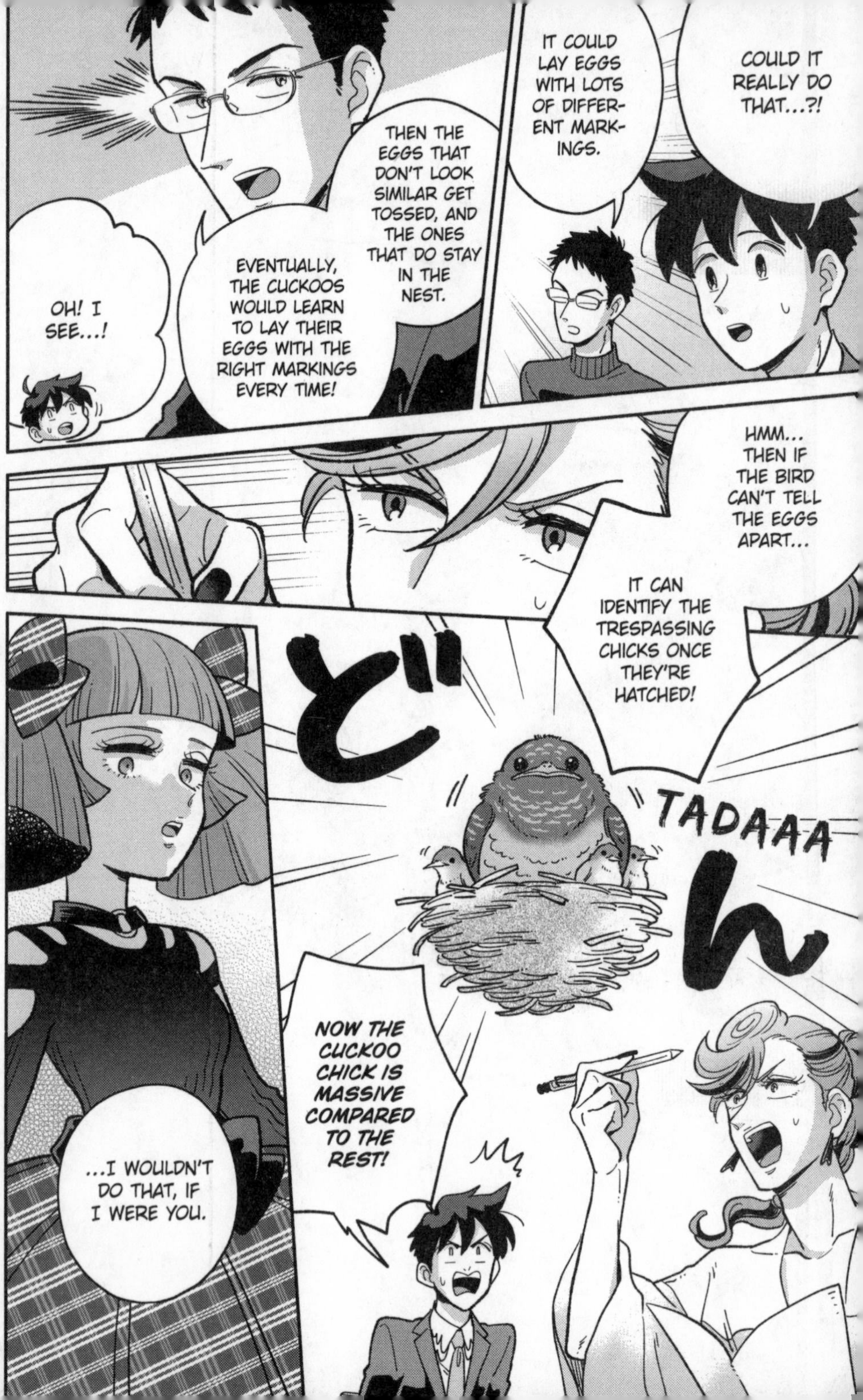
COULD IT REALLY DO THAT...?!
IT COULD LAY EGGS WITH LOTS OF DIFFERENT MARKINGS.
THEN THE EGGS THAT DON'T LOOK SIMILAR GET TOSSED, AND THE ONES THAT DO STAY IN THE NEST.
EVENTUALLY, THE CUCKOOS WOULD LEARN TO LAY THEIR EGGS WITH THE RIGHT MARKINGS EVERY TIME!
OH! I SEE...!
HMM... THEN IF THE BIRD CAN'T TELL THE EGGS APART...
IT CAN IDENTIFY THE TRESPASSING CHICKS ONCE THEY'RE HATCHED!
どん
TADAAA
NOW THE CUCKOO CHICK IS MASSIVE COMPARED TO THE REST!
...I WOULDN'T DO THAT, IF I WERE YOU.

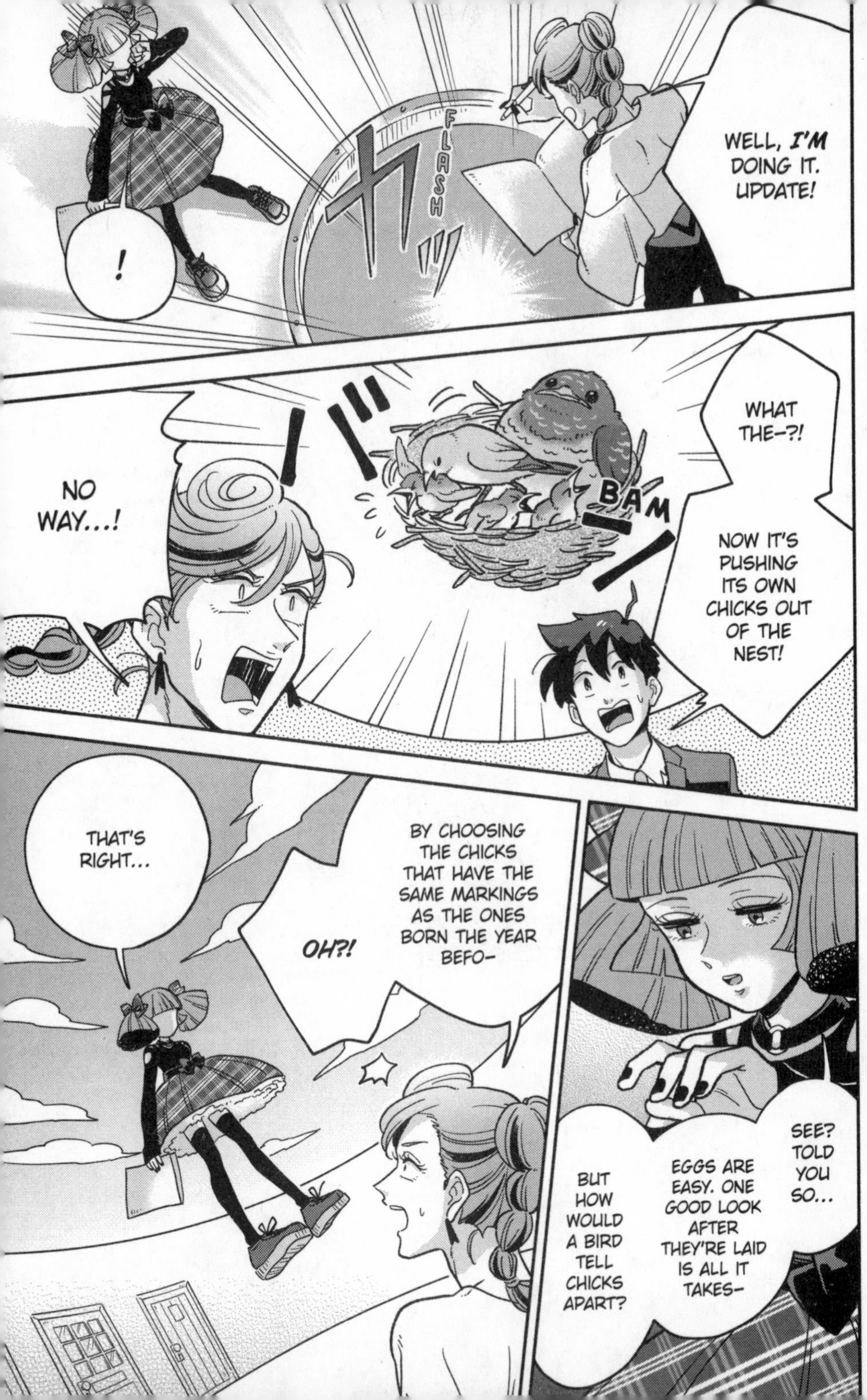
WELL, *I'M* DOING IT. UPDATE!
FLASH
!
WHAT THE–?!
NOW IT'S PUSHING ITS OWN CHICKS OUT OF THE NEST!
BAM
NO WAY...!
SEE? TOLD YOU SO...
EGGS ARE EASY. ONE GOOD LOOK AFTER THEY'RE LAID IS ALL IT TAKES–
BUT HOW WOULD A BIRD TELL CHICKS APART?
THAT'S RIGHT...
BY CHOOSING THE CHICKS THAT HAVE THE SAME MARKINGS AS THE ONES BORN THE YEAR BEFO–
OH?!

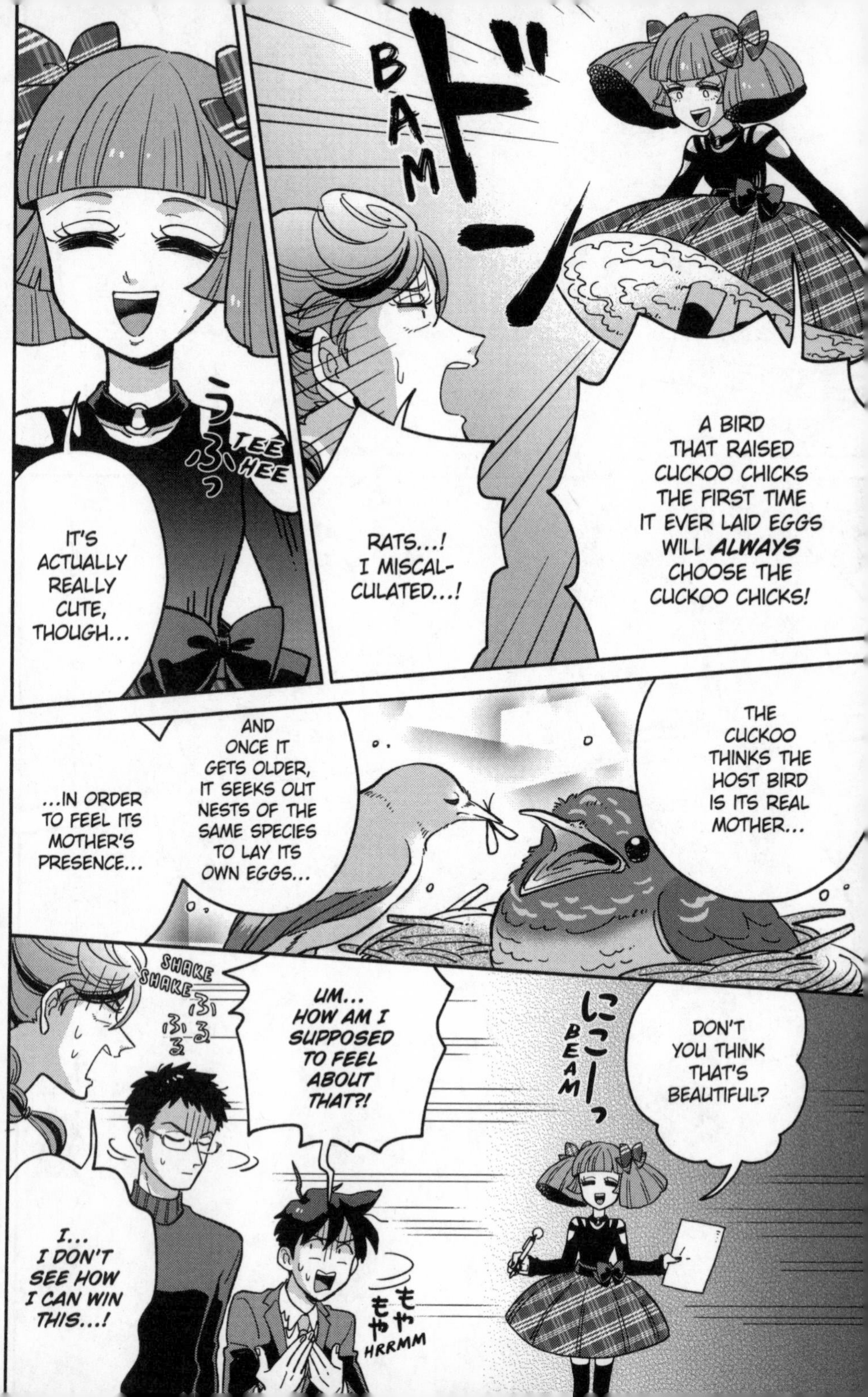
BAM
A BIRD THAT RAISED CUCKOO CHICKS THE FIRST TIME IT EVER LAID EGGS WILL ***ALWAYS*** CHOOSE THE CUCKOO CHICKS!
RATS...! I MISCAL-CULATED...!
TEE HEE
IT'S ACTUALLY REALLY CUTE, THOUGH...
THE CUCKOO THINKS THE HOST BIRD IS ITS REAL MOTHER...
AND ONCE IT GETS OLDER, IT SEEKS OUT NESTS OF THE SAME SPECIES TO LAY ITS OWN EGGS...
...IN ORDER TO FEEL ITS MOTHER'S PRESENCE...
DON'T YOU THINK THAT'S BEAUTIFUL?
BEAM
UM... HOW AM I SUPPOSED TO FEEL ABOUT THAT?!
SHAKE SHAKE
HRRMM
I... I DON'T SEE HOW I CAN WIN THIS...!

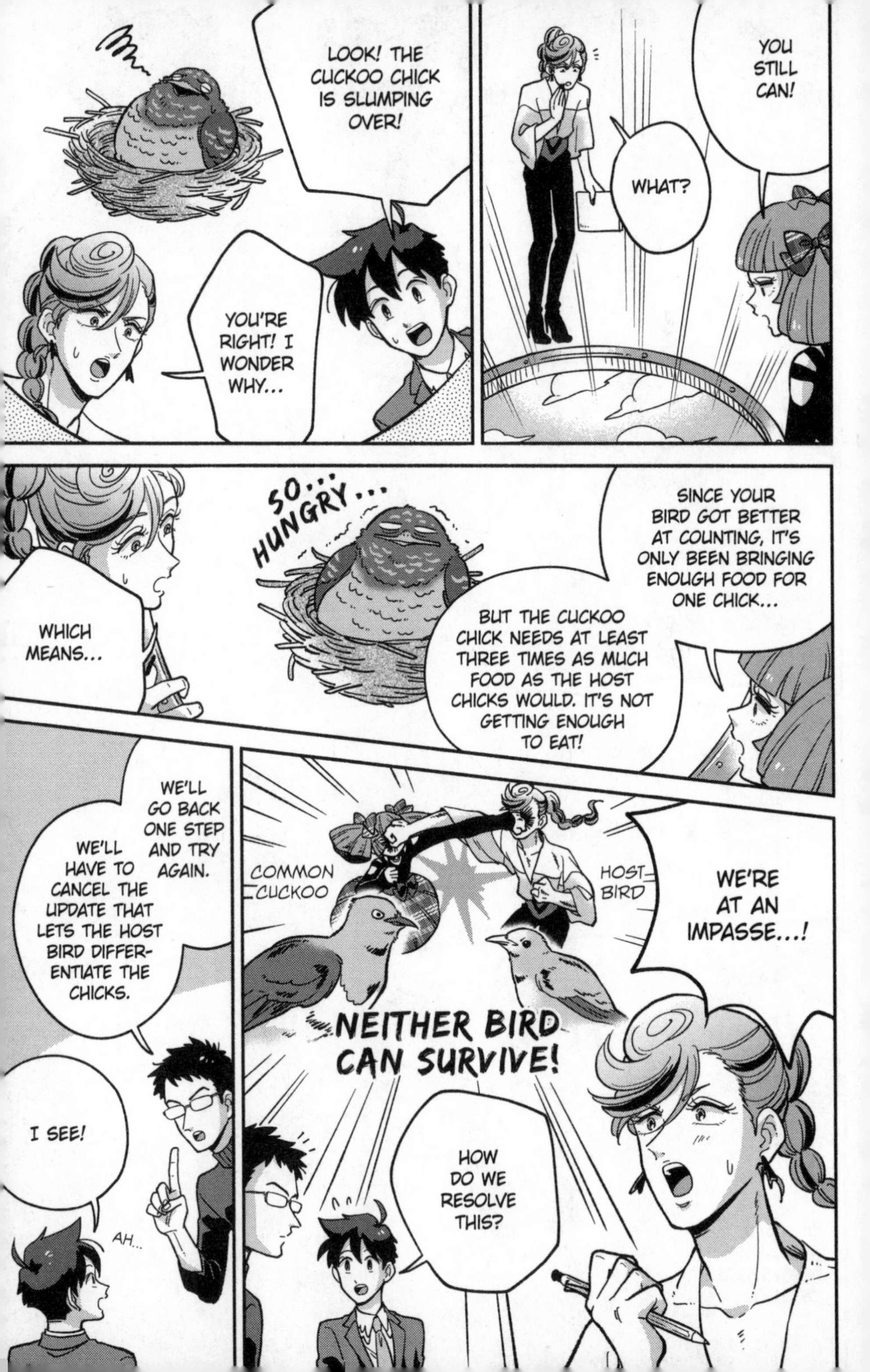
YOU STILL CAN!
WHAT?
LOOK! THE CUCKOO CHICK IS SLUMPING OVER!
YOU'RE RIGHT! I WONDER WHY...
SINCE YOUR BIRD GOT BETTER AT COUNTING, IT'S ONLY BEEN BRINGING ENOUGH FOOD FOR ONE CHICK...
SO... HUNGRY...
BUT THE CUCKOO CHICK NEEDS AT LEAST THREE TIMES AS MUCH FOOD AS THE HOST CHICKS WOULD. IT'S NOT GETTING ENOUGH TO EAT!
WHICH MEANS...
WE'RE AT AN IMPASSE...!
HOST BIRD
COMMON CUCKOO
NEITHER BIRD CAN SURVIVE!
HOW DO WE RESOLVE THIS?
WE'LL GO BACK ONE STEP AND TRY AGAIN.
WE'LL HAVE TO CANCEL THE UPDATE THAT LETS THE HOST BIRD DIFFER-ENTIATE THE CHICKS.
I SEE!
AH...

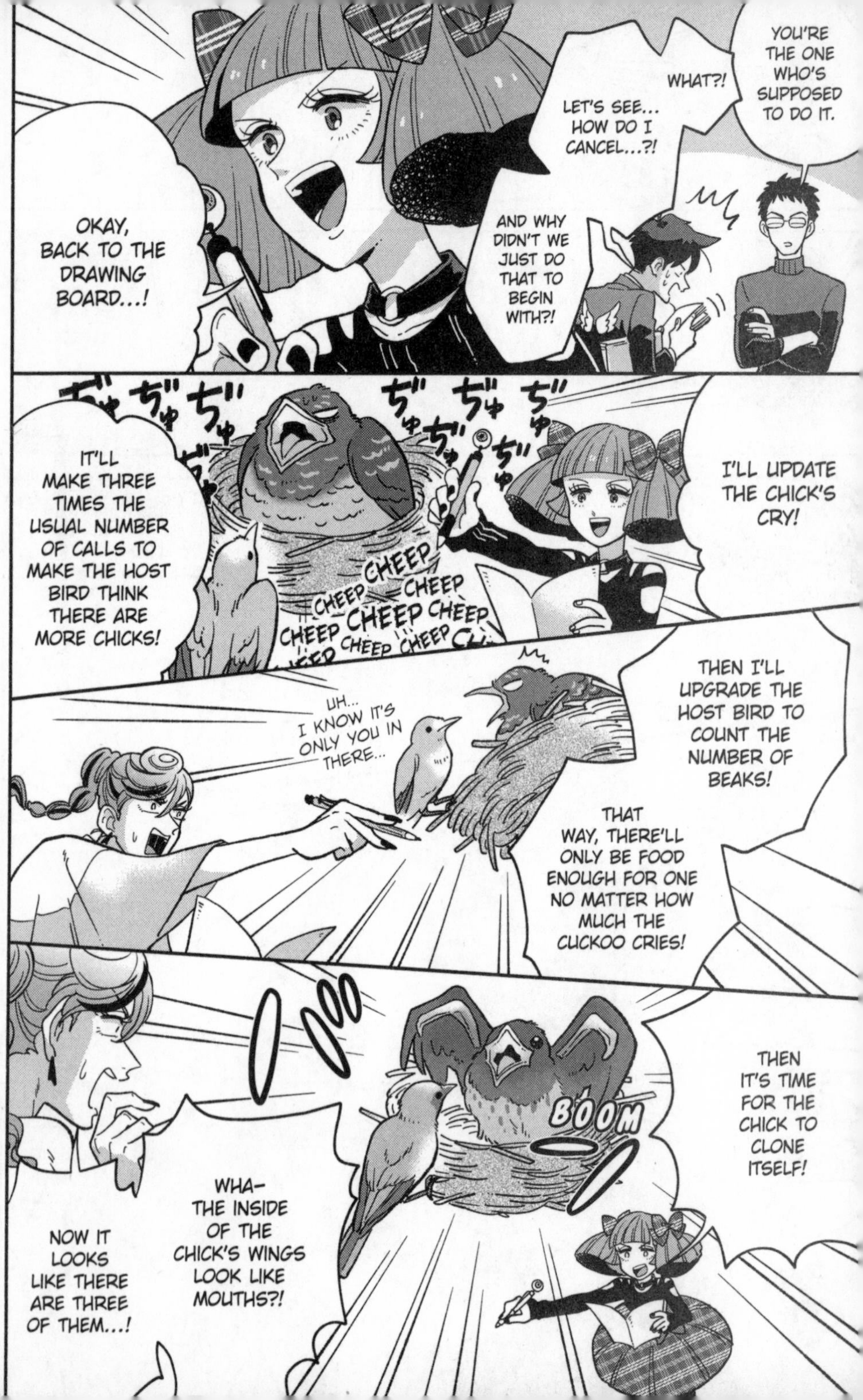

OKAY, BACK TO THE DRAWING BOARD...!
LET'S SEE... HOW DO I CANCEL...?!
AND WHY DIDN'T WE JUST DO THAT TO BEGIN WITH?!
WHAT?!
YOU'RE THE ONE WHO'S SUPPOSED TO DO IT.
I'LL UPDATE THE CHICK'S CRY!
ぢゅ ちゅ ぢゅ ちゅ ぢゅ ちゅ ぢゅ ちゅ ぢゅ ちゅ ぢゅ
IT'LL MAKE THREE TIMES THE USUAL NUMBER OF CALLS TO MAKE THE HOST BIRD THINK THERE ARE MORE CHICKS!
CHEEP CHEEP CHEEP CHEEP CHEEP CHEEP CHEEP CHEEP
THEN I'LL UPGRADE THE HOST BIRD TO COUNT THE NUMBER OF BEAKS!
THAT WAY, THERE'LL ONLY BE FOOD ENOUGH FOR ONE NO MATTER HOW MUCH THE CUCKOO CRIES!
UH... I KNOW IT'S ONLY YOU IN THERE...
THEN IT'S TIME FOR THE CHICK TO CLONE ITSELF!
BOOM
WHA- THE INSIDE OF THE CHICK'S WINGS LOOK LIKE MOUTHS?!
NOW IT LOOKS LIKE THERE ARE THREE OF THEM...!

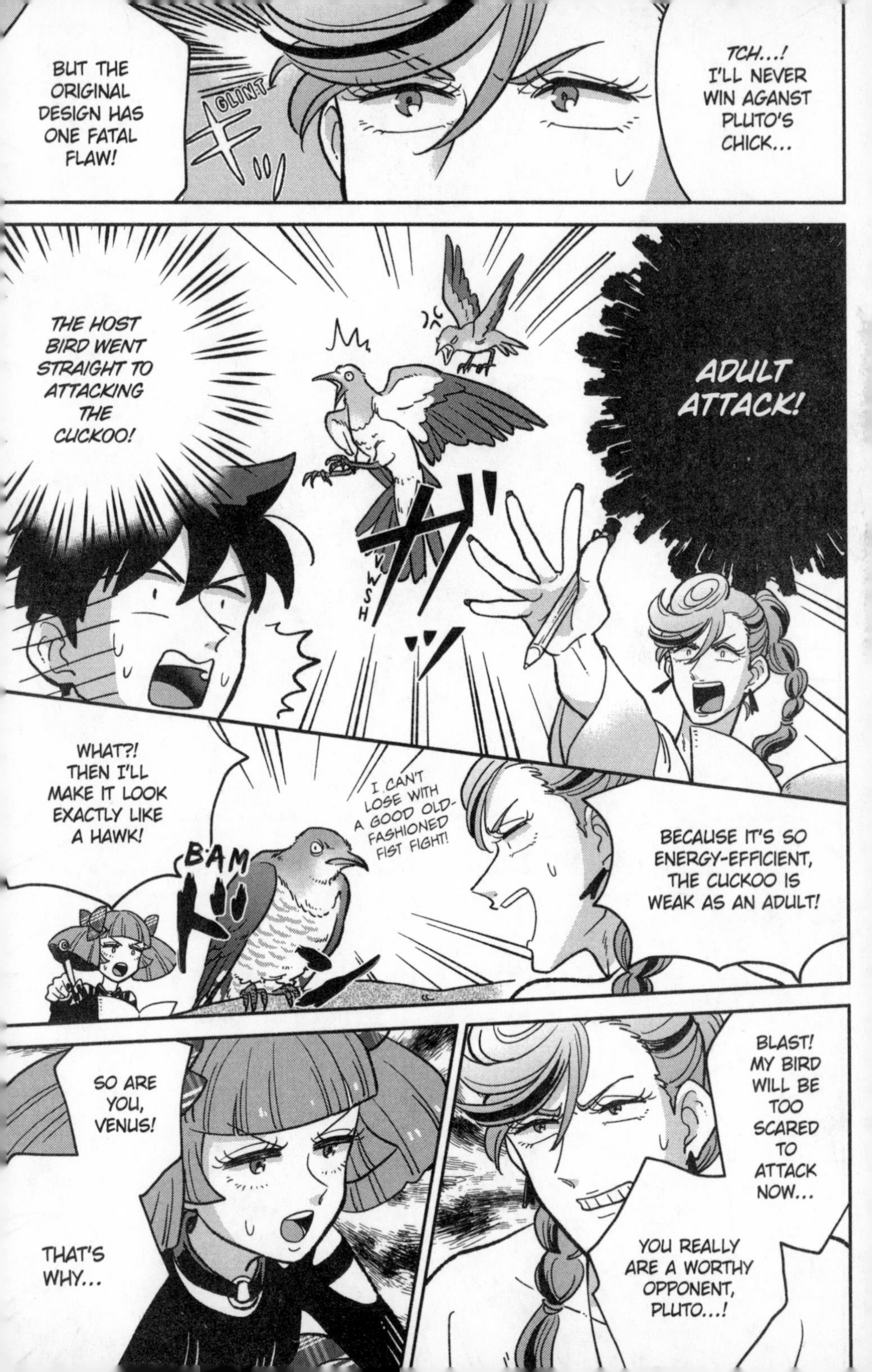
TCH...! I'LL NEVER WIN AGANST PLUTO'S CHICK...
GLINT
BUT THE ORIGINAL DESIGN HAS ONE FATAL FLAW!
ADULT ATTACK!
THE HOST BIRD WENT STRAIGHT TO ATTACKING THE CUCKOO!
VWSH
BECAUSE IT'S SO ENERGY-EFFICIENT, THE CUCKOO IS WEAK AS AN ADULT!
I CAN'T LOSE WITH A GOOD OLD-FASHIONED FIST FIGHT!
WHAT?! THEN I'LL MAKE IT LOOK EXACTLY LIKE A HAWK!
BAM
BLAST! MY BIRD WILL BE TOO SCARED TO ATTACK NOW...
YOU REALLY ARE A WORTHY OPPONENT, PLUTO...!
SO ARE YOU, VENUS!
THAT'S WHY...

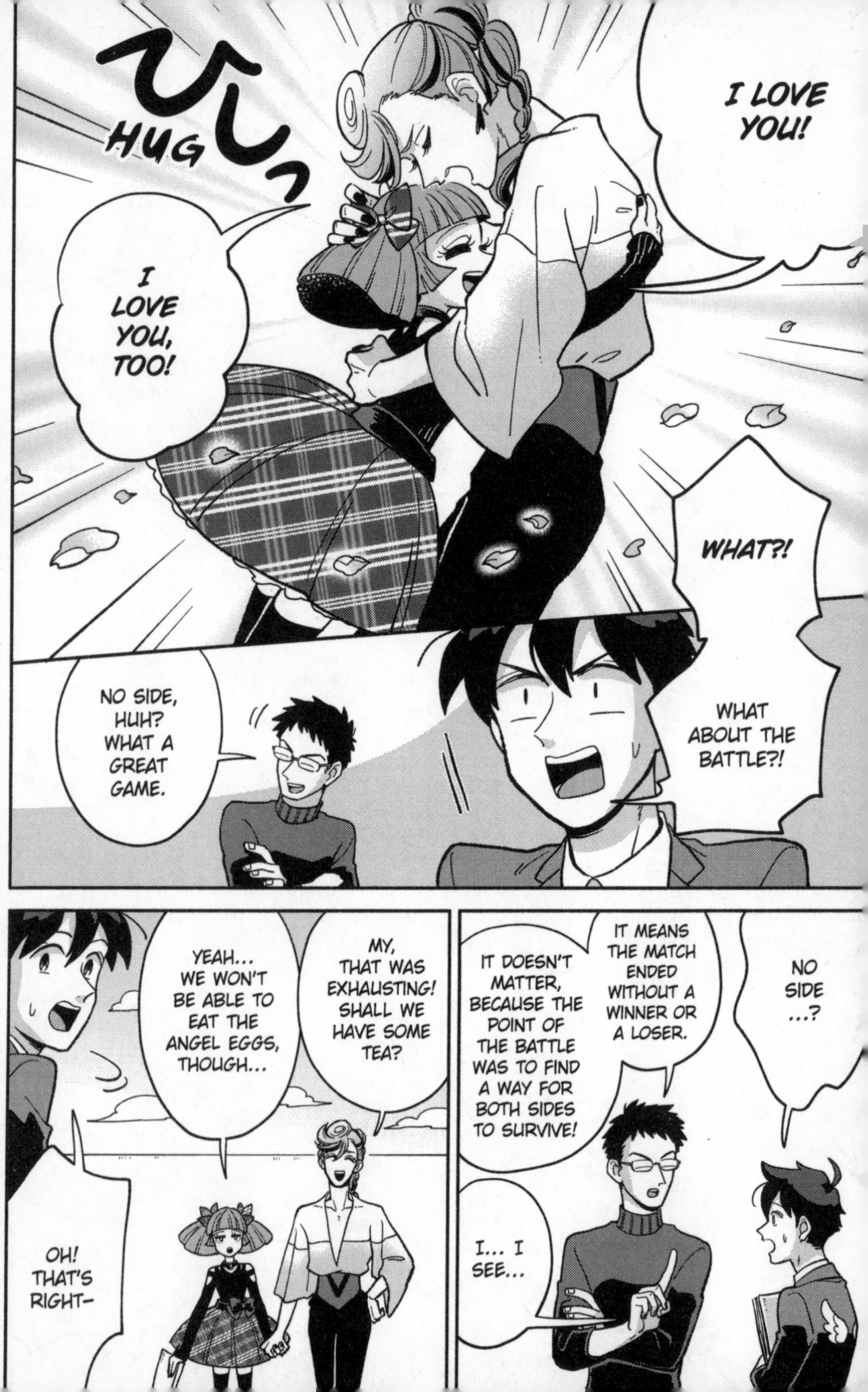
I LOVE YOU!
HUG
I LOVE YOU, TOO!
WHAT?!
WHAT ABOUT THE BATTLE?!
NO SIDE, HUH? WHAT A GREAT GAME.
NO SIDE ...?
IT MEANS THE MATCH ENDED WITHOUT A WINNER OR A LOSER.
IT DOESN'T MATTER, BECAUSE THE POINT OF THE BATTLE WAS TO FIND A WAY FOR BOTH SIDES TO SURVIVE!
I... I SEE...
MY, THAT WAS EXHAUSTING! SHALL WE HAVE SOME TEA?
YEAH... WE WON'T BE ABLE TO EAT THE ANGEL EGGS, THOUGH...
OH! THAT'S RIGHT-

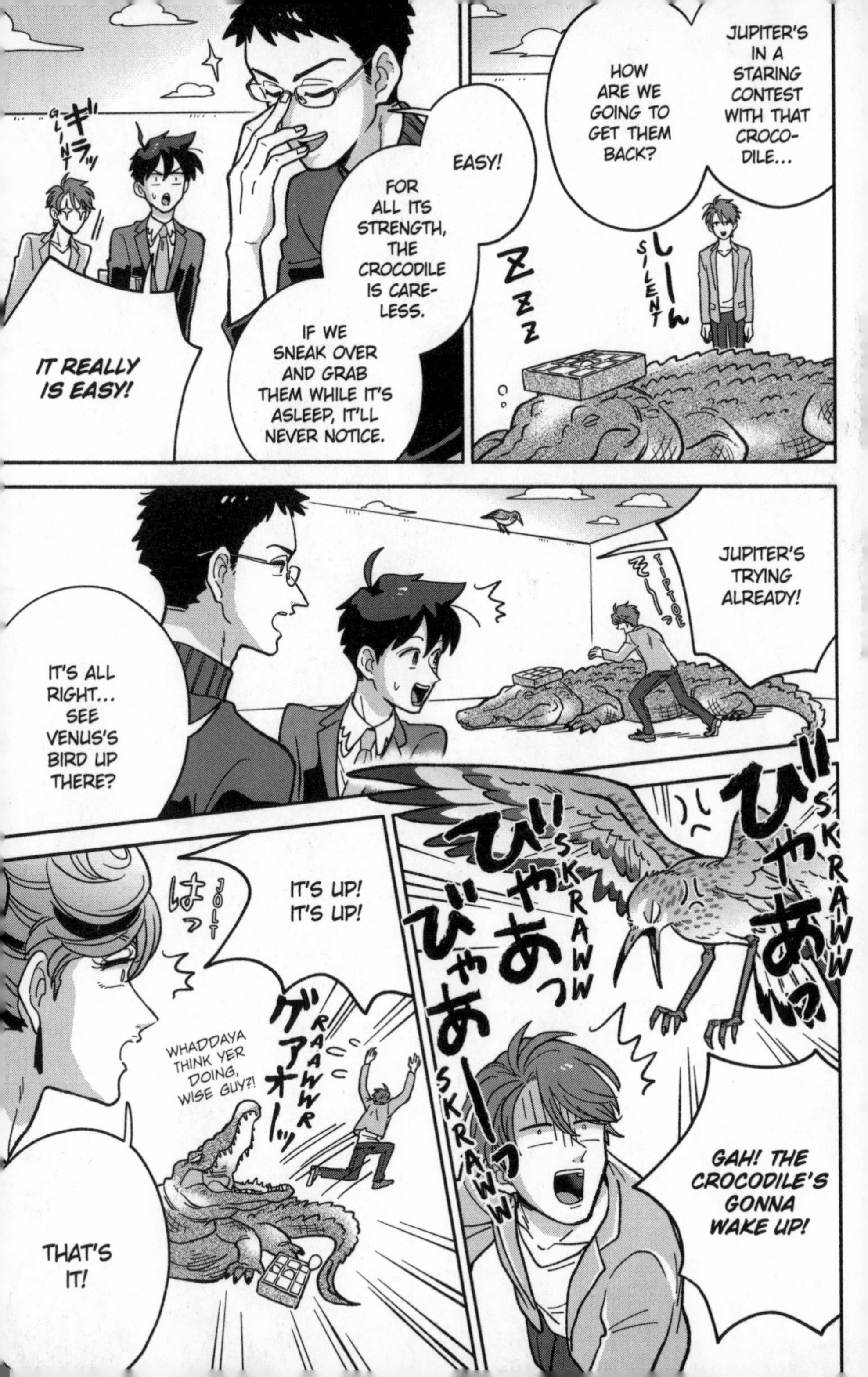
JUPITER'S IN A STARING CONTEST WITH THAT CROCO-DILE...
HOW ARE WE GOING TO GET THEM BACK?
しーん SILENT
Z Z Z
ギラッ GLINT
EASY!
FOR ALL ITS STRENGTH, THE CROCODILE IS CARE-LESS.
IF WE SNEAK OVER AND GRAB THEM WHILE IT'S ASLEEP, IT'LL NEVER NOTICE.
IT REALLY IS EASY!
JUPITER'S TRYING ALREADY!
そ~~っ TIPTOE
IT'S ALL RIGHT... SEE VENUS'S BIRD UP THERE?
びゃあっ SKRAWW
びゃあっ SKRAWW
びゃあーっ SKRAWW
GAH! THE CROCODILE'S GONNA WAKE UP!
はっ JOLT
IT'S UP! IT'S UP!
WHADDAYA THINK YER DOING, WISE GUY?!
グアオーッ RAWWR
THAT'S IT!

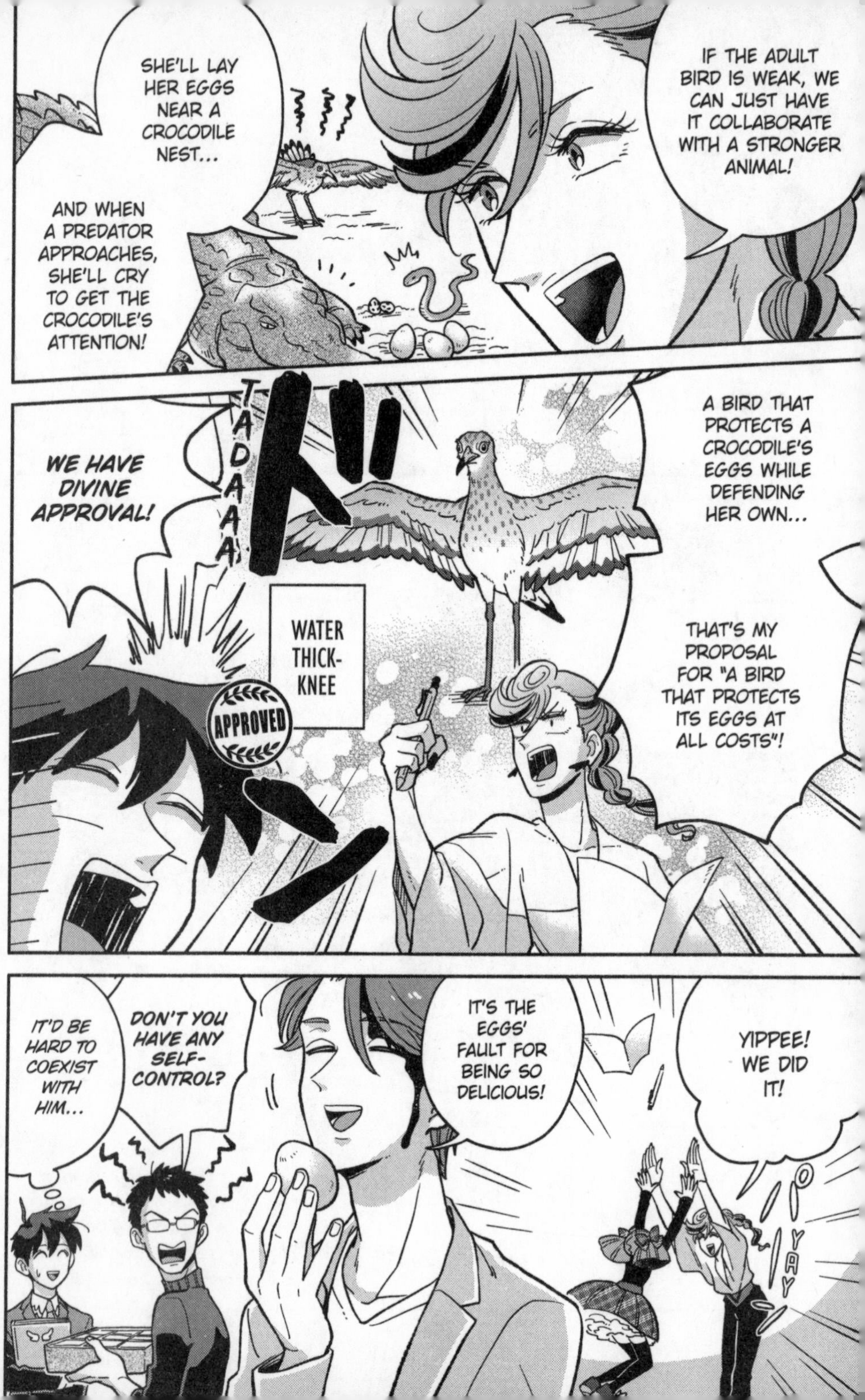
IF THE ADULT BIRD IS WEAK, WE CAN JUST HAVE IT COLLABORATE WITH A STRONGER ANIMAL!
SHE'LL LAY HER EGGS NEAR A CROCODILE NEST...
AND WHEN A PREDATOR APPROACHES, SHE'LL CRY TO GET THE CROCODILE'S ATTENTION!
A BIRD THAT PROTECTS A CROCODILE'S EGGS WHILE DEFENDING HER OWN...
THAT'S MY PROPOSAL FOR "A BIRD THAT PROTECTS ITS EGGS AT ALL COSTS"!
WATER THICK-KNEE
TADAAAA
ドン
WE HAVE DIVINE APPROVAL!
APPROVED
YIPPEE! WE DID IT!
YAY
IT'S THE EGGS' FAULT FOR BEING SO DELICIOUS!
DON'T YOU HAVE ANY SELF-CONTROL?
IT'D BE HARD TO COEXIST WITH HIM...

THE ENCYCLOPEDIA OF REAL ANIMALS 34

ANIMAL 81 | COMMON CUCKOO

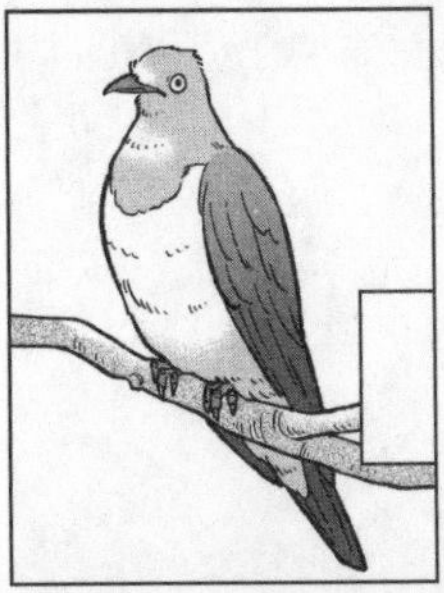

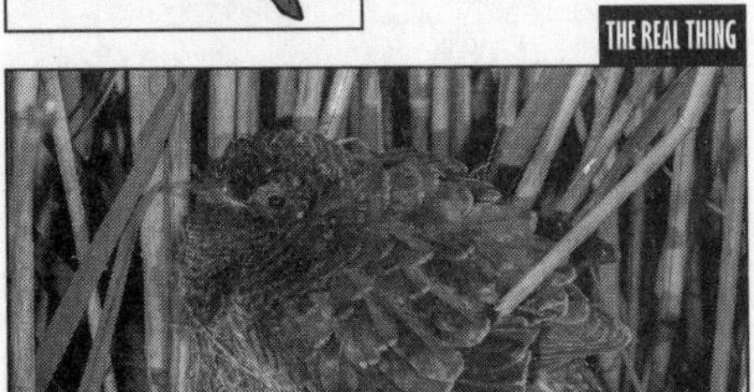
THE REAL THING

The host bird raises a common cuckoo chick larger than itself.

Photo: Minden Piectures/Aflo

[Name] *Cuculus canorus*
[Classification] Class: Aves
Order: Cuculiformes
Family: Cuculidae
Genus: *Cuculus*
[Habitat] Europe, Asia, and parts of Africa
[Length] 35 cm (14 in)

The common cuckoo is a brood parasite, meaning it lays its eggs in other birds' nests and leaves the incubating to the host bird. It is not a strong fighter, so it compensates with a hawk-like appearance.

The cuckoo sometimes lays its own eggs in the nests of birds in the same family, including the Hodgson's hawk-cuckoo and the lesser cuckoo. It has various adaptations to facilitate this, including the ability to lay eggs nearly identical to those of the host bird's and laying eggs extremely quickly. Because cuckoo eggs have a short incubation period, the chicks often hatch before those of the host bird. The chick then pushes the other eggs out of the nest. Hodgson's hawk-cuckoo chicks have markings on the insides of their wings that look like beaks. At feeding time, the chick uses these markings to trick the host bird into giving it more food.

Once existing strategies lose effectiveness with a host species, the common cuckoo will find a new one. When the meadow bunting became too adept at identifying trespassing eggs, the cuckoo began to target the bull-headed shrike.

| # WATER THICK-KNEE

The water thick-knee is found near water in sub-Saharan Africa, and feeds on insects, crustaceans, and mollusks. It is generally nocturnal, but unlike other thick-knees, it is sometimes also active during the day.

The water thick-knee has been observed laying eggs near crocodiles' nests. Some believe this is to protect its young from its natural enemy, the monitor lizard. The monitor lizard also preys on crocodile eggs, but when it approaches an unattended crocodile nest with a water thick-knee nearby, the bird spreads its wings and vocalizes loudly to scare it off. Even if it fails to chase away the predator, the water thick-knee is able to buy enough time for the crocodile to return and intimidate the lizard. In this way, the water thick-knee defends both its own eggs and the crocodile's.

THE REAL THING

It's called a thick-knee, but the part that's thick is actually its ankles.

Photo: Minden Pictures/Aflo

[Name]	*Burhinus vermiculatus*
[Classification]	Class: Aves
	Order: Charadriiformes
	Family: Burhinidae
	Genus: *Burhinus*
[Habitat]	Sub-Saharan Africa
[Length]	Approximately 40 cm (1.3 ft)

HEAVEN'S
DESIGN TEAM

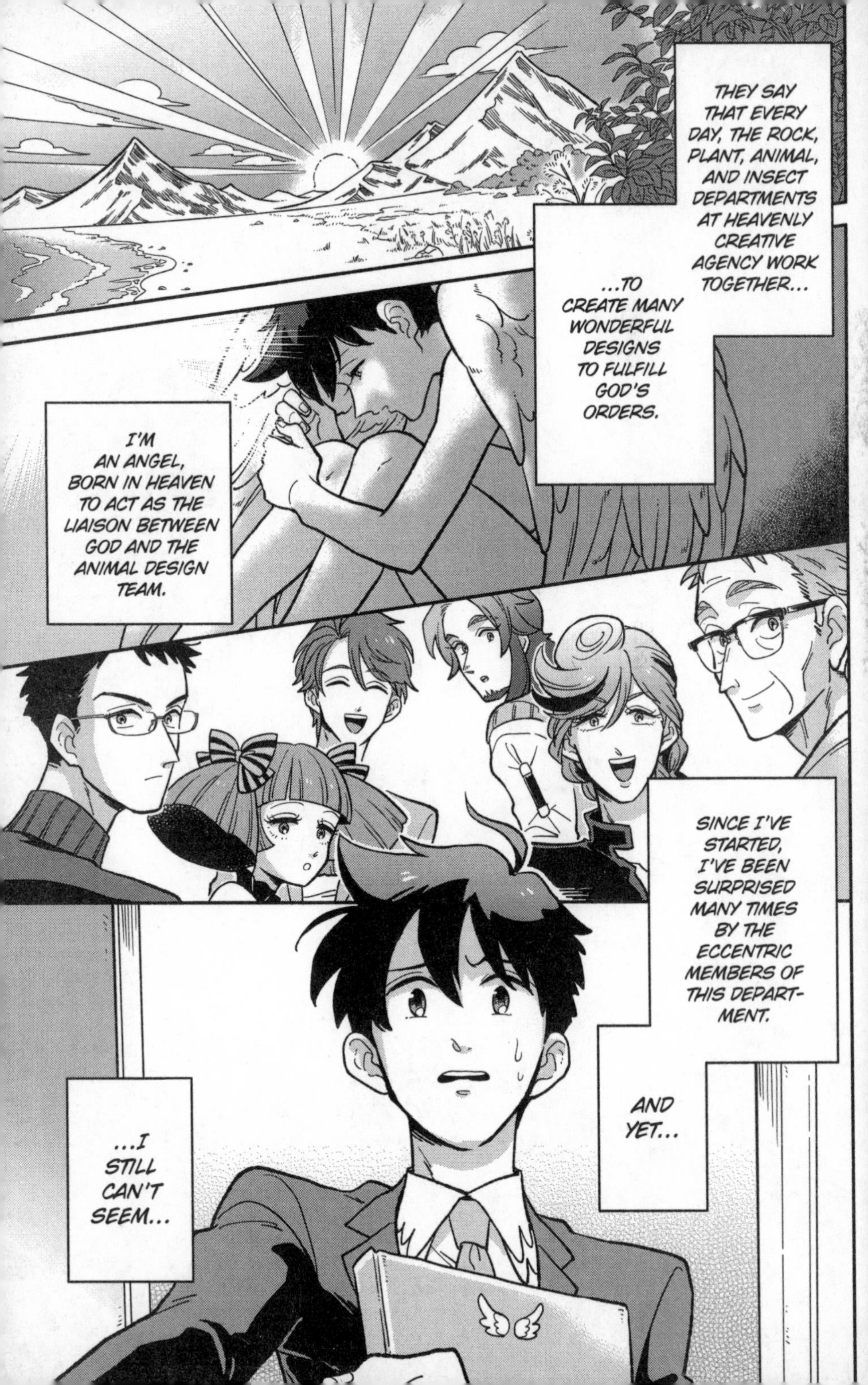
THEY SAY THAT EVERY DAY, THE ROCK, PLANT, ANIMAL, AND INSECT DEPARTMENTS AT HEAVENLY CREATIVE AGENCY WORK TOGETHER...
...TO CREATE MANY WONDERFUL DESIGNS TO FULFILL GOD'S ORDERS.
I'M AN ANGEL, BORN IN HEAVEN TO ACT AS THE LIAISON BETWEEN GOD AND THE ANIMAL DESIGN TEAM.
SINCE I'VE STARTED, I'VE BEEN SURPRISED MANY TIMES BY THE ECCENTRIC MEMBERS OF THIS DEPARTMENT.
AND YET...
...I STILL CAN'T SEEM...

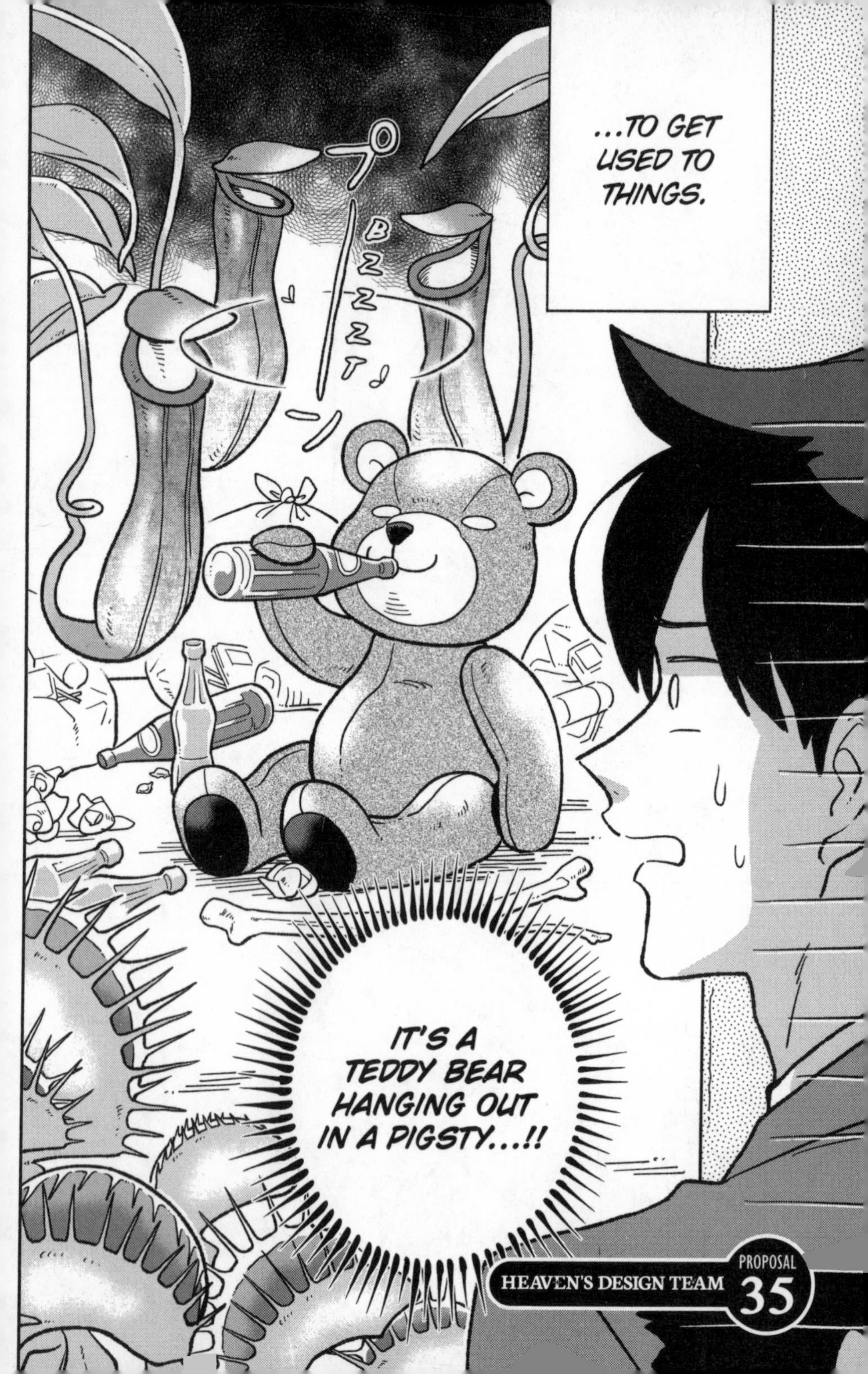
...TO GET USED TO THINGS.
BZZZZT
IT'S A TEDDY BEAR HANGING OUT IN A PIGSTY...!!
HEAVEN'S DESIGN TEAM
PROPOSAL 35

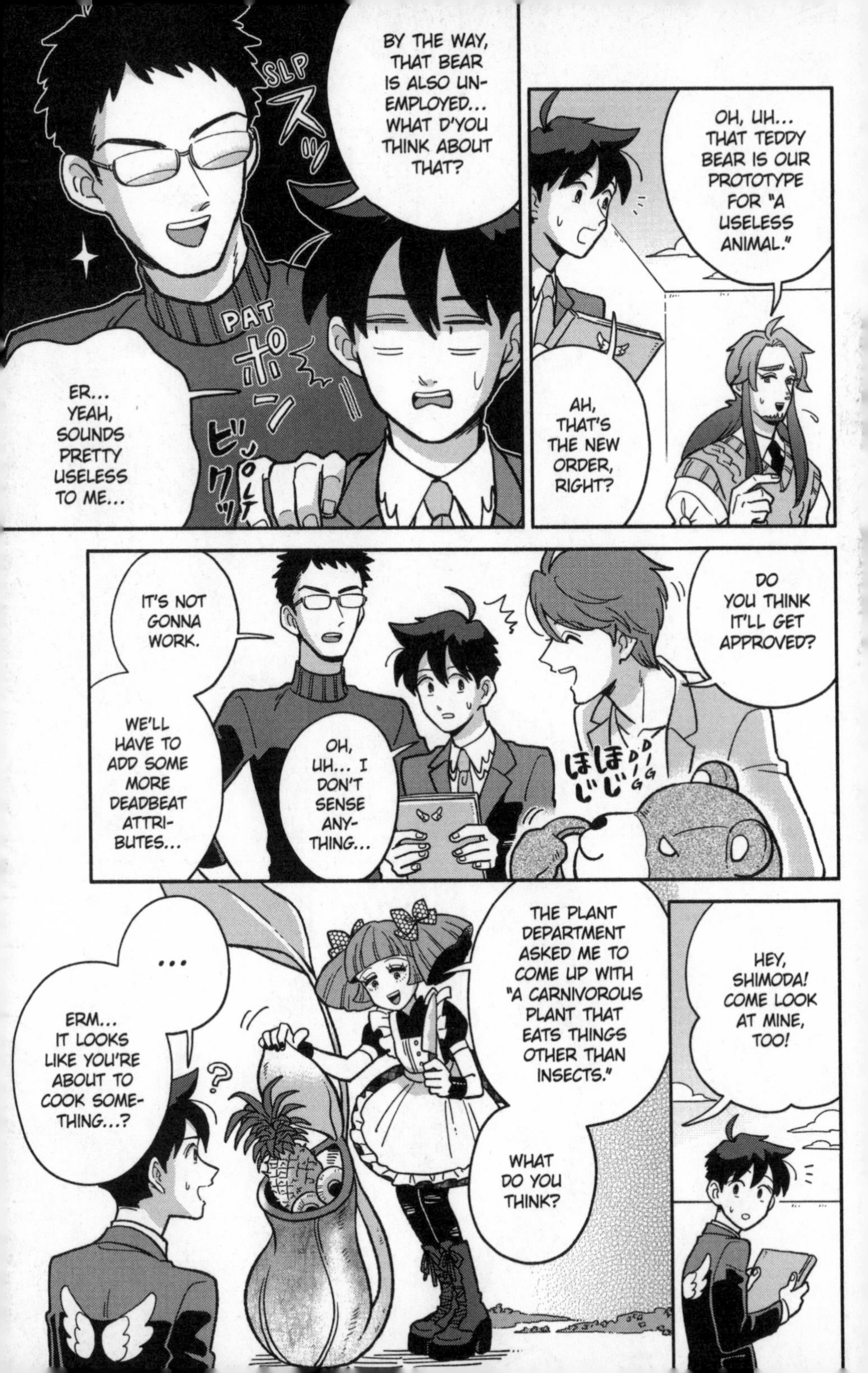
OH, UH... THAT TEDDY BEAR IS OUR PROTOTYPE FOR "A USELESS ANIMAL."
AH, THAT'S THE NEW ORDER, RIGHT?
BY THE WAY, THAT BEAR IS ALSO UN-EMPLOYED... WHAT D'YOU THINK ABOUT THAT?
SLP
スッ
PAT
ポン
JOLT
ビクッ
ER... YEAH, SOUNDS PRETTY USELESS TO ME...
DO YOU THINK IT'LL GET APPROVED?
IT'S NOT GONNA WORK.
ほじほじ
DIG DIG
OH, UH... I DON'T SENSE ANY-THING...
WE'LL HAVE TO ADD SOME MORE DEADBEAT ATTRI-BUTES...
HEY, SHIMODA! COME LOOK AT MINE, TOO!
THE PLANT DEPARTMENT ASKED ME TO COME UP WITH "A CARNIVOROUS PLANT THAT EATS THINGS OTHER THAN INSECTS."
WHAT DO YOU THINK?
...
ERM... IT LOOKS LIKE YOU'RE ABOUT TO COOK SOME-THING...?

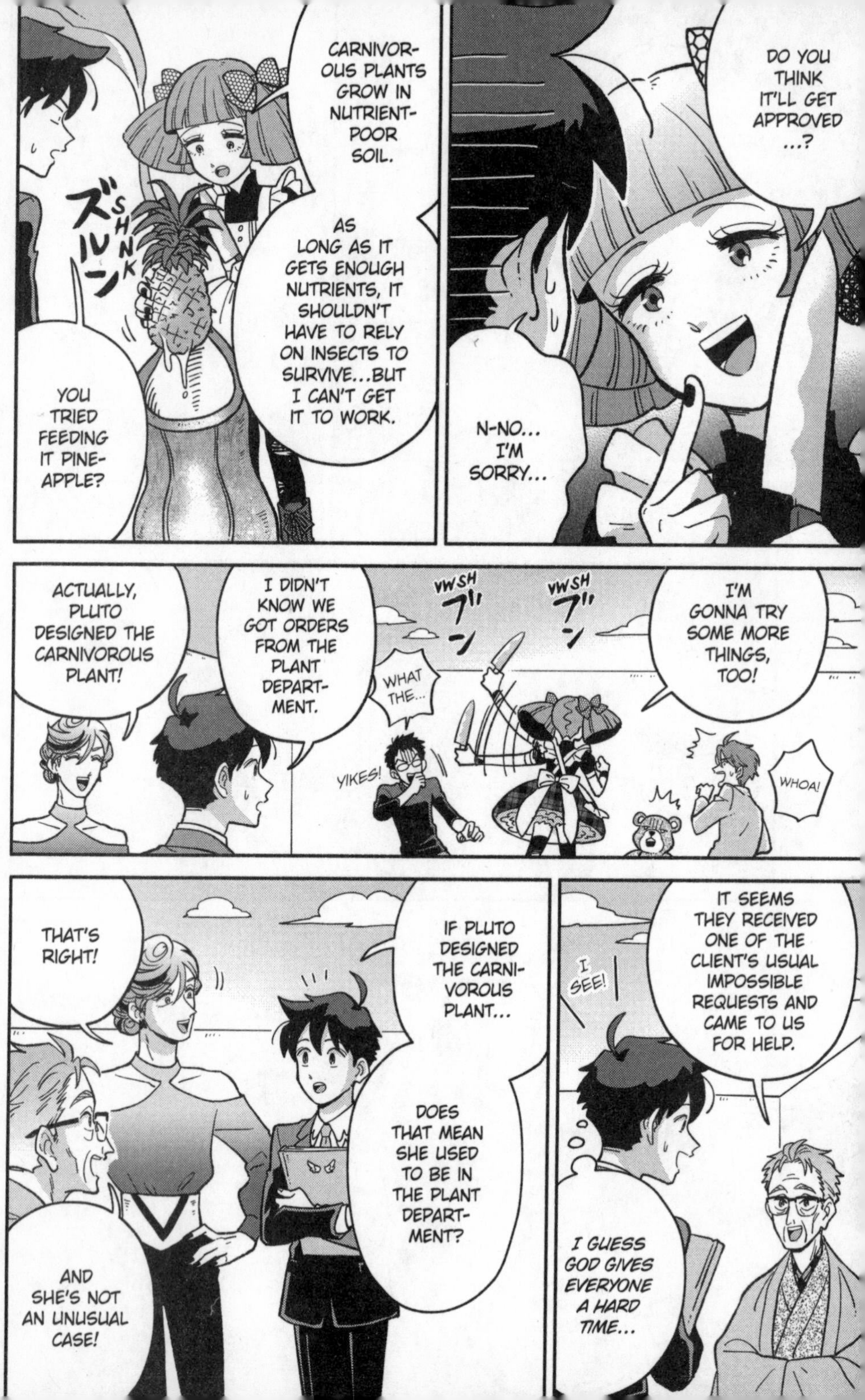
DO YOU THINK IT'LL GET APPROVED ...?
N-NO... I'M SORRY...
CARNIVOR-OUS PLANTS GROW IN NUTRIENT-POOR SOIL.
AS LONG AS IT GETS ENOUGH NUTRIENTS, IT SHOULDN'T HAVE TO RELY ON INSECTS TO SURVIVE...BUT I CAN'T GET IT TO WORK.
ズルーン SHNK
YOU TRIED FEEDING IT PINE-APPLE?
I'M GONNA TRY SOME MORE THINGS, TOO!
WHOA!
VWSH ブン
VWSH ブン
WHAT THE...
YIKES!
I DIDN'T KNOW WE GOT ORDERS FROM THE PLANT DEPART-MENT.
ACTUALLY, PLUTO DESIGNED THE CARNIVOROUS PLANT!
IT SEEMS THEY RECEIVED ONE OF THE CLIENT'S USUAL IMPOSSIBLE REQUESTS AND CAME TO US FOR HELP.
I SEE!
I GUESS GOD GIVES EVERYONE A HARD TIME...
IF PLUTO DESIGNED THE CARNI-VOROUS PLANT...
DOES THAT MEAN SHE USED TO BE IN THE PLANT DEPART-MENT?
THAT'S RIGHT!
AND SHE'S NOT AN UNUSUAL CASE!

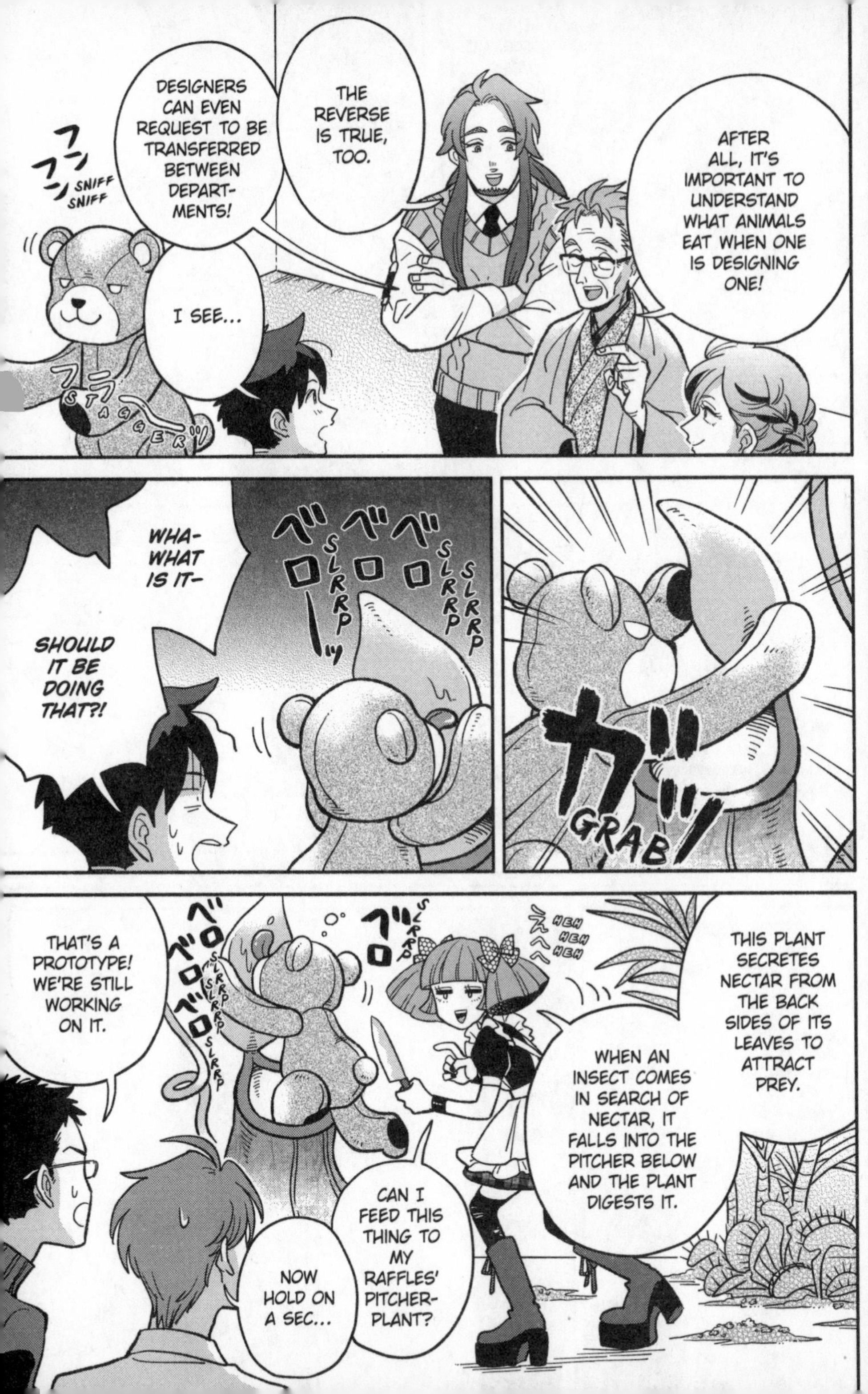
AFTER ALL, IT'S IMPORTANT TO UNDERSTAND WHAT ANIMALS EAT WHEN ONE IS DESIGNING ONE!
THE REVERSE IS TRUE, TOO.
DESIGNERS CAN EVEN REQUEST TO BE TRANSFERRED BETWEEN DEPART-MENTS!
フン フン SNIFF SNIFF
I SEE...
フラ〜ッ STAGGER
ガッ GRAB
ベロ ベロ ベローッ SLRRP SLRRP SLRRP
WHA-WHAT IS IT-
SHOULD IT BE DOING THAT?!
THIS PLANT SECRETES NECTAR FROM THE BACK SIDES OF ITS LEAVES TO ATTRACT PREY.
えへへ HEH HEH HEH
WHEN AN INSECT COMES IN SEARCH OF NECTAR, IT FALLS INTO THE PITCHER BELOW AND THE PLANT DIGESTS IT.
ベロ SLRRP
CAN I FEED THIS THING TO MY RAFFLES' PITCHER-PLANT?
NOW HOLD ON A SEC...
THAT'S A PROTOTYPE! WE'RE STILL WORKING ON IT.
ベロ ベロ ベロ ベロ SLRRP SLRRP SLRRP SLRRP

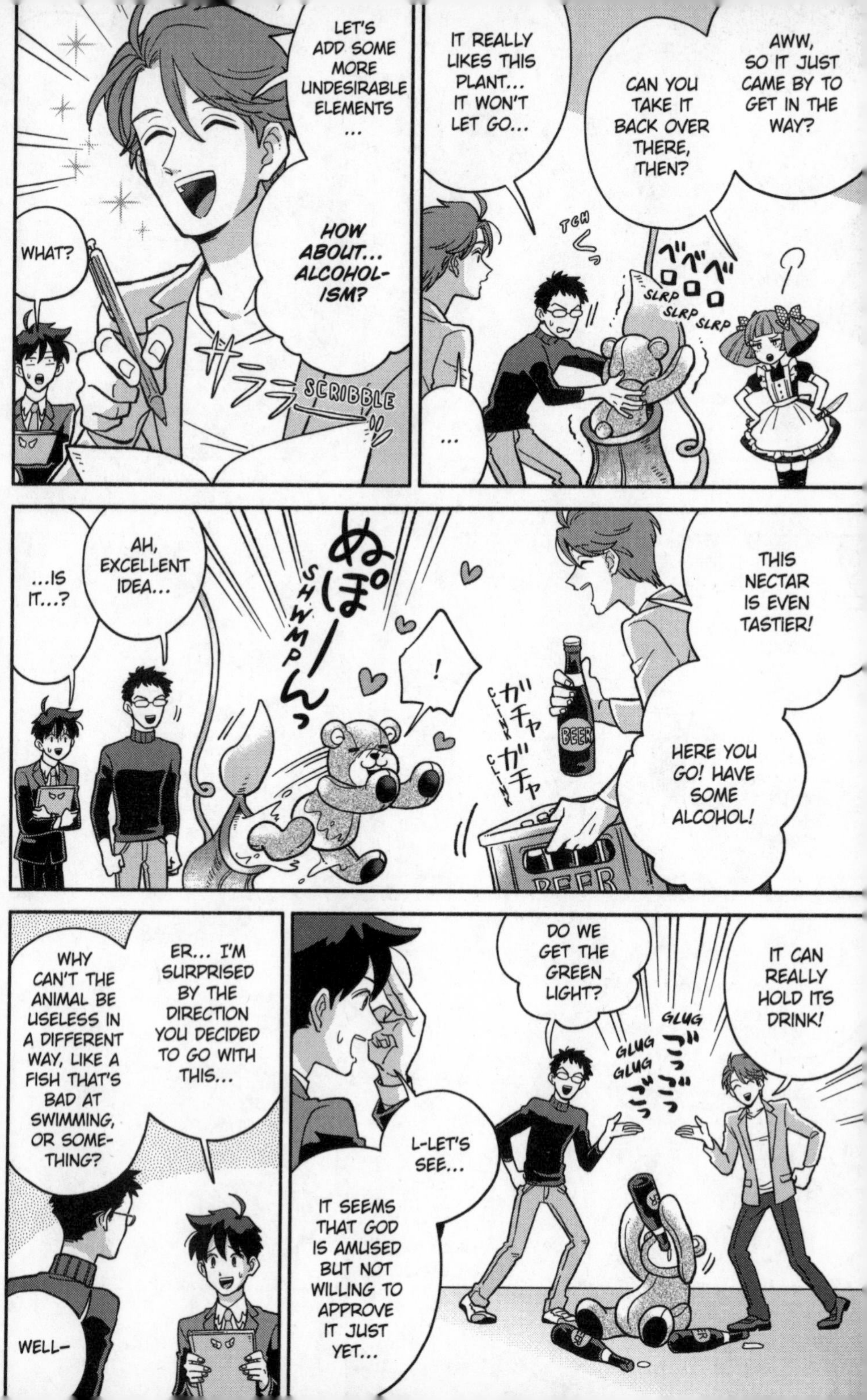
AWW, SO IT JUST CAME BY TO GET IN THE WAY?
CAN YOU TAKE IT BACK OVER THERE, THEN?
IT REALLY LIKES THIS PLANT... IT WON'T LET GO...
TCH
SLRP SLRP SLRP
...
LET'S ADD SOME MORE UNDESIRABLE ELEMENTS ...
HOW ABOUT... ALCOHOLISM?
WHAT?
SCRIBBLE
THIS NECTAR IS EVEN TASTIER!
HERE YOU GO! HAVE SOME ALCOHOL!
CLINK CLINK
!
SHWMP
AH, EXCELLENT IDEA...
...IS IT...?
IT CAN REALLY HOLD ITS DRINK!
DO WE GET THE GREEN LIGHT?
GLUG GLUG GLUG
L-LET'S SEE...
IT SEEMS THAT GOD IS AMUSED BUT NOT WILLING TO APPROVE IT JUST YET...
ER... I'M SURPRISED BY THE DIRECTION YOU DECIDED TO GO WITH THIS...
WHY CAN'T THE ANIMAL BE USELESS IN A DIFFERENT WAY, LIKE A FISH THAT'S BAD AT SWIMMING, OR SOME-THING?
WELL-

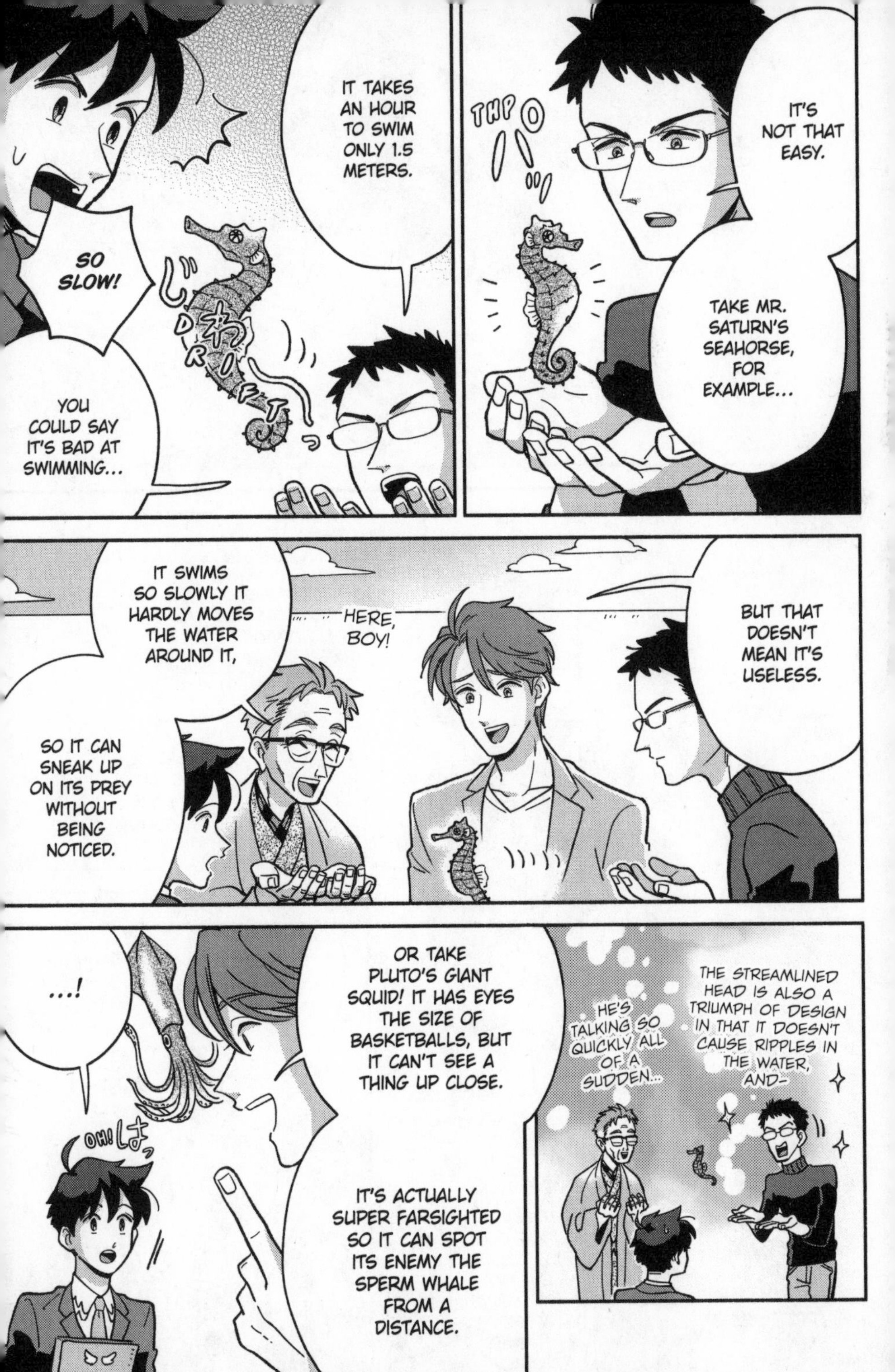
IT'S NOT THAT EASY.
THP
TAKE MR. SATURN'S SEAHORSE, FOR EXAMPLE...
IT TAKES AN HOUR TO SWIM ONLY 1.5 METERS.
SO SLOW!
じわ DRIFT
YOU COULD SAY IT'S BAD AT SWIMMING...
BUT THAT DOESN'T MEAN IT'S USELESS.
HERE, BOY!
IT SWIMS SO SLOWLY IT HARDLY MOVES THE WATER AROUND IT,
SO IT CAN SNEAK UP ON ITS PREY WITHOUT BEING NOTICED.
THE STREAMLINED HEAD IS ALSO A TRIUMPH OF DESIGN IN THAT IT DOESN'T CAUSE RIPPLES IN THE WATER, AND—
HE'S TALKING SO QUICKLY ALL OF A SUDDEN...
OR TAKE PLUTO'S GIANT SQUID! IT HAS EYES THE SIZE OF BASKETBALLS, BUT IT CAN'T SEE A THING UP CLOSE.
...!
OH! はっ
IT'S ACTUALLY SUPER FARSIGHTED SO IT CAN SPOT ITS ENEMY THE SPERM WHALE FROM A DISTANCE.

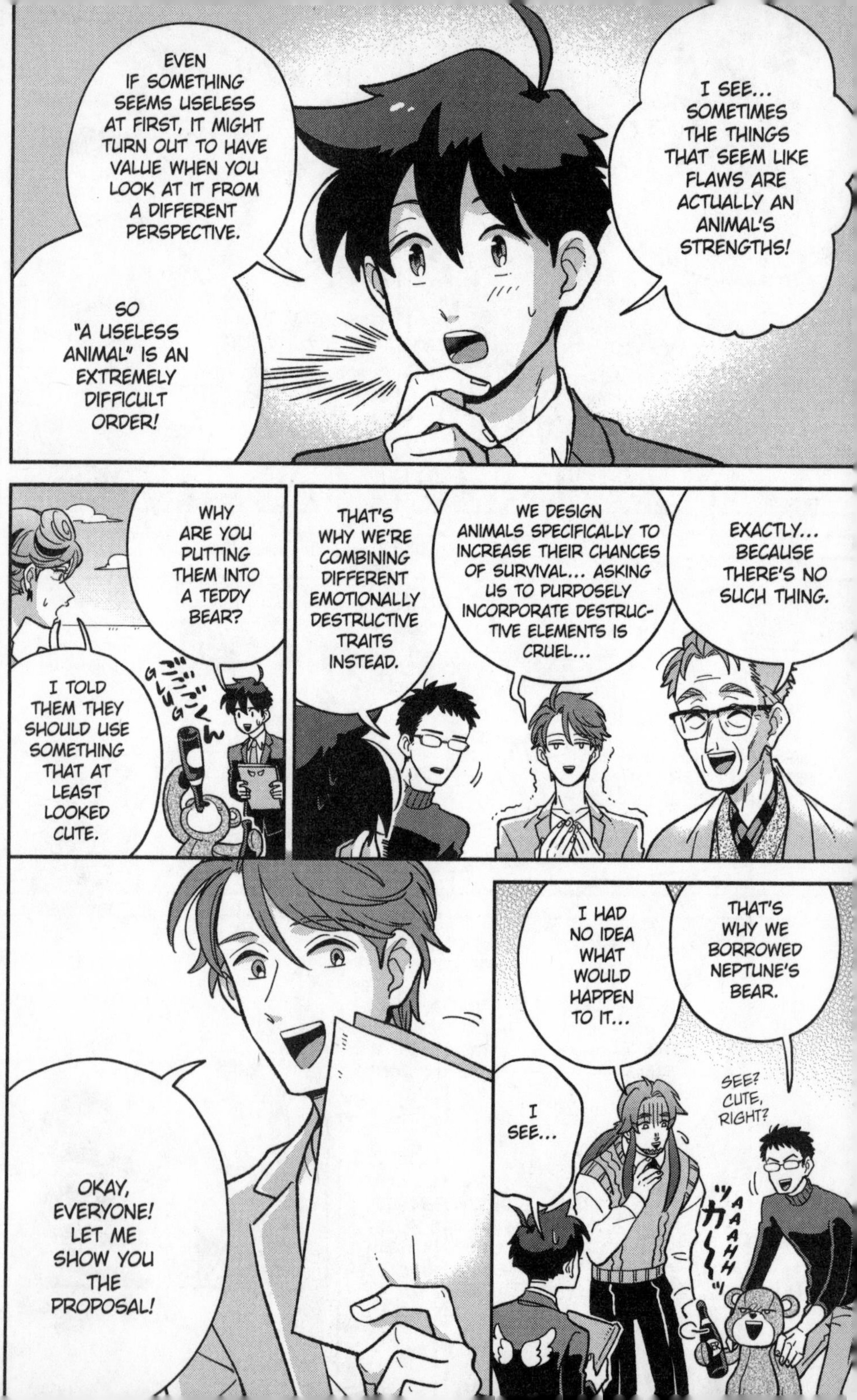
I SEE... SOMETIMES THE THINGS THAT SEEM LIKE FLAWS ARE ACTUALLY AN ANIMAL'S STRENGTHS!
EVEN IF SOMETHING SEEMS USELESS AT FIRST, IT MIGHT TURN OUT TO HAVE VALUE WHEN YOU LOOK AT IT FROM A DIFFERENT PERSPECTIVE.
SO "A USELESS ANIMAL" IS AN EXTREMELY DIFFICULT ORDER!
EXACTLY... BECAUSE THERE'S NO SUCH THING.
WE DESIGN ANIMALS SPECIFICALLY TO INCREASE THEIR CHANCES OF SURVIVAL... ASKING US TO PURPOSELY INCORPORATE DESTRUCTIVE ELEMENTS IS CRUEL...
THAT'S WHY WE'RE COMBINING DIFFERENT EMOTIONALLY DESTRUCTIVE TRAITS INSTEAD.
WHY ARE YOU PUTTING THEM INTO A TEDDY BEAR?
GLUG
I TOLD THEM THEY SHOULD USE SOMETHING THAT AT LEAST LOOKED CUTE.
THAT'S WHY WE BORROWED NEPTUNE'S BEAR.
I HAD NO IDEA WHAT WOULD HAPPEN TO IT...
SEE? CUTE, RIGHT?
AAAHH
I SEE...
OKAY, EVERYONE! LET ME SHOW YOU THE PROPOSAL!

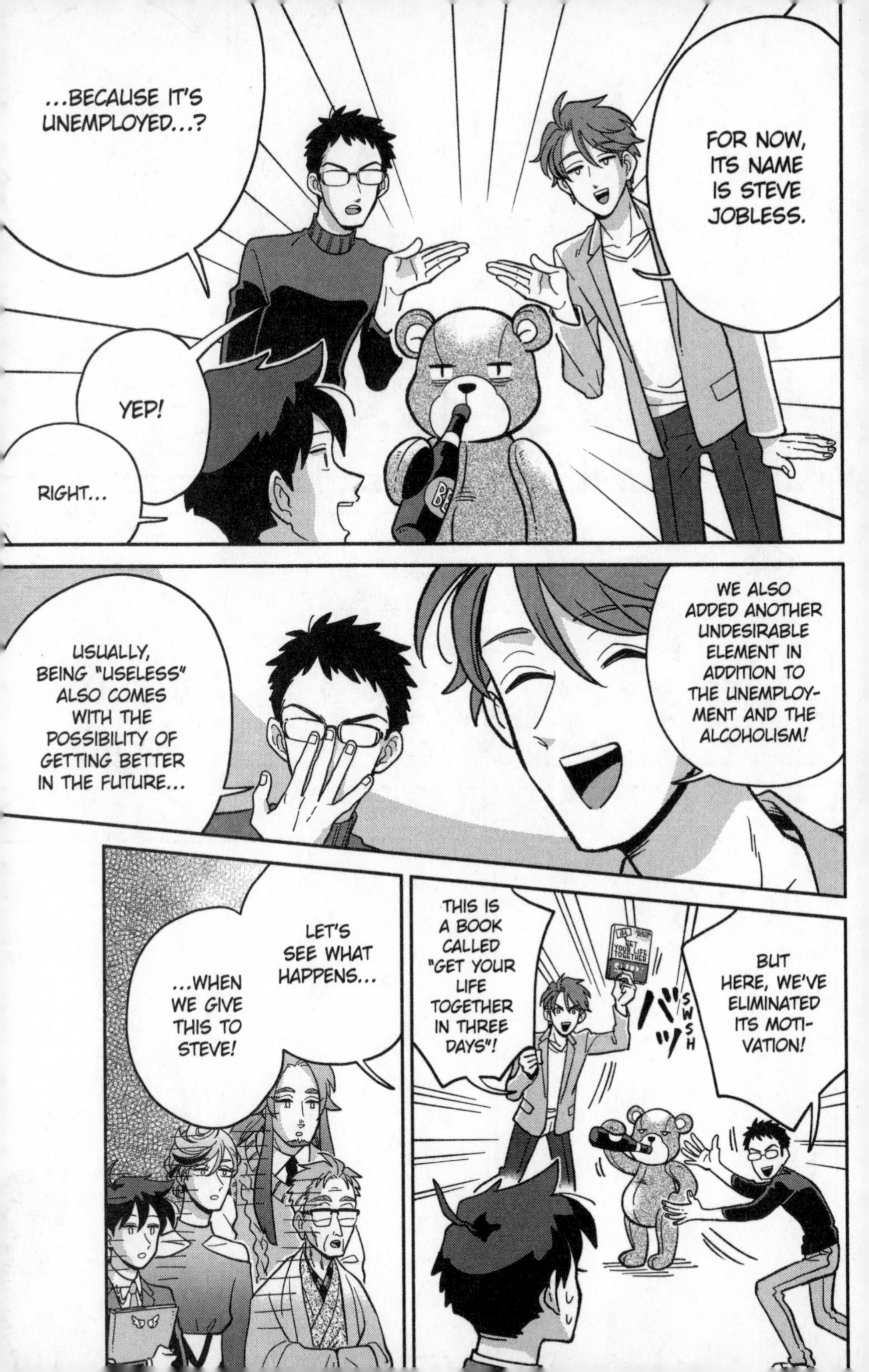
FOR NOW, ITS NAME IS STEVE JOBLESS.
...BECAUSE IT'S UNEMPLOYED...?
YEP!
RIGHT...
WE ALSO ADDED ANOTHER UNDESIRABLE ELEMENT IN ADDITION TO THE UNEMPLOY-MENT AND THE ALCOHOLISM!
USUALLY, BEING "USELESS" ALSO COMES WITH THE POSSIBILITY OF GETTING BETTER IN THE FUTURE...
BUT HERE, WE'VE ELIMINATED ITS MOTI-VATION!
THIS IS A BOOK CALLED "GET YOUR LIFE TOGETHER IN THREE DAYS"!
SWSH
LET'S SEE WHAT HAPPENS...
...WHEN WE GIVE THIS TO STEVE!

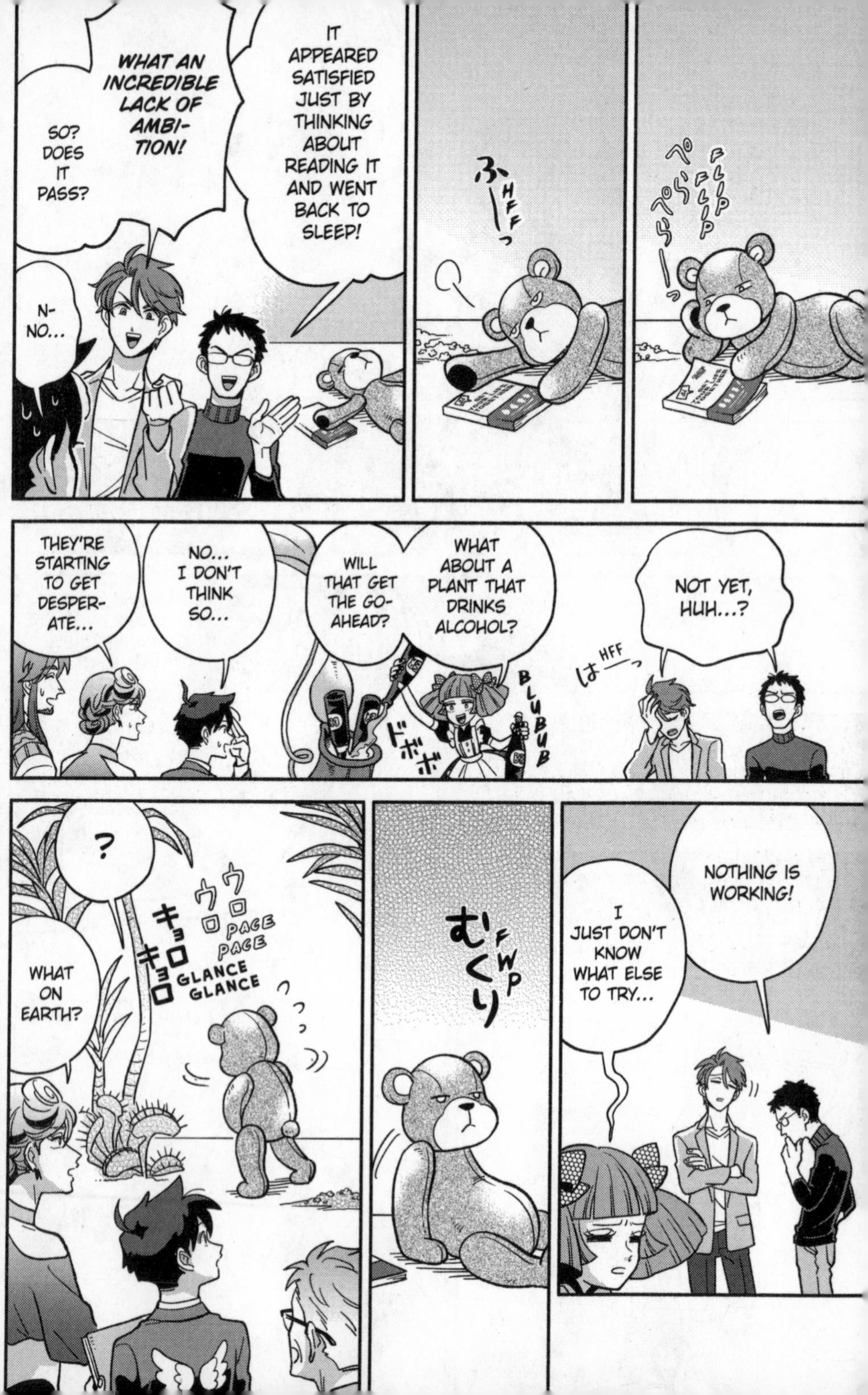
ぺらぺらーっ
FLIP FLIP
ふーっ
HFF
IT APPEARED SATISFIED JUST BY THINKING ABOUT READING IT AND WENT BACK TO SLEEP!
WHAT AN INCREDIBLE LACK OF AMBITION!
SO? DOES IT PASS?
N-NO...
NOT YET, HUH...?
は―っ
HFF
WHAT ABOUT A PLANT THAT DRINKS ALCOHOL?
WILL THAT GET THE GO-AHEAD?
ドボボ
BLUBUB
NO... I DON'T THINK SO...
THEY'RE STARTING TO GET DESPERATE...
NOTHING IS WORKING!
I JUST DON'T KNOW WHAT ELSE TO TRY...
むくり
FWP
?
WHAT ON EARTH?
ウロウロ
PACE PACE
キョロキョロ
GLANCE GLANCE

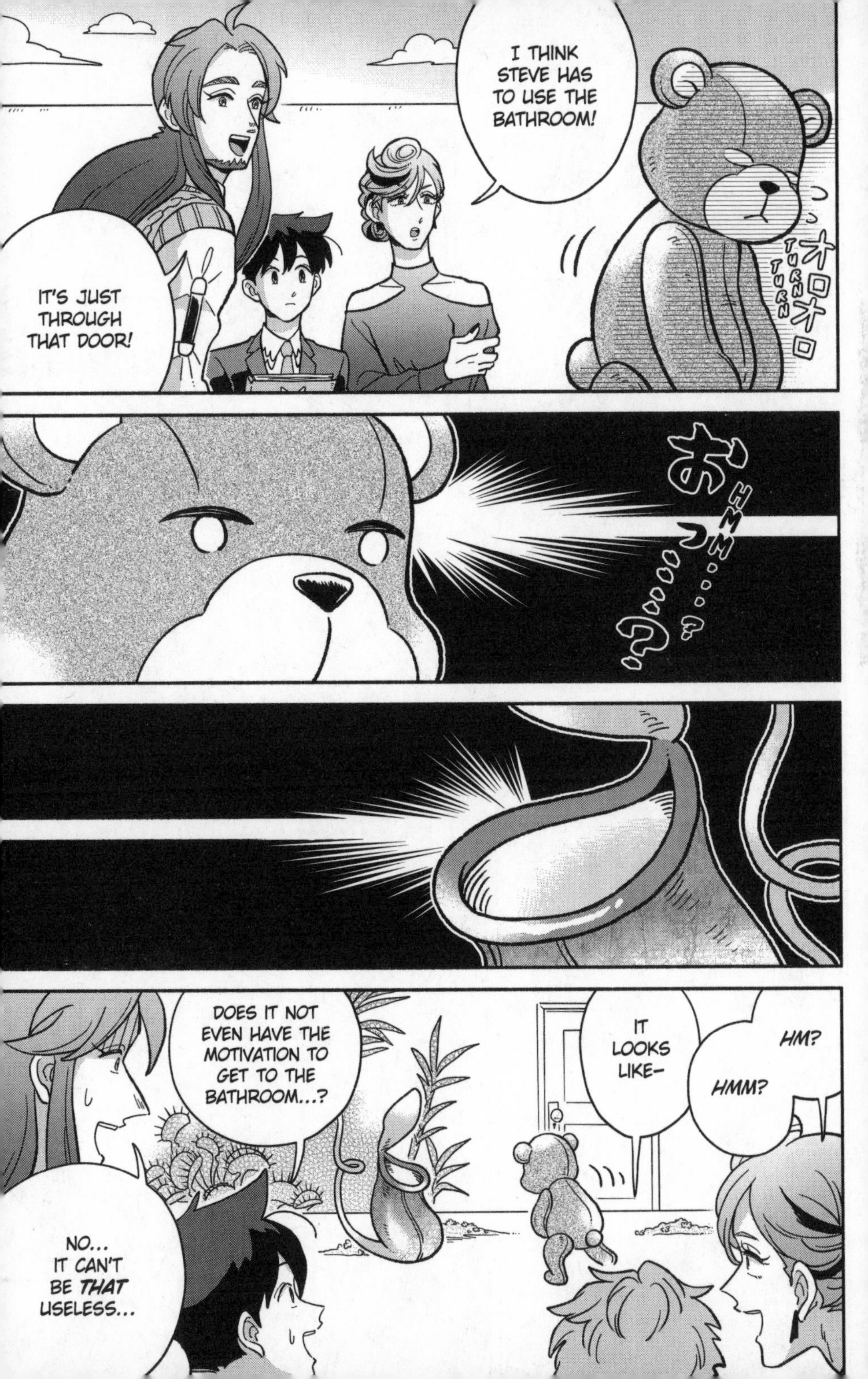
オロオロ
TURN TURN
I THINK STEVE HAS TO USE THE BATHROOM!
IT'S JUST THROUGH THAT DOOR!
おっ…？
HMMM…?
HM?
HMM?
IT LOOKS LIKE-
DOES IT NOT EVEN HAVE THE MOTIVATION TO GET TO THE BATHROOM…?
NO… IT CAN'T BE *THAT* USELESS…

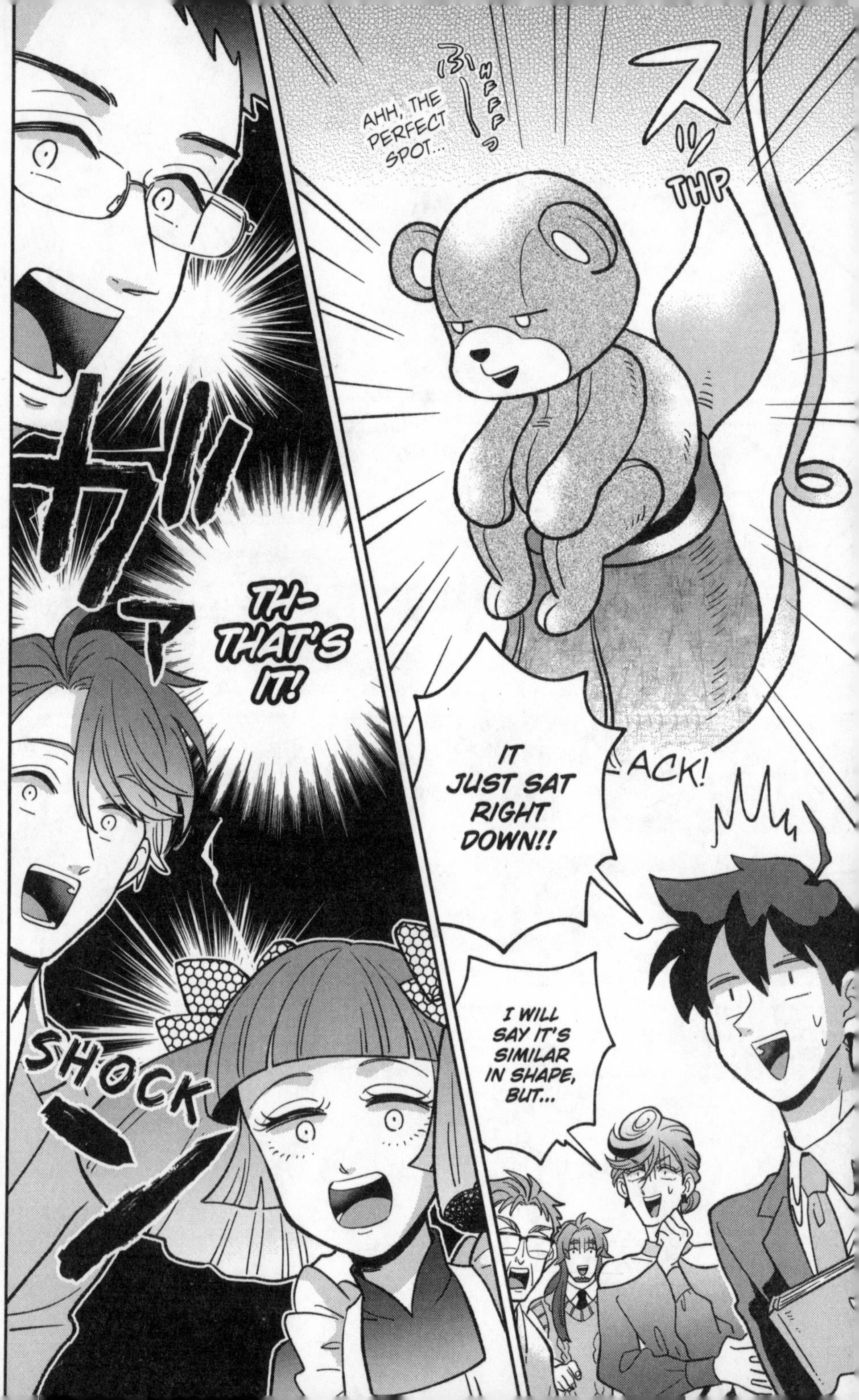
THP
HFFFF
AHH, THE PERFECT SPOT...
ACK!
IT JUST SAT RIGHT DOWN!!
I WILL SAY IT'S SIMILAR IN SHAPE, BUT...
TH-THAT'S IT!
SHOCK

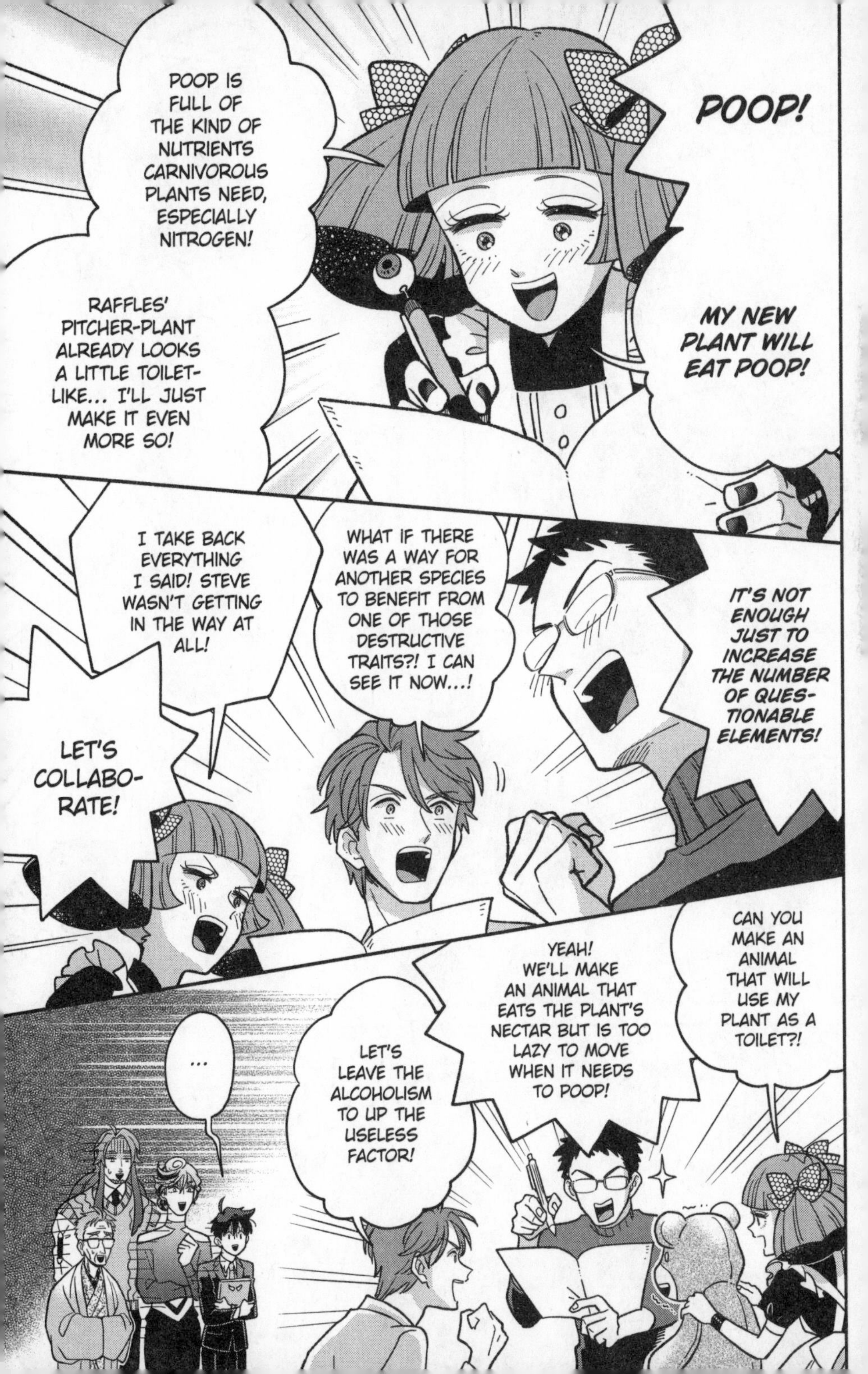
POOP!
MY NEW PLANT WILL EAT POOP!
POOP IS FULL OF THE KIND OF NUTRIENTS CARNIVOROUS PLANTS NEED, ESPECIALLY NITROGEN!
RAFFLES' PITCHER-PLANT ALREADY LOOKS A LITTLE TOILET-LIKE... I'LL JUST MAKE IT EVEN MORE SO!
IT'S NOT ENOUGH JUST TO INCREASE THE NUMBER OF QUES-TIONABLE ELEMENTS!
WHAT IF THERE WAS A WAY FOR ANOTHER SPECIES TO BENEFIT FROM ONE OF THOSE DESTRUCTIVE TRAITS?! I CAN SEE IT NOW...!
I TAKE BACK EVERYTHING I SAID! STEVE WASN'T GETTING IN THE WAY AT ALL!
LET'S COLLABO-RATE!
CAN YOU MAKE AN ANIMAL THAT WILL USE MY PLANT AS A TOILET?!
YEAH! WE'LL MAKE AN ANIMAL THAT EATS THE PLANT'S NECTAR BUT IS TOO LAZY TO MOVE WHEN IT NEEDS TO POOP!
LET'S LEAVE THE ALCOHOLISM TO UP THE USELESS FACTOR!
...

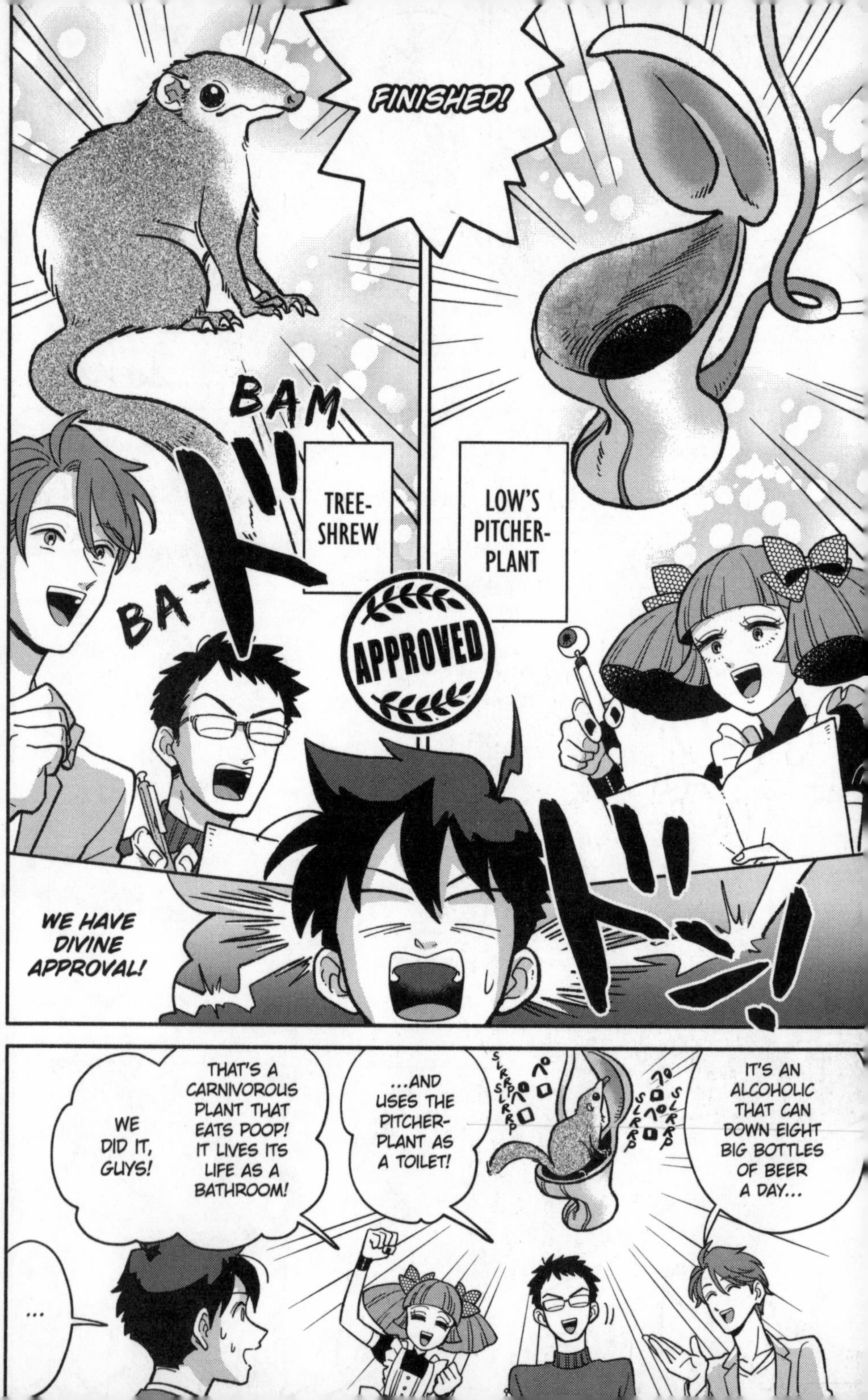
FINISHED!
LOW'S PITCHER-PLANT
TREE-SHREW
BAM
BA-
APPROVED
WE HAVE DIVINE APPROVAL!
IT'S AN ALCOHOLIC THAT CAN DOWN EIGHT BIG BOTTLES OF BEER A DAY...
SLRRP
SLRRP
...AND USES THE PITCHER-PLANT AS A TOILET!
THAT'S A CARNIVOROUS PLANT THAT EATS POOP! IT LIVES ITS LIFE AS A BATHROOM!
WE DID IT, GUYS!
...

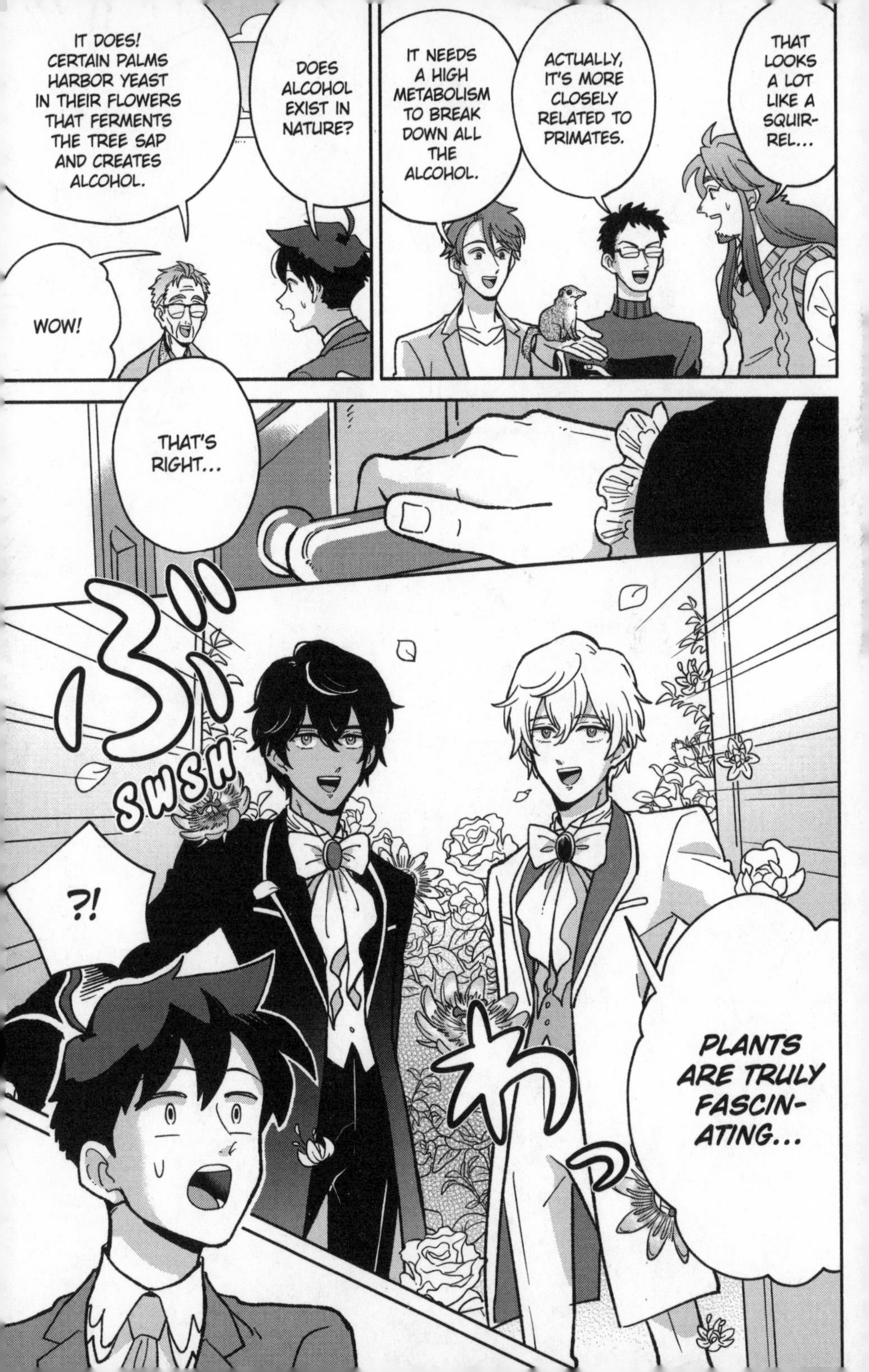
THAT LOOKS A LOT LIKE A SQUIR-REL...
ACTUALLY, IT'S MORE CLOSELY RELATED TO PRIMATES.
IT NEEDS A HIGH METABOLISM TO BREAK DOWN ALL THE ALCOHOL.
DOES ALCOHOL EXIST IN NATURE?
IT DOES! CERTAIN PALMS HARBOR YEAST IN THEIR FLOWERS THAT FERMENTS THE TREE SAP AND CREATES ALCOHOL.
WOW!
THAT'S RIGHT...
SWSH
PLANTS ARE TRULY FASCIN-ATING...
?!

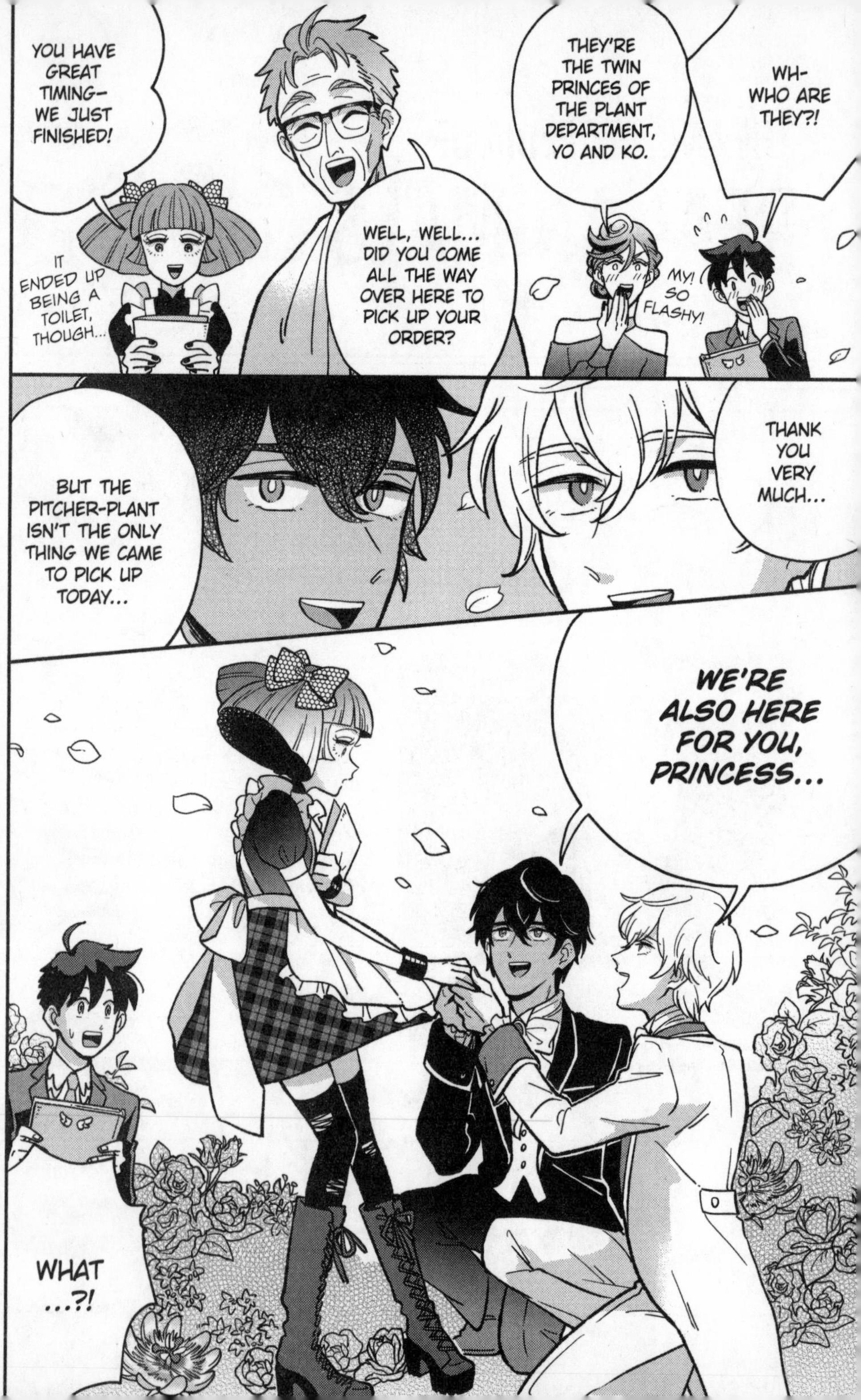
WH- WHO ARE THEY?!
THEY'RE THE TWIN PRINCES OF THE PLANT DEPARTMENT, YO AND KO.
MY! SO FLASHY!
WELL, WELL... DID YOU COME ALL THE WAY OVER HERE TO PICK UP YOUR ORDER?
YOU HAVE GREAT TIMING— WE JUST FINISHED!
IT ENDED UP BEING A TOILET, THOUGH...
THANK YOU VERY MUCH...
BUT THE PITCHER-PLANT ISN'T THE ONLY THING WE CAME TO PICK UP TODAY...
WE'RE ALSO HERE FOR YOU, PRINCESS...
WHAT ...?!

THE ENCYCLOPEDIA OF
REAL ANIMALS 35

ANIMAL 83	TREESHREW

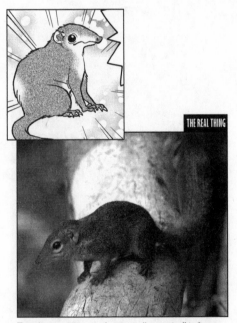

THE REAL THING

Treeshrews were once known as "tree mice" in Japanese. The one pictured above is a *Tupaia glis*.

Photo: Minden Piectures/Aflo

Though the treeshrew looks like a squirrel, it is actually more closely related to primates and retains some very primitive mammalian traits. The species that uses Low's pitcher-plant as a toilet is the *Tupaia glis*. It enjoys licking the nectar off of the pitcher-plant's lid, and because its rear end is placed perfectly above the entrance of the plant's pitcher when it does this, the treeshrew's feces become the plant's meal.

The species that loves a good party is known as the pen-tailed treeshrew. Certain species of palm produce a nectar fermented by the yeast present in its flowers that has an alcohol content of up to 3.8%. The pen-tailed treeshrew drinks the human equivalent of eight large bottles of beer per night. A cute animal that drinks like a fish and licks toilet lids—that is the treeshrew.

[Name] Treeshrew
[Classification] Class: Mammalia
Order: Scandentia
[Habitat] Tropical rainforests of Southeast Asia
[Length] 11-30 cm (4.3 in-12 in)

The pitcher-plant is a carnivorous evergreen species. Where most plants get their nutrients from photosynthesis or the soil, the pitcher-plant absorbs nutrients from the prey it catches, and can therefore thrive in areas with low light or poor soil. It captures its meals in a variety of ways, but most species lure insects with nectar and digest them after they fall into their pitchers.

The species that are known to feed on treeshrew feces are the Low's pitcher-plant and the *Nepenthes rajah*. The Low's pitcher-plant in particular looks very much like a toilet. *Tupaia glis* favors the Low's pitcher-plant for relieving itself, while the *Nepenthes rajah*, which has the biggest pitcher in the genus, is the preferred spot of the larger mountain treeshrew. To create a more comfortable seat for the treeshrew, the pitcher of the *Nepenthes rajah* has a protruding rim, which brings to mind a toilet with an extra-wide seat.

These species make the rational choice of getting their nutrients from animal feces, which, unlike insects, doesn't run away or resist.

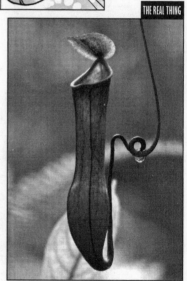

THE REAL THING

Nepenthes distillatoria is endemic to Sri Lanka.

Photo: Aflo

[Name]	Nepenthes
[Classification]	Clade: Eudicots
	Order: Caryophyllales
	Family: Nepenthaceae
	Genus: *Nepenthes*
[Habitat]	Tropical regions, mostly in Southeast Asia
[Length]	Larger specimens have stems that reach more than 10 m (33 ft) long

References

Conniff, Richard. *Swimming with Piranhas at Feeding Time: My Life Doing Dumb Stuff with Animals.* Translated by Kei Nagano and Maki Akamatsu. Japan: Seidosha, 2010.

Kobayashi, Michinobu. *The Piranhas: Nikushokugyo no Shiiku to Tanoshimikata (Aquarium Series).* Japan: Seibundo Shinkosha, 2009.

"New Fossil Tells How Piranhas Got Their Teeth." *Science Daily.* Sourced from National Evolutionary Synthesis Center (NESCENT), 2009. https://www.sciencedaily.com/releases/2009/06/090625201822.htm.

Nettaigyo·Mizukusa 1500 Shu Zukan. Japan: Pisces, 1999.

Wildlife of the World. Supervised by The Smithsonian Institution and Masao Kosuge. Translated by Atsushi Kurowa. Japan: Nittou Shoin Honsha, 2017.

Genshoku Wide Zukan Doubutsu Shinsouban. Japan: Gakken Asoshie, 2016.

Shinkai no Fushigina Seibutsu - Kakokuna Shinkai de Ikinuku Tame no Kimyou na Sugata to Seitai. Edited by Kodomo no Kagaku Henshuubu. Supervised by Katsunori Fujikura. Japan: Seibundo Shinkosha, 2010.

Sato, Takako. *Shinkai Seibutsu Daijiten.* Japan: Seibido Shuppan Co., Ltd., 2014.

Yoshioka, Motoi and Naoki Kamezaki. *Iruka to Umigame - Umi wo Tabi suru Doubutsu no Ima (Gendai Nihon Seibutsu Shi 4).* Japan: Iwanami Shoten, 2000.

Kuratani, Shigeru from Riken Rikagaku Kenkyuusho. "Kame no Koura wa Douyatte Dekiruka Shitteimasuka. Sekitsuidoubutsu no Itanji Datta?!" *Bluebacks Outreach.* Published by Kodansha Ltd., 2018. https://gendai.ismedia.jp/articles/-/55786.

Matsui, Masafumi, Tsutomu Hikida, and Hidetoshi Ota. *[Shinpan] Ryouseirui· Hachuurui (Shougakukan no Zukan NEO).* Japan: Shougakukan Inc., 2017.

Obara, Hideo, Hidetoshi Ota, Masanori Uramoto, and Masafumi Matsui. *Doubutsu Sekai Isan, Red Data Animals 7 - Australia, New Guinea.* Japan: Kodansha Ltd., 2000.

Yamashito, Hideyuki. *Sango Shirarezaru Sekai.* Japan: Seizando-Shoten Publishing Co., Ltd., 2016.

Waldbauer, Gilbert. *How Not to Be Eaten: The Insects Fight Back.* Translated by Kyoko Nakazato. Japan: Misuzu Shobo, 2013.

Mattison, Chris. *300 Frogs: A Visual Reference to Frogs and Toads from Around the World.* Supervised by Masafumi Matsui. Japan: Neko Publishing, 2008.

"Kiwi facts & characteristics." *Kiwis for Kiwi.* 2020. https://www.kiwisforkiwi.org/about-kiwi/kiwi-facts-characteristics/.

"New Zealand no Kokuchou." *National Geographic Nihonban.* Published by the National Geographic Society, Nikkei National Geographic Inc. https://natgeo.nikkeibp.co.jp/nng/feature/0211/f_5_zoom1.shtml.

Metzler, Christian. *Home ranges and dispersal patterns of Great Spotted Kiwi (Apteryx haastii) subadults.* Vienna, Austria: University of Natural Resources and Life Sciences and Lincoln, New Zealand: Lincoln University, 2011.

Yunoki, Osamu. *[Shinpan] Tori Kyouryuu no Shisontachi (Shougakukan no Zukan NEO).* Supervised by Keisuke Ueda. Japan: Shougakukan Inc., 2015.

Tori (Kodansha no Ugoku Zukan MOVE). Supervised by Kazuto Kawakami. Japan: Kodansha Ltd., 2011.

Suzuki, Katsumi. *Sakana no Kosodate no Himitsu.* Japan: Yama-kei Publishers Co., Ltd., 2005.

Nakaya, Kazuhiro. *Sekai no Utsukushii Same Zukan.* Japan: Takarajimasha Inc., 2015.

Okutani, Takashi. *Nihon Kinkaisan Kairui Zukan.* Japan: Tokai University Press, 2017.

Takashige, Hiroshi. *Nihon no Kai 629 Shu - Ontai Iki· Senkai de Mirareru Shu no Seitai Shashin + Kaigara Hyouhon (Nature Watching Guidebook).* Japan: Seibundo Shinkosha, 2019.

"Tsumetagai (Bladder moon snail)." *Bouz-Konnyaku no Ichiba Gyokairui Zukan.* Published by Bouz-Konnyaku, 2007. https://www.zukan-bouz.com/syu/ツメタガイ.

Mizuno, Tomomi. "Asari no Tenteki 'Tsumetagai' to 'Sakigurotamatsumeta' ni Tsuite." *Suzuka Suisen Kenkyuushitsu,* 2006. http://web.archive.org/web/20060919212030/http://www.sea.pref.mie.jp/mirainet/h18/asarinotenteki.PDF.

"Tsumetagai no Shoutai." *Shijou Saikyou no Shiohigari Choujin, S.S.S.Superman,* 2002. https://harady.com/shiohigari/teki2.html.

"Tsumetagai -Tamagaika-." *Kai no Zukan.* KAINOZUKAN. https://kai-zukan.info/tsumetagai.php.

DeVries, P. J. "Singing Caterpillars, Ants and Symbiosis." *Scientific American,* Vol. 267, Issue 4, 1992, pp. 56-62.

Motokawa, Tatsuo. *Uni mo Sugoi Batta mo Sugoi Design no Seibutsugaku (Chuukou Shinsho 2419).* Japan: Chuokoron-Shinsha, Inc., 2017.

Maruyama, Munetoshi, Takeshi Yoro, and Yuta Nakase. *Konchuu wa Motto Sugoi (Kobunsha Shinsho).* Japan: Kobunsha Co., Ltd., 2015.

Ikeda, Kiyohiko and Takeshi Yoro. "Mushi to no Taisetsu na Jikan." *Kangaeru Hito.* Published by Shinchosha, 2018. https://kangaeruhito.jp/interview/5995.

Sarashina, Isao. *Kaseki no Bunshi Seibutsugaku - Seimei Shinka no Nazo wo Toku (Kodansha Gendai Shinsho).* Japan: Kodansha Ltd., 2012.

Red Data Oitsumerareru Yasei Doubutsu Honyuurui Koushite Zetsumetsushita 5 Shu, Soshite Ayabumareru 20 Shu. Newton Mook. Newton Press, 2006.

Davies, Nick. *Cuckoo Cheating by Nature.* Translated by Hiroshi Nakamura and Atsuko Nagayama. Japan: Chijinshokan Co., Ltd., 2016.

Higuchi, Hiroyoshi. *Akai Tamago no Himitsu.* Japan: Komine Shoten, 2011.

Yasuma, Shigeki. "Vol.39 Tsupai no Nakama." *Doubutsu-no-Kuni,* 2013. http://www.doubutsu-no-kuni.net/?p=16620.

Wiens, Frank, Annette Zitzmann, Marc-André Lachance, Michel Yegles, Fritz Pragst, Friedrich M. Wurst, Dietrich von Holst, Saw Leng Guan, and Rainer Spanagel. "Chronic intake of fermented floral nectar by wild treeshrews." *PNAS,* 2008. https://www.pnas.org/content/pnas/early/2008/07/25/0801628105.full.pdf.

Clarke, Charles M., Ulrike Bauer, Ch'ien C. Lee, Andrew A. Tuen, Katja Rembold, and Jonathan A. Moran. "Tree shrew lavatories: a novel nitrogen sequestration strategy in a tropical pitcher plant." *Biology Letters, The Royal Society,* 2009. https://www.ncbi.nlm.nih.gov/pmc/articles/PMC2781956/.

Hasebe, Mitsuyasu. "Shokuchuu Shokubutsu no Tekiou Shinka - Shoudoubutsu kara no Eiyou de Hineiyou Chi de Seiiku." *Seibutsu no Kagaku Iden,* Vol. 70, No. 4, 2016, pp. 274-278. http://www.nibb.ac.jp/~evodevo/pdf_JP/2016_Hasebe_iden.pdf.

Discovery Henshuubu. "Jungle ni Hisomu Shokuniku Shokubutsu...! Honyuurui mo Toraeru Utsubokazura." *DISCOVERY.INC,* 2018. https://www.dplay.jp/article/0000028772.

"Shokuchuu Shokubutsu no Sekai Wamyou vs. Gakumei Daiouhyou." *E-COTTAGE,* 1998-2020. http://www2f.biglobe.ne.jp/~e-cottag/nature/cp/atoj/atoj.html.

Kondo, Katsuhiko and Masahiro Kondo. *Color Ban Shokuchuu Shokubutsu Zukan.* Japan: Ie-no-Hikari Association, 2006.

Nam. "Crypto ~Sekai no Kimyou na Juunintachi: Mimic Toilet~*Nepenthes rajah*." *CRYPTO Mysterious Creatures, Plants & Dishes,* 2020. https://www.crypto-f.com/2020/01/blog-post_25.html.

*All websites were accessed on March 23, 2020.

Special thanks:

Editor/Yoshimi Takuwa-san (Institution for Liberal Arts, Tokyo Institution of Technology)
Illustration Production Collaboration/Izumi Kanchiku-san (Team Pascal)
Kamome Shirahama-san
Saba-san
Ame Toba-san
Tomato-san

A Kodansha Comics Trade Paperback Original
Heaven's Design Team 5 copyright © 2020 Hebi-zou&Tsuta Suzuki/Tarako
English translation copyright © 2021 Hebi-zou&Tsuta Suzuki/Tarako
All rights reserved.

Published in the United States by Kodansha Comics, an imprint of
Kodansha USA Publishing, LLC, New York.

Publication rights for this English edition arranged through
Kodansha Ltd., Tokyo.

First published in Japan in 2020 by Kodansha Ltd., Tokyo
as *Tenchi sozo dezainbu*, volume 5.

ISBN 978-1-64651-154-9

Original cover design by SAVA DESIGN

Printed in the United States of America.

www.kodansha.us

9 8 7 6 5 4 3 2 1
Translation and lettering: JM Iitomi Crandall
Additional translation: Jacqueline Fung
Additional lettering and layout: Belynda Ungurath
Editing: Jesika Brooks, Vanessa Tenazas
YKS Services LLC/SKY Japan, INC
Kodansha Comics edition cover design by My Truong

Publisher: Kiichiro Sugawara

Director of publishing services: Ben Applegate
Associate director of operations: Stephen Pakula
Publishing services managing editors: Alanna Ruse, Madison Salters
Production managers: Emi Lotto, Angela Zurlo
Logo and character art ©Kodansha USA Publishing, LLC